◁ **W9-CUF-975**

Here are comments about To The Top Canada!!!

"From encounters with bears to Big City Life including the stark challenges of solo biking through the Arctic, a priceless "Canadian" narrative. Chris has a huge passion for Canada, courage in spades and an unrivaled adventure spirit! Tie him down!"

Roy Green
Award-Winning Talk-Radio Host of The Roy Green Show
Corus Radio Network

"We can all learn from an already Proud Canadian who was willing to go out and learn more about the very fabric of our great country! Well done Chris!!!"

Brian Williams
The Dean of Canadian Sports Commentators
CTV/TSN Television

"To The Top Canada teaches us that one person can not only make a difference but also inspire others to act on their dreams. It's like reading someone's diary, someone who turns out to be just an ordinary Canadian who did something extraordinary! It happens to all of us all the time: we are moved by an event or situation, but Chris Robertson belongs to that rare breed who do something about it…"

Connie Smith
News Anchor
CH Global Television

"When I read To The Top Canada, I was mesmerized by this great adventure story, and truly moved by Chris' total commitment to citizenship and service to his country.   His personal challenge, to go out and do something for Canada, inspired me and helped shape the vision for completing Chicken Soup for the Canadian Soul.   To The Top Canada is the wake up call to make Canada great in the 21st Century, and Chris Robertson is a real Canadian Legend!"

Janet Matthews
Canadian Co-Author of National Bestselling Book
Chicken Soup For The Canadian Soul

"You are an inspiration to all of us."

Robert Bateman
Wildlife Artist-Environmentalist-Naturalist

To The Top Canada
20th Anniversary Special Edition

This special 20th Anniversary edition of the Canadian bestselling book To The Top Canada celebrates 20 years after the successful completion of the 1997-1998 To The Top Canada Expedition. This book includes a NEW CHAPTER by Chris Robertson entitled:

Two Decades Later...

You'll learn how the To The Top Canada Expedition affected the life of Chris Robertson and the lives of other Canadians. Chris Robertson is the "first" person in history to travel from the bottom of mainland Canada 6,520 kilometres to the top under his own power or by any means of transportation over land. Enroute in media appearances and Canada Rallies he challenged and encouraged millions of Canadians to make Canada better. In this new chapter of this special 20th Anniversary edition you learn that Chris Robertson has dedicated his life to promoting positive citizenship and a better Canada. Chris' most remarkable achievement since the completion of the To The Top Canada Expedition is speaking in over 1000 schools from coast to coast to coast. Students across Canada have been enpowered with glowing hearts that they can achieve any goal to make Canada better. Chris Robertson is truly Canada's Ambassador of Positive Citizenship!!!

To The Top
Canada

The incredible true story of the very first journey from the bottom of mainland Canada to the top by a proud Canadian to save his country!

CHRIS ROBERTSON

EXCEEDING
EXPECTATIONS
PUBLISHING™

Canadian Cataloguing in Publication Data

ISBN 0-9684952-0-6

Cover Design and Layout by Absolute Advertising
Maps by James Loates/VisuTronx
Printing by Webcom

Eighth printing March 2014

An Important Word From Chris' Lawyer

The information conveyed in this book is the sole opinion and perspective of Chris Robertson alone and should not be taken as a basis in fact. Many of Chris Robertson's observations during the period reported in this book were made after only a very brief period and often in a fatigued and malnourished state. All readers are strongly encouraged to do their own independent research and form their own independent conclusions before deciding on any facts in relation to this book.

Dedication

The success of the very first journey from the very bottom of mainland Canada 6520 kilometres to the top was only possible because of the loving support of two people. My wife, Carol and my son, James gave their total commitment to the To The Top Canada expedition. This book is dedicated to them because, in my eyes, they are the greatest Canadians I have ever met...

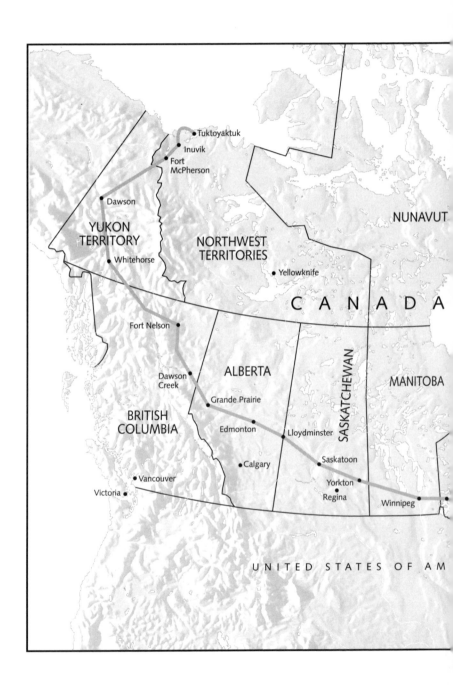

NUNAVUT

YUKON
TERRITORY

NORTHWEST
TERRITORIES

C A N A D A

Tuktoyaktuk
Inuvik
Fort
McPherson

Dawson

Whitehorse

Yellowknife

Fort Nelson

ALBERTA

Dawson
Creek

SASKATCHEWAN

MANITOBA

Grande Prairie

BRITISH
COLUMBIA

Edmonton

Lloydminster

Calgary

Saskatoon

Yorkton

Vancouver

Regina

Victoria

Winnipeg

UNITED STATES OF AM

Iqaluit

NEWFOUNDLAND

St
John's

QUEBEC

ONTARIO

PRINCE
EDWARD
ISLAND

NEW
BRUNSWICK   Charlottetown

Quebec   Fredericton

Halifax

NOVA SCOTIA

Sudbury   Montreal

Thunder
Bay

Sault Ste.
Marie   Ottawa

C A   Barrie

Toronto
Hamilton
London

Leamington
Point Pelee

Saturday, March 1, 1997

It was after midnight. I stared quietly at the ceiling so as not to waken my wife Carol and son James who were with me in the room donated by the Leamington Comfort Inn. It was ten hours till the Media Conference that would launch the To The Top Canada expedition, when, at 41, I would attempt to be the first person in history to travel from the very bottom of mainland Canada 6,520 kilometres to the top. Like a racehorse in the starting gate, I was ready to go now. Throughout the months of training and preparation, I had encountered many cynics and critics who thought I would never make it past the starting post. I was ready to prove them wrong with a vengeance. I didn't fall asleep until 2:30 am which meant my 6:00 am wake up call would come all too soon.

After breakfast we all headed out to the Point Pelee National Park Visitor Centre, the site of our To The Top Canada Media Conference. Point Pelee, Canada's southern-most mainland point, is located at the southern tip of Ontario at a latitude on par with that of northern California. My destination: Tuktoyaktuk, in the Northwest Territories nestled on the Arctic Ocean. The magnitude of the undertaking was overwhelming to me, and yet I was filled with the excitement of anticipation for the adventure which lay ahead. Driving to Point Pelee it occurred to me that I was so excited I'd forgotten to shave.

When I pulled into the parking lot, I took a quiet moment to speak to my family before we began a day that would be full of activity. "I want to thank you both for helping me get to this point..." My voice cracked and I fought back the tears. We are an incredibly close family who does everything together, and I knew Carol, James and even our dog Smooch, would miss me, and would also be making an enormous sacrifice for the cause of making Canada a better country. I knew that very soon on this weekend we would have to say our first "goodbye". That thought tore me up inside. Carol didn't say a word, as she knew I was about to start the most challenging episode of my life. I would be tested physically, mentally, emotionally and spiritually.

Arriving in advance of the staff at the Point Pelee National Park Visitor Centre, I discovered an open washroom and quickly shaved before the staff arrived. Once the building was opened, I carried in a large stereo system and immediately started playing fast tempo music. Listening to music was a pregame ritual I use to carry out before high school and college football games. As people entered the Visitor Centre they were greeted by music not normally heard in a nature reserve - pulse-racing music, suggesting that, momentarily, something very important was about to begin. Just before the Media Conference, Carol passed me a message that CBC-TV were enroute but running late, so please don't leave Point Pelee until they arrived. In the next moment I was approached by CBC-Radio who told me they needed to hurry so it would be helpful to begin as soon as possible. I decided to start at exactly the scheduled time and proceed with the Media Conference as planned. There was a large contingent of media including television, radio and newspapers. Also present were 30 area cyclists who had come out to support my To The Top Canada expedition, by riding 19 kilometres from Point Pelee, to Leamington the first official stop of the To The Top Canada expedition. Also present were many people who are part of a volunteer organization called "Friends of Point Pelee". The Media Conference began.

"I'd like to introduce myself. My name is Chris Robertson and during the To The Top Canada expedition, I hope to become the first person in history to travel from the bottom of mainland Canada 6,520 kilometres to the top of mainland Canada under my own power. The reason I am undertaking the To The Top Canada expedition is to get Canadians' attention and to ask them this one, very important question:

What will you do before the year 2000 to make Canada a better country than when you found it?"

Applause filled the room. Inside, I breathed a sigh of relief that my message was being positively received. I explained that Canadians enjoy the greatest privilege on the planet Earth. We are citizens of the country which the United Nations ranked as Number One, three years in a row, as the best country in terms of income, health care and education.

"I suggest that if you have never taken on a personal project to make Canada a better place, NOW is the time to really think about what your special gift is and what personal project you should do for Canada."

I explained that I believe we as individuals can make a difference. My 11-year-old son James and I were in Montreal in 1995 with tens of thousands of Canadians for the Rally held before the Quebec Referendum. Individual efforts came together, to create an event that brought the federalist forces back from a ten point deficit in the polls to win a victory by a razor sharp margin. I knew that in the not-too-distant future, Quebec Sovereignists would again bring Canada to another fork in the road with another referendum. But this time, a last minute rally would not save the day. So, I explained, it is what we do right here and right now that will determine the destiny of Canada. The bottom line was that, despite the personal cost of cashing in $36,928.69 in RRSP's of my life savings to allow the expedition to go forward, spending several months away from my family and pushing my body to the limit beyond pain, the most important objective was to do everything in my power to ensure that there would be a Canada in the 21st century for my son James.

Reverend Gary Boyes of the St. Paul's & Trinity Anglican Church said the following special blessing for the To The Top Canada expedition:

Heavenly Father, your Son, our Saviour was born into this world so that our sad divisions will be overcome and that all things will be reconciled through him with you. May this endeavour which has begun in you have success and go in safety. May this expedition for Unity be a visible sign that creates an inward love of Canadians of every race, colour, and nation for each other. Que Dieu benisse le Canada, and may God Almighty, the Father, the Son, and the Holy Spirit bless this cycling expedition. Amen.

At the end of the indoor portion of the Media Conference we moved outside and I cycled down the last 2 km to the tip of mainland Canada. This was my first time seeing the tip in the winter time. There was snow, ice, fog and sand. It was desolate. I kidded the reporters that once they developed their pictures, they could use them for a To The Top Canada expedition skill testing question: "Was this picture taken in Point Pelee or Tuktoyaktuk?" Everyone laughed, as it seemed to look more like what we would imagine Tuk would look like. I had never been to Tuk so, aside from my research, this would be an expedition into the unknown for me. As I pushed forward with my bike to the tip, a Point Pelee official pointed out to me that I was past the tip and actually on an iceberg. "That's good enough for me," I replied, and turned my bike around to face north. (My son later kidded me, if the iceberg had broken off and floated south on Lake Erie, I might have had to rename the expedition To The Top USA).

I then leaned down facing my bike, on one knee, to say a prayer. I prayed for my family to be safe and for the Lord to watch over them. I prayed for the safety of the 30 cyclists who would be part of our parade to Leamington. I prayed for Canada to be strong and united and that Canadians would discover a new pride, passion and patriotism for their country. I then stood up and said, "I ride for all Canadians and for the glory of Canada". The journey of a lifetime began.

I took my bike from the beach to the road where I was joined by my son James on his bicycle, and by an army of local cyclists. There were bicycles built for two and one bicycle that looked more like a tricycle with a six foot front wheel and a one foot back wheel. Where do they get these bikes? Canadian Tire? My wife Carol followed in the car with Barry Shainbaum, a freelance photojournalist as her passenger. Barry had taken a special interest in chronicling the To The Top Canada expedition. As we rode the 9 km through Point Pelee National Park to the front gate, we were passed by the four television vans leap frogging past each other to shoot the first kilometres of the To The Top Canada expedition.

While we were in the park a large group of scouts was cheering us on. At the front gate of the park, two police cars waited for us to act as escorts for us into Leamington. Riding along the top of Lake Erie we hit a very heavy fog. I slowed the pace so we would not lose any cyclists. Turning onto Erie Street, the main street of Leamington, I pulled out my large Canadian flag which I bought for the Montreal Rally before the October 1995 referendum in Quebec. I was as energetic today as I had been on that day.

On the morning of the rally, Friday, October 27, 1995, my son James and I were scheduled to fly to Montreal. We both wore identical Canadian red sweats with the word "Canada" emblazoned across our chests. Being Hamilton Tiger Cat fans we take our cheering very seriously with an "in-your-face" approach. We painted our faces red on one side and white on the other. Our hair was also spray painted half red and half white. Our six foot long Canadian flag was on an aluminum pole making it easy to carry. James and I ran through Terminal 2 at Pearson International Airport in Toronto at warp speed.

The group of Sikh Canadians manning airport security looked shocked when we ran straight into the security checkpoint. I'm sure they had never seen anything like us in their lifetime. We checked in at the Air Canada counter at 8:55 am for our 10:00 am flight. The attendant said she could get us on the 9:00 am flight if we could run. Can we run? Do the Maple Leafs play hockey? With the blessing of the Air Canada attendant, we ran as if the building was on fire.

All the regular business travellers were seated on the plane, seat-belted, ready for departure. Then we walked on the plane, looking like the Spirit of Canada, surprising the passengers. As we walked down the aisle with our Canadian flag, to the back of the plane where our seats were, all eyes were on us. I commented to all the passengers in a loud voice, "Can you believe they bumped us from business class?" The plane shook with roars of laughter. We put our Canadian flag in the overhead compartment. My son was thrilled to get a day off school and to fly along with Dad to save Canada at the Montreal Rally.

On my bike in Leamington I smiled with the memories of that day. Glancing back at James, who was right behind me on his mountain bike, I thought, today is another day he will remember the rest of his life.

People cheered and waved as we went by and cars honked their horns. We arrived at Leamington Town Hall two minutes ahead of schedule for our 1:00 pm presentation. I presented the Mayor with a certificate commemorating the To The Top Canada expedition passing through Leamington. The Mayor presented me with a Leamington hat and a Leamington Pin. I remarked on the enthusiastic turnout in Leamington and assured the Mayor that the spirit of Canada is alive and well in Leamington. I thanked all the town officials, the cyclists, the police and the media. I posed for pictures with everyone.

The official schedule of our first day was now over. The kickoff of the To The Top Canada expedition had gone perfectly, just as it had been planned (a rare blessing indeed - such special events usually harbour some glitches). Angels were truly watching over us today.

After having lunch at a local restaurant with my family, I cycled over to the Leamington Hospital. I wanted to visit people in the hospital and give mementoes to the patients and staff - Canadian flags to children and Canadian flag pins to adults. The nurses at shift change were all at the nursing station and they recognized me as that Canadian unity guy on television. As if they had practiced, they broke into song with the most rousing version of "O Canada" I have ever heard. Patients who had never gotten out of bed before were coming down the hall to see what was going on. I visited the patients and tried to lift their spirits, by letting them know that they would be better and out of the hospital, long before I would make it to Tuktoyaktuk.

For one patient, the conversation turned serious. He was being transferred the next day to London, Ontario, to have triple by-pass heart surgery. I told him I would pray for him. He was afraid. I tried to comfort him with my confidence. I told him he would be fine and that he would see the finish of the expedition. I told him I was riding for Canada and all Canadians, especially for him.

After visiting all the patients, my family and I went back to the Comfort Inn where we ordered pizza for dinner. We all felt elated and exhausted. I fell asleep early and slept soundly all night.

Sunday, March 2, 1997

Waking up after a deep sleep, my family and I went down for the complimentary breakfast provided by the people at the Leamington Comfort Inn, who were also kind enough to donate a room for two nights.

After packing up, I wrote a long letter to the Editor of the Leamington Post. I thanked everyone in Leamington and Point Pelee who had welcomed me and had promised to remember me in their prayers.

We dropped off the letter to the Leamington Post and then drove to St. John The Evangelist Anglican Church. It was 10:30 am by my watch when we entered the front door. We noticed the choir were at the back of the church ready for the processional hymn. The minister was at the front of the church, addressing the congregation, and we tried to inconspicuously sneak into a pew. I tried. As a person who is built like a Tiger-Cat linebacker, and wearing a bright fluorescent yellow winter jacket, I was not all that inconspicuous. The minister finished his sentence and immediately spoke my name and asked me to stand up. Now I'm in trouble, I thought. He proceeded to introduce me and talk about the To The Top Canada expedition for the benefit of those who had not seen me on television. The congregation clapped and I nodded in appreciation. During the service, the lay minister leading the prayers of the people prayed for a safe journey for me.

After the service Carol, James and I spoke to the people of the church for over an hour in the parish hall. We went for lunch at a local restaurant and then we pulled the car into a Petro Canada gas station beside Leamington Town Hall where I had finished the previous day. I strapped my gear onto my bike, which swayed unsteadily under the tremendous weight, and tied my huge backpack onto my back. It was time to say goodbye to my family.

My son James was already hurting inside knowing I would be away. We are closer than father and son. To each other we are the brother neither of us had, doing everything together. My son is too brave to say he'd miss me, but I knew what he was feeling when he exclaimed that "Smooch" was going to miss me badly. (Smooch is our family dog, a black and white Shih Tzu - very big for his breed, hence his nickname "the Shack of Shih Tzus".)

My wife Carol, who is my very best friend in the whole world, also was under strain at this moment. Here she was, leaving me having to return home to Hamilton, where James had to go back to school and she had to return to her job as Director of Nursing at Idlewyld Manor, a long term care facility. Not only was she leaving me, but she was leaving me to conquer an impossible challenge that no one had ever attempted before. Carol knows me better than anyone and she knew that I compete to win and never accept defeat.

Despite that, she hugged and kissed me, and cried as she said "If you need us, just call and we'll come right away and get you and bring you home". I was so choked up I couldn't speak. I hugged and kissed my wife and son, both of whom I love dearly. Riding away from Leamington Town Hall I watched our family car drive from my sight. I rode my bike towards Wheatley. It was five to ten degrees below zero. When I came to Wheatley I turned north towards Tilbury, my destination for the day. Along the flat terrain speckled with farm houses, several people darted from their homes and ran beside me for a couple of kilometres. Riding further in the cold weather I learned my first lesson of the expedition.

1. Never Trust The Weather!

In the preparation for the To The Top Canada expedition, I had ridden my bike extensively in January in cold winter conditions, with temperatures well below zero. I was quite comfortable when I dressed properly for the cold weather. Before driving down from Hamilton to Point Pelee, I watched the Weather Channel to know what weather I could expect. The Weather Channel report indicated I would see temperatures of 16°C or 62°F. I hadn't brought my winter boots for my first week. Now my toes grew numb, as the cold air seeped into my running shoes. As I left late from Leamington, twilight was just beginning as I pulled into Tilbury. I rode my bike over to the only motel in town and asked if they could donate a room for the evening to support my Canadian Unity expedition. Despite the fact that, judging from the parking lot, it looked as if they did not have any customers, the manager said "no!". Due to the freezing temperatures, there were only a few people to be seen outdoors in the town. One by one I rode up to them, explained my Canadian unity expedition and asked if they knew where I might find a home that would put me up for the night. When everyone said no, I came to the conclusion I would be sleeping outside sooner than I had expected. I rode to the Tilbury Police Station to find it locked up, so I called the Police on an outside phone on the wall. I knew that in the Canadian Criminal Code there is a law about trespassing on private property between 9:00 pm and 6:00 am. I wanted to check with the Police to ensure that I was camping in the proper spot. It would put a poor light of my expedition, if I was arrested on the second day. A friendly officer drove up in a cruiser and I followed her on my bike to the south east end of town. The officer left me with a warning that there were some trouble makers in town, so she would check on me later. There were only a few minutes of daylight left so I hurried to set up my base camp. I planted my Canadian flag pole on the ground, put up my tent, moved my gear inside the tent and locked my bike to a hydro pole for the night. I got into my sleeping bag. My sleeping bag is rated for 30° below zero. It was the first warmth my toes had felt in hours. More tired than hungry, I ate a few oatmeal cookies and had a Pepsi for my supper. It was completely dark now and I turned on my lantern flashlight so I could read my Bible. I had decided before my expedition I would read the Bible from beginning to end during my expedition. I had been working with my son James since he was a year away from the age of his confirmation into the Anglican Church.

Despite attending church all my life, including four years of church every day at Appleby College, which also included weekly scripture classes, I found that my knowledge of Christianity was not strong enough to make me a good teacher for James.

James is extremely bright. The previous June at his school, he'd won the achievement award in academics for being the best student in Grade Four. I would like to say he gets it from his Dad, but, to be honest, he probably gets it from his mother. I graduated from Appleby as the Top Student with the General Proficiency Award, but Carol is the only one I ever met who was Valedictorian in her Public School, High School and University. With no brothers or sisters, James has a lot of adult company. He asks very tough questions and has a razor sharp wit. I was no match for him to be a knowledgeable instructor. I would come prepared to teach him the Beatitudes and he would change the conversation to "Why does God exist?"

I had never read the Bible from start to finish at one time and I felt the expedition was the perfect time to start this spiritual journey. I started reading from my Good News Bible.

"In the beginning, when God created the universe, the earth was formless and desolate. The raging ocean that covered everything was engulfed in total darkness, and the power of God was moving over the water. Then God commanded, "Let there be light" - and light appeared. God was pleased with what he saw."

After reading the first ten chapters in Genesis, I turned off my lantern flashlight and went to sleep.

Monday, March 3, 1997

I had slept quite well and was very warm. At one point I even had to open my sleeping bag zipper to cool off. That all changed when I was greeted by 20° below zero temperatures in the morning. You may be reading this and thinking "Oh, that's not so cold". But I'm here to tell you I was not dashing from the house to the car to the office or to the mall. I was putting on clean clothes that had their surface temperature reduced to 20° below zero. It felt like wearing ice cubes on my body. I emerged from my tent to be greeted by a reporter from the Tilbury newspaper snapping my picture. He told me that he'd received calls from homes overlooking the park "that the unity guy on television is camping in the park." I proceeded to pack up my base camp which included:

1. Rolling up my sleeping bag
2. Rolling up my Slumberjack
3. Pulling up tent pegs frozen into the ground
4. Untying tent ropes
5. Packing gear in bags
6. Folding up the tent
7. Tying the gear to my bicycle
8. Unlocking the bike from the pole
9. Taking down the Canadian flag pole I had set up

The reporter continued to snap pictures during all this "exciting" activity. I offered my mittens to the reporter because he was shivering uncontrollably. I enjoyed watching the expression on the reporter's face when this "guy on a bicycle" who was roughing it in sub-zero temperatures reached into his bag and pulled out a professionally typed media release to make his job easy.

The reporter drove off and I got on my bike and rode to the Town Hall where I presented the Tilbury Certificate to the town. Just before cycling out of town I pulled into the Truck Stop. I grew up around trucks. My father got out of World War II with a hundred dollars and bought a truck with that down payment and built a successful company called Robertson Transport Ltd. He later sold his terminal and fleet to retire. Ever since I was a young boy I loved the smell of diesel fuel, the roar of large truck engines and the large portions served at truck stops. I ordered the Truckers Special which was 5 pancakes, 4 pieces of bacon, 4 sausages, 4 toast slices and coffee, which I switched to hot chocolate. I do not drink coffee and occasionally I get a waitress who will exclaim, so the whole restaurant will hear "YOU DON'T DRINK COFFEE?" All the noise stops, absolutely everyone looks at you and you can hear a pin drop. . . Over time, I've learned a surefire response that closes the subject every time: "I don't believe you should drink a beverage grown as a cash crop in the third world, on farm land that could be used to feed starving children!" All the coffee drinkers feel embarrassed instead of me and I pleasantly enjoy my meal.

As I chowed down my trucker's breakfast, the waitress came over and told me the boy working the gas bar had paid for the breakfast of the Unity Guy he'd seen on TV. His kind act single-handedly made me love the community of Tilbury.

I shaved and washed up in the washroom. Leaving the restaurant I went out to my bike and got out a "Friend of Canada" certificate and presented it to the Gas Bar boy. On this certificate under the headline "Friend of Canada" and the Canadian Flag, there is the following inscription on the left side of the certificate.

Canadian Chris Robertson, the first person in history to travel 6520 kilometres under his own power from the bottom of mainland Canada to the top, would

like to thank you for your service to the "To The Top Canada" expedition! Your dedication to making Canada a better place is appreciated. Your good deed is saluted by Chris Robertson as a symbol of your national pride in our great country of Canada!

On the right side of the certificate there is a picture of me holding my bike up with one arm in front of the Canadian flag. Under the picture is poetry I wrote to capture how I feel about Canada.

Canada's Prayer

I'm dreaming of Canada tonight.
A country where mountains and hopes touch the sky
A country where an ocean of kindness fills all hearts
A country where ideas are a forest of wisdom
Oh God let me wake up in Canada!

I'm dreaming of Canada tonight.
A country where compassion is as tall as a douglas fir
A country where understanding is as deep as a great lake
A country where confidence grows like grain
Oh God let me wake up in Canada!

I'm dreaming of Canada tonight.
A country where happiness flows like the water of a river
A country where love is a breath of fresh air
A country where peace covers the land like snow
Oh God, please let me wake up in Canada, tonight...

I headed out from Tilbury on Highway #2 towards Chatham having learned my second lesson of the expedition.

2. Kindness is an important characteristic of Canada.

Riding through the flat farm land on my way to Chatham I encountered something for the very first time. Most of my training had been in the city so I was always partially protected from strong winds. Now I had 80 kilometre per hour head winds blowing straight at my chest. To put this in perspective, I am not built like a cyclist. I weighed 272 pounds, my bike weighed 30 pounds, and I carried 250 pounds of gear. I was pedaling for 500 pounds, which is challenging enough with no wind. According to the speedometer on my bike, even though I was pedaling much harder than I usually do, my speed had been cut to less than half my usual cruising speed.

An Ontario Provincial Police cruiser stopped and the female officer rolled down the passenger window to ask me if I was alright, as the winds against me, were now in excess of a 80 kilometres per hour. The wind then shook the cruiser as if with anger and the OPP officer had to grab her hat as the wind tried to snatch it off her head. I yelled into the wind that I was fine and kept my legs turning, struggling against the blast. After an afternoon of fighting the wind all the way to Chatham I pulled off highway #2 into the first payphone located at a Journey's End Motel. I went in and called Jim Hundt to let him know I had arrived. Jim was the first of many kind Canadians to open their homes to me during the expedition. When I went out to my bike I discovered that my bike had fallen over, after the kickstand had buckled from the weight and the wind pushing on it. As I set my bike upright I saw there had been another casualty of the wind and the weight. My rear saddlebags had ripped open. I secured the saddlebags with some electrical tape and headed towards Jim Hundt's house.

I'd first met Jim Hundt on Saturday, an avid cyclist who had come to Point Pelee, to be there for Canada and to ride with me to Leamington. I'd spoken on the phone with Jim before the expedition, after he'd heard on the radio that I was looking for a home to put me up while I was in Chatham. He called my home in Hamilton immediately to offer a pull out bed in his basement. Jim said he hoped I wasn't one of those vegetarian guys because they were having steak for dinner. I told Jim that I was a Steel City meat and potatoes guy. Steak sounded just wonderful after the day I'd had. Jim and his wife, Marian, and their boys were like a family of angels, making me feel at home. After supper, Jim asked if he could work with my bike to try to design a carrier that would take the heavy weight of my backpack off my body. Jim was a manager of an engineering department and this assignment was right up his alley. I told him I was very tired and I wanted to call it an early night, but he was welcome to work on my bike. Who was I to argue with an engineer and an avid cyclist, especially since I was neither. Going to bed early after an exhausting day, I was asleep by 8 o'clock.

Tuesday, March 4, 1997

In the morning I rode to the Anglican Christ Church in Chatham. One of my goals was to visit Anglican churches during the To The Top Canada expedition. If I asked you to name a famous Anglican person who was not an Archbishop, Bishop, minister or a member of the Royal Family, you might be hard pressed to name anyone - especially a famous Anglican Canadian. I wanted to visit Anglican churches across Canada and let local parishioners know that I was an Anglican and proud of it. We need more people to stand tall and publicly let others know that they believe in Jesus Christ. At Christ Church, I met the Rev. Ken Anderson, who kindly gave me $50.00 to help with my expedition. He also called the minister in Thamesville to arrange for my overnight accommodation on Wednesday. Christ Church is a beautiful church founded in 1819. I made an interesting discovery while reading the church's records. At one point in the early history of this Chatham parish, it was part of the diocese of Quebec. I was baptized and confirmed in the diocese of Niagara. This diocese of Niagara, east of Chatham, must have also been formerly part of the diocese of Quebec. This was another important reason that my Canada had to include Quebec. Quebec is an part of my culture and my heritage.

Cycling over to City Hall, I was greeted by a Town Crier in full colonial dress. In front of television cameras, a radio station reporter and a newspaper reporter, the Town Crier opened his scroll, read his proclamation, officially welcomed me to Chatham, and wished me good luck on my mission for Canada. The Mayor presented me with a Chatham sweatshirt and a Chatham golf shirt that were actually in my size - extra large. I gave my To The Top Canada speech and asked the Mayor to pass on my question: "What will you do before the year 2000 to make Canada a better country than when you found it?" He promised me he would introduce my question at their next televised council meeting and would pass it on to all the citizens of Chatham. I posed for pictures in the local paper holding up my Canadian flag proudly. The Mayor then invited me into City Hall and offered me a hot chocolate to warm me up.

Afterward, I headed to a local bike shop to purchase two new saddle bags and a new kickstand to replace the ones that were already casualties of the expedition. The bike shop owner had heard me speaking on the radio and, to help me out, sold the items to me at cost.

At John Uyen Roman Catholic School, I spoke to all of the elementary students in their large library. With younger children I didn't do my full story which detailed recent Canadian political history. I did tell them where the To The Top Canada expedition had started, in Point Pelee, and about my 6520 kilometre route to Tuktoyaktuk, NWT. Then I repeated the question I was asking all Canadians: "What will you do before the year 2000 to make Canada a better country than when you found it?" I inquired whether anyone there had ever done something to make Canada a better country? One boy told how he picked up garbage on the school ground. Commending his effort, I explained that when we make our school better, we make Canada better. Another young girl said her family tries to recycle. I commended their effort and reiterated that when we make the community of Chatham better, we make Canada better as well. I encouraged everyone to talk about my question in their classrooms and to come up with more ideas to make Canada a better country. I told the students it was okay to get excited about Canada. A good reason to get excited was the fact that Canada was chosen by the United Nations as the best country in the world, not just once, but three years in a row! Dividing the audience down the centre, I asked the children on the left side of the room to stand. I asked the children to shout in their loudest voices three times "I am Canadian!" Patriotic shouts filled the school. Next I asked the children on the right side to stand. They had to do the same thing but were competing with the first group and had to be even louder! I counted to three. The noise was deafening. Then I asked everyone to remain standing. Going to the centre of the room, I told everyone that we were on one team and our team was Team Canada! I wanted everyone in the room to shout in their loudest voices, "I AM CANADIAN!" I counted "ONE, TWO, THREE!" The sound was off the scale! I had just granted every student the chance to fulfill the dream of making as much noise as they could in school, and they seized the opportunity. The sheer power of the collective shout even surprised the students. They thought this was awesome. This was the excitement I wanted them to show for Canada, not just today but for the rest of their lives.

Later that day I decided to visit St. Joseph's Hospital in Chatham. Many of the patients were young children. It was late afternoon and I wasn't sure when visiting hours were, but the children I dropped in on really enjoyed my visit. I found most were alone in their rooms, with no one keeping them company. I gave each of the kids paper Canadian flags as a remembrance of my visit. I tried to talk to each child as long as I could. It wasn't my role to discuss religion or God with these children without the consent of the parents, but, out of the blue, one child asked, "If Jesus loves me, why am I in the hospital?" Not wanting to dodge the question, I told the little girl that one of the gifts of God was our freedom to let the future happen. This means good things happen to people and bad things happen to people. Even when something bad is happening, she should know that Jesus loves us with all His heart. When life is tough, one of the things we can do to find comfort is pray to Jesus and ask Him to help us. Not always right away, but in time, I find my prayers are usually answered. The little girl smiled. I think just she needed someone to tell her that Jesus still loved her.

Back at Jim's house, I asked his son Richard what the kids at school had thought of my presentation. He said they thought I was "cool". I took that as an endorsement. Jim's older son Byron was on the family's personal computer surfing the Net. I heard his mother, Marian Hundt, call down from upstairs, "I want you to try to get outdoors!" She was concerned about the time her son was spending in cyberspace with no fresh air or exercise. Her son yelled back, "Okay Mom". Then with a click of his mouse, he went to www.outdoors.com. It seems to me he missed his mother's point.

When Jim came home he was excited. He wanted to take me over to the local bike shop. He'd been doing some research and had found that there was a trailer available that could take all the weight off my back. At the bike shop, I was shown a catalogue for a BOB trailer. BOB stood for Beast of Burden. It was manufactured by a California company, and if I wanted the trailer it could be couriered to me overnight. The owner of the bike shop said he would catch up to me on my To The Top Canada expedition route to install the trailer once it arrived. The cost of the trailer was over $600.00. Using my Interac expedition card, I paid for the trailer. This money was meant for food and lodging but I knew that Jim's recommendation would be a great benefit in the long run.

We came home and had dinner at Jim's house. Afterward, we went over to a relative's house. Jim's nephew Hans was having his birthday party. We arrived in time to share birthday cake and ice cream. I gave Hans a birthday gift - one of my books, *Exceeding Expectations: The Strategy of Personal & Organizational Excellence*.

Jim and his wife talked privately to me about Byron. They were concerned that he didn't have any significant goals and his life seemed to be without focus. I suggested that, with their permission, I could speak to Byron and do some personal potential planning with him. They were pleased and said they'd hoped I would do just that. I sat down with Byron at the kitchen table. On a blank piece of paper I wrote out the six life areas into which I divide personal planning. These include family, adventure, finances, career, health and faith. We spent an hour discussing different life choices. At the end of the process, Byron had a comprehensive plan taking him right into adulthood. We put the plan on the refrigerator so he would see it everyday and stay focused on what to do next. Byron had developed this plan that took him right into adulthood and eventually working in a respectable career area. In one evening, he had gone from no set future to an organized life plan. Jim and his wife were amazed at the progress and were thrilled. Jim remarked that I was like a Canadian Tony Robbins. I told him maybe Tony Robbins was like an American Chris Robertson.

Wednesday, March 5, 1997

Waking at 5:30 am, I didn't want to awaken anybody else in the house, so I quietly read my Bible. The next time I looked at my watch it was just after 7:00 am. I was due at Chatham radio station CKSY-FM with morning man Mitch O'Conner at 7:30 am. I turned into a tornado of action. I packed my gear and ran out to strap everything to my bike. Jim had already left for work and was scheduled to pop over and meet me at the radio station. I said my goodbyes to the family and thanked them for their hospitality. It was windy and there was snow blowing that morning. When I arrived Jim was already at the station. He had never been on a radio show before. At home, his family was taping the show so they could listen to Dad on the radio. I kidded program host, Mitch, that we had a news scoop to announce on his show this morning. Mitch had done an earlier telephone interview with me before the expedition began. This interview was to be a discussion on how the Hundts had first heard of me and decided they wanted to support my effort to help Canada. Jim found the technology of the radio station control room fascinating as he sat down in front of the visitor microphone. On Mitch's show I announced the expedition would soon be going from two wheels to three wheels with the addition of the BOB trailer I had ordered in Chatham. I thanked Mitch and said publicly on the air that if kindness makes you a great Canadian, then Jim and his family deserved a badge of honour. After camping in freezing cold weather and fighting punishing winds enroute to Chatham, I found their home to be a sanctuary for me. We stayed on the show for the next half hour talking about the To The Top Canada expedition, introducing songs and announcing birthdays. After the show I said goodbye to Jim, who had been a guardian angel. A call had come into the radio station from a teacher who asked if I could speak at her school in Thamesville. She was delighted to learn that I could speak at her school the next morning after cycling there today. I cycled over to the Anglican church and attended the communion service which was taken from the Book of Common Prayer. It was the service I grew up with and felt very comfortable with. Still, I prefer the newer Anglican communion service from the Book of Alternative Service, because it is written in the contemporary English of today. If we are going to follow the teachings of Jesus and invite people to join the Christian community, we need a service that the newcomer will feel comfortable with on their first visit to a church. The newer service achieves this goal. An older lady gave me fifteen dollars. I thanked her especially warmly, as I knew she was on a fixed income but wanted to help Canada. After church I had another experience. A big Cadillac pulled up to me on my bike in Chatham and a lady gave me fifty dollars. I stopped to pick up the Chatham News and found that my story had made the front page.

Heading east on Highway #2 out of Chatham, I listened on my Discman to the music soundtracks from the different "Rocky" movies. Soon, I was out in the countryside again. I saw a country store with a small lunch counter, so I decided to pull over. As I walked in the front door, I glanced at the store clerk who looked at me as if she had seen a ghost. I smiled warmly and she still looked shocked. After a pause she said, "You're Chris Robertson!" I sheepishly replied "Yes". She explained that a moment ago she had been talking about me to the regulars in the small restaurant. She wondered what route I would be riding on. She had just wished out loud "I hope he comes this way because I'd like to meet him", when I walked through the door! After my lunch I went to pay my bill. She would not take any money. I thanked her very much and posed while she took pictures of me. Before I left, she gave me a big hug. Her warmth and affection brought tears to my eyes.

I rode into Thamesville. Riding through the small downtown area, I eventually found Jack and Diane Beedle's house. There was no one home so I sat down against a tree in the front yard and rested. After a short time, Jack and Diane drove into their drive-way. Jack had made the decision to become an Anglican Minister when his job was transferred. He made a commitment to go to theology school and get a Bachelor of Arts degree from the university in London. It was a commitment that lasted the next six years of his life with no guarantee of a position when he completed his education. Jack's faith was rewarded and he achieved his goal of entering the Anglican ministry. His easy-going, fatherly approach reminded me of Mr. C, Richie Cunningham's father on the old TV series "Happy Days".

Jack and Diane invited me to attend a community dinner, but because this was the day that UPS would be delivering my new BOB trailer, I stayed back. I read my Good News Bible while waiting for the courier. When it was clear that it was past the hour when my trailer might arrive, I went to bed. Tired, I fell asleep early. Riding in the wet weather had drained me.

Thursday, March 6, 1997

I went for breakfast with Rev. Jack Beedle at a coffee shop downtown. As we drove in Jack's car, he pointed out a small manufacturing plant. At this plant in Thamesville they manufacture the steel wool used in most homes across Canada. During breakfast we talked about the inspirational stories in the book *Chicken Soup for the Soul* . After I hustled to pack my gear as I was due at Thamesville Public

School to address the students. I delivered a rousing program in the school gym that had all the children cheering for Canada! Afterwards, during the morning recess, I was invited into the staff room to enjoy freshly baked hot cinnamon rolls. Sitting at the table, I ate my sticky cinnamon bun and talked about the To The Top Canada expedition and how every Canadian has their own special gift they can use to make Canada better. Personally, I can't write music but I hope there is a Canadian who takes up the challenge of the To The Top Canada expedition to make Canada better by writing the great Canadian song. Americans have so many songs celebrating their country. Canada needs songs like "America The Beautiful" that will give Canadians goosebumps. In Canada we have only our national anthem and our unofficial anthem which is the music track for Hockey Night in Canada. For example, I think the most inspirational Canadian of this century is Terry Fox, but to my knowledge (with the exception of Rod Stewart, who is Scottish) no one has written a song to tell his story of courage and bravery. We have world class recording artists like Celine Dion, Bryan Adams, David Foster, Shania Twain, Alanis Morrisette, Gordon Lightfoot, Neil Young, and Anne Murray but we need the great Canadian song for them to sing. A teacher across the table announced, "I've got the song..." I was surprised.

"What do you mean, you've got the song?"

"I've written a great Canadian song" he replied. The other teachers jumped in and said I should hear this song! This music teacher had written the song which was chosen to be the theme song of Canada's 125th birthday! I had to apologize and say I had never heard the song. He didn't have the money to promote the song and make it famous. That is why I'd never heard of it. The revelation left a bad taste in my mouth.

At the end of recess I said goodbye as I had to leave to ride to the town hall and present a certificate. The teachers asked if I was leaving town right after the presentation. I told them I was. At the town hall where they were expecting me, I presented my certificate to the people of Thamesville. Afterwards I set out on my bike to my next destination, Glencoe. On my way out of Thamesville, all the students and all the teachers had left their classrooms and lined the street to cheer for me as I rode by. I raised my large Canadian flag as high as my right arm would stretch as I passed by the students. I could feel the good wishes of each and every one. I knew I had to go the distance and not let them down.

As I pedaled to Glencoe, I pondered why a great Canadian song written by the Thamesville Public School music teacher did not become a part of our popular Canadian heritage. Was this the fault of Canada's music industry or Canada's radio industry or Canadians themselves for not asking for songs that show pride in Canada? Some way, some how, I would try to tackle this problem when the To The Top Canada expedition was over.

I was treated to a very late lunch donated by a local diner just on the west side of Glencoe. Arriving in Glencoe, I met the Rev. Billy Graham. This Billy Graham was the Anglican minister in Glencoe. He had a Canadian Flag tattooed onto his arm. Bill was excited that I was coming and had arranged for me to speak to three groups that evening including the After School Youth Group, the Rotary Club and the Venturers troop. I enjoyed a roast beef dinner cooked by Mrs. Graham. Later in the evening my BOB trailer arrived and we hooked it up to my bike. I'd never seen anything like it before but in a moment I knew that it would be a Godsend. There was a single tire for the trailer which actually locked onto my rear bicycle axle. With the weight off my back, I would be able to ride much faster. We put the bike in the church basement safely for the night. A retired minister, the Rev. George Hamilton, was going to let me spend the night as he had a spare bed. His wife was named Margaret. They had spent time living up in Canada's Arctic where they'd lived for some time. Margaret indicated she knew the Dempster Highway well, and told me if I took the Dempster Highway I wouldn't survive. I'd never been in the Arctic. The strong conviction of Margaret's warning scared me. I took a long time to fall asleep.

Friday, March 7, 1997

I was up early, anxious to try out my new BOB trailer. My morning began with a University of Toronto radio interview over the phone for a program called "Caffeine Free". I rode down to the Glencoe school where Bill had set up another assembly for me. I walked my whole bike, now with three wheels, into the school for all the children to see. After the presentation I rode to the local Presbyterian church for the 6th World Day of Prayer service. All the community churches were represented. Their focus was to pray that the starvation that was expected to unfold very soon in North Korea be prevented. I cycled out of Glencoe after the service enjoying the first day of blue sky on the expedition. The batteries in my CD player had died after 2 1/2 days of use. I rode to the small community of Mount Brydges. Here, the Kozy Corner restaurant donated a late lunch. Pete and Shelley Aarssen, who were London Life acquaintances of the Hundts, in Chatham had offered to act as my hosts on the Sunday night. They would keep my bike's new BOB trailer and all my equipment in their garage. The first week of the expedition was now over and I had ridden a bicycle farther than ever before, which made me proud. Despite this incredible achievement I knew that it was only a drop in the bucket compared to the distance and challenges that lay ahead. To lessen the pain of separation on my family, I planned to spend weekends with them while I was still in Southern Ontario. This was my first weekend. While waiting for my wife Carol and son James to drive to Mount Brydges, I was treated to a delicious supper of pizza and salad by Pete and Shelley. They are a wonderful family in a warm Christian home. When Carol arrived, I thanked them and headed home for a weekend with my family. It had only been one week away but I missed them terribly. Missing my family would be one of the toughest challenges of the To The Top Canada expedition!

Monday, March 10, 1997

I had arrived in Mount Brydges ahead of schedule which was good news. The

Southern Ontario leg of the *To The Top Canada* expedition would take me through population centres that totalled over 3 million people. At every City Hall, presentations and media conferences were scheduled. Having a Mayor take time out of his or her busy day to greet me only to find themselves in front of the media not knowing why the unity cyclist was late would be a disaster for the *To The Top Canada* expedition. To quote the famous line from the movie "Apollo 13", "Failure Was Not An Option!" In my planning, I knew I could never be late. This meant being on time even if Ontario had a late March snowstorm. I had contingency time built into my schedule in for just such an event. Mount Brydges was a few kilometres from London, so I treated myself to a three day weekend with my family.

Late Monday afternoon I returned to Mount Brydges to stay overnight there, ready for my next day's ride into London. Carol dropped me off after work at the Aarssen home and then drove back to Hamilton that evening, with James and our family dog Smooch keeping her company. My host Pete worked at the Head Office of the London Life insurance company. He gave me a London Life pin to wear. Their logo was a Maple Leaf and they were proud to be a Canadian company. Just after nine o'clock there was a telephone call and they told me it was Carol. My heart jumped into my throat thinking there might have been a car accident. Thankfully, this was not the case. Carol and James were at home watching the CBC television hit comedy show: "This Hour Has 22 Minutes". Rick Mercer had featured me on his satirical "newscast". I was treated with the same respect usually reserved for Prime Minister Jean Chretien, President Bill Clinton, Queen Elizabeth and Mother Teresa. I took the news in a positive light because it meant the *To The Top Canada* expedition now had a truly national profile. It meant the nation was watching Chris Robertson. Once again, I felt the weight that was now on my shoulders - I had to go the distance for Canada.

Tuesday, March 11, 1997

I was up early so I quickly made up the pull-out couch I had been sleeping on and used the remaining time to read my Bible. With permission to use the family computer, I typed a letter to the CBC program "This Hour Has 22 Minutes". My letter was short and tongue in cheek:

Dear Friends At This Hour Has 22 Minutes,

What made you think I am cycling 6520 kilometres from Point Pelee to Tuktoyaktuk for "Canadian Unity"? I'm trying to escape Revenue Canada!

Yours sincerely,

Chris Robertson
To The Top Canada expedition
(Pedaling through London with 190 kilometres down and 6330 to go!)

P.S. I love your show and my bike has 21 speeds.

This morning my official responsibility was to speak to children attending the home school at the Aarssen house. In the large recreation room I spoke to what seemed like all the kids in the world. The line from the Mother Hubbard poem went through my head:

"She had so many children, she didn't know what to do."

After my speech Shelley thanked me, saying it was an honour to have me in their home. We went upstairs and I finished packing up my bike. It was time to head out. All the children were on their bikes and ready to follow me as I flew the Canadian flag proudly. They circled me and I had to try hard not to hit any of them. I had taken my son to see the movie Independence Day where aliens attack the Earth. The countless children's bicycles were like the swarms of alien spacecrafts that blackened the skies in the movie. I crawled in my slowest gear. I felt like a bull in a china shop. The armada of children's bicycles followed me to the town's limits.

For the second time on the journey, it was a very windy day. Only today was different, the wind was at my back. I came upon my first gulley and with all my weight, I quickly accelerated. With my trailer in tow, I could feel I was being pushed down the hill. It felt like sitting in the front car of a roller coaster. You start going over the first dip but you don't feel the push until the majority of weight is going downhill and then you feel you've been shot out of a sling shot. I was going so fast down the hill, a vibration was building from the trailer right through the entire bike. The bike shook violently. I hit the brakes as fast as possible but it took all the strength in my hands and arms to stop my bike, my trailer, my gear and myself as I accelerated downhill. My heart was racing. Just as my heart calmed down, a funeral procession passed by going west. I took it as a message that I had to be more careful.

I arrived in London early that afternoon. Would I be able to find a hotel that would be willing to donate a room for the night? My first stop was the Delta Hotel. I politely asked if they could donate a room in support of my Canadian Unity mission. They couldn't because they were "almost" full. Given a choice between maximizing profit and showing pride in your country, they chose profit. I approached three other hotels with no luck. I remembered the story of American Billionaire Ross Perot who started his own company. He had to make over 70 sales calls before he made his very first sale. If he'd given up at 69, Ross Perot would not be the billionaire he is today. He didn't give up and neither would I. At my fifth hotel, the Best Western on Wellington Road, they said "yes" - they would donate a room for two nights. The Business Depot on Wellington Road donated the use of their fax machine to send my letter to CBC Halifax where the program This Hour Has 22 Minutes is produced. I called home and left Carol a message that I had a place to stay and I would be going to sleep early. In my room, I stowed my gear away and then fell into a deep sleep.

A loud knock at the door awakened me. The door opened. I jumped up. It was a bell boy. I had to call my wife right away. I called immediately. Carol got my message and had called my room but there was no answer. She was worried I'd had a heart attack and she called the hotel to have them check on me. The truth was, I was so tired I'd just slept through, not hearing the phone!. After reassuring Carol I was fine, I went back to sleep to ready myself for a busy day tomorrow - my "official arrival" in London.

Wednesday, March 12, 1997

It was a beautiful day and I had my Canadian Flag flying high as I cycled along. I had some time to kill before my mid morning arrival at London City Hall so I rode through all the streets of downtown London. Cars and busses were honking at me and giving me the thumbs up. Checking my watch, I noticed I was due to arrive at City Hall in five minutes. As I looked at my watch, my right hand steadying my bicycle handle bars, the flag pole in my left hand shifted position. The result was my Canadian flag got pulled into my rear wheel and jammed in my spokes, chain and wheel. My bike came to a sudden stop. Heart pounding, I had to race against the clock to reclaim my flag from the wheel and then travel the two kilometres to City Hall. Arriving just in time, close inspection would reveal I had a touch of bicycle grease on my Canadian flag. Following my official presentation, I was interviewed by television, radio and newspaper reporters. The television reporter and I both laughed when we shook hands because we had identical cycling mittens that were even the same colour, both of us attempting to contend with the cold weather. We were kindred spirits.

After the full presentation, I cycled over to St Paul's Anglican Cathedral where I was given the royal tour. They even took me up almost vertical steps into the bell tower. I was shown how hymns are played on the bells that can be heard throughout the City of London. Asked if I would like to play the bells, I accepted the offer. There was only one hymn to which I knew all the notes - this was a prerequisite to play the bells. That song was "Kumbaya". I played and listened to the giant bells chiming out all over the city. At the end of my song one bell player said to the other: "Do we put him on the wall?", to which the other bell player replied: "Yeah, I think we should!" They showed me the wall in the Bell Tower. Ever since St Paul's Cathedral was built back in the 1800's, everyone who played the bells in the Cathedral has signed a brick in the Bell Tower to be immortalized forever. I was given a pencil in order to sign a brick on the Bell Tower wall. It was an honour to be included with those who had served St Paul's by their personal ministry playing the bells. I stayed for the afternoon service and the kind Rector Bruce Howe invited me to a reception afterward.

My next stop was London Life headquarters where I was being interviewed for a newsletter article. So far on my journey, I had stayed in the home of two London Life employees. I noticed that the security in the building was incredible. What was so important that they needed this level of security. They must have a shipment of Wayne Gretzky hockey cards inside. Although I already had one, they gave me another Maple Leaf company pin to wear on my expedition jacket.

On receiving my BOB trailer, I had attached a fluorescent safety flag to it for greater visibility. The wind had blown the flag so hard it had snapped and been left behind on some country road. At the local Cyclepath store I bought a new one and installed it on my trailer. On my way back to the Best Western, I stopped into McDonald's who donated my supper. That evening I was visited by Jim Hundt and his family from Chatham. It was a day off and they decided to go shopping in London. Jim really wanted to see my new BOB trailer. I let him go for a spin on my bike pulling the trailer. Before leaving, Jim thanked me again for the planning session I'd done with his son. It had been my pleasure to help a family that had made me feel so welcome. I went to bed, as another busy day awaited me tomorrow.

Thursday, March 13, 1997

This morning I had scheduled a cable television interview on Roger's Cable London community access station. The studio was conveniently located on the east side of town, right on my way out of town. I cycled over to the studio where I was able to bring my bike, trailer and gear right inside for the interview. It was difficult to navigate my equipment down the narrow halls. One technician tried to help by grabbing the back of my trailer to help it swing around a corner. His face grimaced when he felt the weight of the trailer. In the studio we set up the bike and trailer just behind the two chairs set out for me and the interviewer. The interview was in two segments with a small break for a video public service announcement. During the break a young woman, another studio technician, came over to my bike and adjusted the handlebars so that the front wheel was at a better angle for the camera shot. Just before the end of the break she made the final adjustment which destabilized the balance. The bike and over 250 pounds of weight shifted forward, pinning the studio technician down just as we came back on the air. Forgetting about the interview, I jumped out of my seat and lifted the bike to free the studio technician. The cameras were filming so I just looked at them and said "Kids, don't try this at home!" That got a belly laugh from everyone in the studio, giving me time to steady the bike and sit down to finish the interview.

Afterwards I thanked everyone and headed out. I wanted to reach Ingersoll quickly because the weather forecast was predicting that a bad snow storm would hit south-western Ontario later in the day. A city bus passed me and honked as it went by. I thought it was a warning but then the bus raced by me, pulled to the right and came to a sudden stop. The bus driver jumped out and ran back to me. He declared: "I just wanted to shake your hand and tell you what you are doing is great". I appreciated this strong show of support. I could see there was a bus full of people and I hoped none of them were in a hurry. After our conversation, the bus driver ran back to his city bus and sped off.

I continued cycling towards Highway 2 where I later stopped at a roadside diner to warm up, and ordered a hot roast beef sandwich. The waitress read my To The Top Canada shirt and asked what I was doing. After hearing my explanation, she remarked that this was incredible and that it should be on television! I told her television coverage had been good but I hoped there would be some more. With my marketing background, I knew that some people had to see a message as many as three times on television before it would register in their memory. That is why media buyers tried to get at least 300 GRP's (Gross Rating Points are the units of which television reach is measured) in their television media buys. I knew that the challenge of securing sufficient media coverage was almost as awesome as cycling to the top of mainland Canada! I pray that when Jesus returns for the second coming that God gives Him a good publicist so people know He is here.

At the Thamesford Mac's Milk, the lady in the store told me it would be mostly downhill to Ingersoll. In a car you don't notice the hills and inclines that your car effortlessly glides over, but on a bicycle hills can mean the difference between a good day or a bad day. It was mostly uphill to Ingersoll! Along the way I stopped at a little Town Office out in the country for the community of Zarr. I was happy to warm up in the building and rest for a few moments. The staff gave me a community pin and wished me good luck.

In Ingersoll, I rode to St. James Church which is a deceptively huge building. On the outside it doesn't look that large but on the inside it is massive. I met the Rev. Bill Welch. He was a kind minister who helped me by locking my bike and gear in the church for the weekend and then offering to put me up overnight on Sunday evening. It was now the end of the week and Carol was on her way to pick me up. I was looking forward to the three day weekend with my family. Just as my wife pulled up, I could see the storm that was predicted was starting. Snow flurries were blowing horizontally but I didn't care because I knew the car was warm and tonight I would sleep in my own bed.

Monday, March 17, 1997

Reading my Bible each day, I had worked my way up to the Book of Exodus. The challenges I was going to face in the coming week were small compared to the challenges of the people of Israel. In the rectory of St. James Church, I put on my green City of Chatham sweatshirt to celebrate St. Patrick's day. This was also my first day with my GPS 4,000 which I had ordered in the mail. GPS stands for Global Positioning System. It looks like a television remote control and can receive signals from U.S. military satellites that would tell me my exact location on the planet. After paying the U.S. Exchange, it cost about $600.00 Canadian. It was another of those purchases that I thought was important because, especially in the Arctic, my life might depend on knowing exactly where I was and that I was heading in the correct direction to reach help. An early morning reading in Ingersoll indicated it was exactly 81 kilometres as the crow flies to my house in Hamilton.

I thanked Rev. Bill for his hospitality and then headed off to the Ingersoll Town Hall where I did my presentation and an interview with the local newspaper. I did two more presentations - one at Victory Memorial School and one at Princess Elizabeth School. In the Princess Elizabeth school lobby, a couple of things caught my attention. First was a framed page of the Ministry of Education's Essential Outcomes. I was proud to see that one of the essential outcomes was that students "Practice Responsible Citizenship". I was puzzled by the second item, a carved wooden plaque depicting a young boy about age seven holding a long rifle, a man standing behind him with his arm on the boy's shoulder, a look of pride on the man's face. It seemed out of place with my vision of Canada. One of the reasons we have a lower violent crime rate in Canada is that we don't share the United States belief in the right to bear arms. Less access to guns means fewer deaths, when emotions like anger and fear rear their ugly heads. Now I'm sure in some parts of Canada there are "dangerous areas" with bears and other animals that may require a gun for self defence. I knew I would be riding through the heart of some of these dangerous areas, but I had no plans to carry a gun. One thing I did know was there was no bear problem in south western Ontario.

My lunch was kindly provided by McDonald's of Ingersoll. That afternoon, I rode to Woodstock. Enroute, as I cycled I passed through the community of Beachville - the Lime Capital of Canada. A deep quarry trench ran parallel to the side of the road for several kilometres.

There was a sign in Beachville that caught my attention. "Home of the first recorded baseball game in 1838". The first recorded baseball game was played in Canada! If the people in the United States knew about this it would drive them nuts. Mother, apple pie and baseball are institutions of pride in the United States. If Canadians were really the first to play this incredible game, why is this fact not known by every citizen? I wondered, if one day, Canadians would remember Chris Robertson was the first person to travel from the very bottom of mainland Canada to the top under his own power or would the memory of Chris Robertson remain obscure like Beachville, Ontario with no national tributes or celebrations. It is not that I wanted fame or acknowledgement but I knew in my heart that if Canada is to survive as a nation we have to develop a spirit of pride where we celebrate everything Canadian. Let's pay tribute to every great Canadian, glorious Canadian deeds and Canadian trail blazers, whatever their accomplishments! We need to put humility for our nation in the backseat. We need to shout for joy, celebrating Canada at every turn in life. We need pride that will allow us to steer our ship of Canada safely through the toughest crises of nationhood. I want to live in a country where Canadians get goose-bumps every time they see the Maple Leaf!

I cycled on to Woodstock, where I went into a large Bingo Hall and used a pay phone to call the home of Mike and Virginia Goneau. They had offered to accommodate me for two nights. This was London Life watching out for me again, as Virginia worked in the local Woodstock office. I cycled to their address just north of town and was able to leave my bike in the garage for the night.

Tuesday, March 18, 1997

My presentation at City Hall in Woodstock wasn't scheduled until Wednesday morning. This was an easy day for me. The weather had been on my side all week with sunny skies but as was my habit, I had allowed extra time for poor weather conditions so I would never be behind schedule. Mike had the day off from his job. As a police officer, he was fascinated with my journey and asked me about my route. He was very knowledgeable about the highways across Canada. I found out why. On his holidays Mike would supplement his income by delivering school busses that were manufactured nearby to communities across North America. It might be fun to drive a school bus to some community far away - once - but the novelty would soon wear off and I wouldn't want to do this every vacation. I came to the conclusion that we need to pay our police officers more so they can enjoy their vacations. Mike had more experience than I, with highway flares (considering I had never even lit one before). I was carrying three flares with me to use in the event of an emergency. I wanted to get some practice so I would know what I was doing, in advance, rather than trying to read the instructions somewhere up north with no light at midnight. Mike offered to show me how they worked and as I pulled out my flares he told me to save them and pulled out a couple of his own. He showed me how they worked and let me try one myself. I timed one with my watch and they really do burn for 20 minutes. I appreciated Mike's help because I knew this would be an important skill to have under my belt. After our modest fireworks display I decided to head into town.

I visited the local school and thought I'd pop by the local Anglican Church. In this small community there was an old St. Paul's Anglican Church and a new St. Paul's Anglican Church, both active. Now I thought that either there was a dramatic story of political disagreement in this Anglican community or we had a shortage of saints' names to choose from. At the new St. Paul's Church, there was a meeting of area Anglican clergy. My host from Ingersoll, Rev. Bill Welch, was present. The group of ministers said a prayer for me, taken from the Anglican Book of Alternative Services.

God whose glory fills the whole creation, and whose presence we find wherever we go, preserve those who travel in particular your servant Chris; surround them with your loving care; protect them from every danger; and bring them in safety to their journey's end; through Jesus Christ our Lord.

I appreciated the prayers of the ministers. My life was in God's hands, everyday. Only God's grace would keep me safe. I felt a comfort from sharing prayers with my brothers and sisters in Christ.

Swiss Chalet treated me to a delicious lunch. They couldn't do enough for me. They even insisted I have hot soup along with my chicken dinner, followed by pecan pie and ice cream for dessert! I appreciated their kindness. Most of all I appreciated that they were there standing tall and proud without hesitation, when there was an opportunity to use their resources to help Canada.

After visiting different groups in town, I cycled back to the home of Mike and Virginia Goneau. I spoke about my family and how my son James had become a tornado fan after seeing the movie "Twister". Mike pulled out a photograph of a twister he had taken. It looked to be a closeup. I remember being very impressed and

I asked Mike where he was when he took this picture. I thought perhaps Mike had come across this twister when he was on one of his long driving trips delivering a school bus to a community. You can imagine my surprise when he told he me "the front lawn..." Shocked I exclaimed: "THE FRONT LAWN! Weren't you scared having a twister this close to your house?" Mike told me he once had a twister level his house. He flipped to some pages in his photo album and I could see a big beautiful country home landscaped with flowers. The picture beside it showed the same house totally flattened. Splintered wood and debris was strewn everywhere on the ground. It looked like someone had taken a bulldozer to Mike's house. He explained that this area of Southwestern Ontario was Canada's Tornado Alley. I kidded Mike and told him: "I'm glad I'm leaving tomorrow!"

Mike, Virginia and I enjoyed a wonderful steak supper. During the meal, Virginia's son, Robin, from her first marriage, arrived home from his factory job. I asked him how his day was, and his answer caught me off guard. "I hate my job and hate my life", he replied with remorse and then headed downstairs to wash up. Virginia's expression told me she was concerned. These words of despair were like a red flag waving in front of me. Virginia's son needed help. I explained to Virginia that I was really one of Canada's top personal potential trainers and with her permission I would talk to her son tonight. She immediately said "Yes!"

Later, that evening, I sat down with Robin. I reminded him of his comments when he came through the door. I questioned why he had said this. One of my professional speaking colleagues, Dr. Linda Abbott, has an expression I believe in. Dr Abbott says: "People can't be helped, until they're heard..." I patiently listened as he told me how he felt he had a dead end job that he didn't enjoy and how his life was in a rut. After he completely finished I asked him this question: "If I could wave a magic wand and give you one billion dollars, so money would never be a problem, what would you do with your life?" He'd never been asked this question before... After a pause, he said he would buy a motorcycle and go on a long trip. I reminded him of his wealth, and told him he could go on his trip in an executive Learjet if he wanted to. Did he still want to go on a motorcycle? The answer was yes. I then changed the scenario and told him the only money he had was what was in his bank account right now. He had just come from a second doctor, who had confirmed a prognosis giving him only six months to live. What was the one thing he wants to do in his last six months. The answer was the same - buy a motorcycle and go on a long trip. This confirmation question told me that riding motorcycles was what his heart was telling him to do. In my interactive Personal Excellence seminar, I interview the audience. Many people tell me they want to build their dream home or start their own corporation. Next I ask the second question that totally removes the power of money and increases the pressure of time. I usually find that people change their answers and instead of wanting material things, they become relationship oriented and want to be closer to the people they love or closer to God. I challenge people to discover their true life's calling, what they would do, regardless of which of these soul searching questions are being asked. When I encounter the rare person who answers these questions identically, I know there is a focus or passion in their heart.

Robin loved motorcycles. I encouraged him to go to Canada's major motorcycle tradeshow and make a list of the companies he would like to work for in his perfect life. Contact the President and offer to buy him breakfast, lunch or dinner, and just say you respect him as a senior executive in Canada's motorcycle industry and would like to use the meal as an opportunity to benefit from his wisdom and ask his advice. Most executives have big egos and can't refuse an offer like this from a "fan". I explained to Robin that he needed to ask what training and education he would need to be a preferred candidate for employment in the industry and be hired by their company. Many times I've seen an executive offer an enthusiastic advice seeker a job right on the spot. I also explained to Robin that the interpersonal skills used in a meeting are "real" and he would have to practice them to come across as a confident, effective communicator. I told him to expect that his first meeting with an executive might be a "disaster", because of mistakes he would make, but to use the meeting as a learning experience. Identify each mistake and develop better answers to the questions he was not expecting. Now he would be ready to approach an executive with another motorcycle firm and put his best foot forward. The eyes of Virginia's son sparkled as he could now see a strategy that would make his dream come true. My job was done.

Wednesday, March 19, 1997

While Mike and Virginia made my breakfast, I kidded them that they must have cornered the bacon futures market. I like bacon and they gave me a mountain of it. I was off early as I had to cycle to the "Home of the Huskies", Huron Park High School. The Principal had invited me to do the morning announcements and tell my story over the Public Address System. Seizing the moment, I gave a fiery speech for Canada in place of the usual monotonous announcements. Next, I had to head to City Hall right away but teachers and students came out of classrooms to get a glimpse of this wild, passionate Canadian who had just spoken to them about loving their country. At City Hall I learned that the Mayor had declared today "Chris Robertson Day" in Woodstock! This special honour was truly appreciated. After meeting with the media, I had to visit radio station K104 FM for a scheduled interview. The Assistant Mayor walked to the middle of the main street stopping traffic both ways so my bicycle could cross to proceed to the radio station. I told him I didn't realize Assistant Mayors had this power under the Highway Traffic Act... A group of cyclists joined me in support of my Canadian Unity effort. After the radio interview our posse of cyclists including Mike, Kris, Jeff, Clayton, Benny and Chris started on the 30 kilometre journey to Paris. As we drove along the country road, I led the convoy of cyclists pulling my BOB trailer with all my gear. At one point, a mean, angry dog came running at the pace of a cruise missile from behind a barn, and I was the target. The dog barked as he ran and by the tone of the bark, it seemed as if he was saying: "I"m going to rip your leg off, I'm so mad!" Even though I pedaled faster, the dog was gaining on me. When he was about fifteen feet from me, the other mountain bikes behind me broke formation, flew over the ditch and put themselves between me and my pursuer. Immediately, the dog backed down and returned to the barn. Canadians working together had overcome adversity, saving my hide. Once we arrived in Paris, the cyclists gave me high fives and then turned back towards home to complete what would be a 60 kilometre round trip for them.

I went to the little motel in Paris. Asking if they would provide a room for me, the owner indicated he would reduce the price from $25 to $20 for me. I took it. After stowing my heavy gear in my small motel room, I visited the Paris News and did a lengthy interview. Then I called on the patients at the Paris Hospital. Many of them knew me already from television. Late in the afternoon, I cycled back to my motel as it was getting dark. I fell asleep quickly.

Thursday, March 20, 1997

It was the first day of spring but I woke to be greeted by several centimetres of snow. The Mayor of Paris didn't seem very excited that I was coming to town and asked me to hand in my *To The Top Canada* certificate at the office. Now normally this would bother me because Canadians were passing up a chance to celebrate Canada, but in this case it was a blessing in disguise. Today was my wife's birthday. I was very aware of the sacrifice she was making for Canada as I would be away from home for almost an entire year. This being the case, I wanted to make her birthday special. A tall order this year, because I had a track record of making her past birthdays special. We have a tradition in our family where I take Carol on a weekend to a special place she has never been in her life before. These weekends are usually planned with military precision. I wanted this year to be special, as well. Standing in the snow, I smiled because of my plan. Before the day was done, I would whisk Carol off to Dallas, Texas... Air Canada had just started flying to Dallas and they had these incredibly low introductory fares that I'm sure were well below their cost. My plan was to spend tonight, Friday and Saturday in Dallas before flying home Sunday evening. On Monday morning I would continue the *To The Top Canada* expedition. I didn't know what the public would think if they knew the Canadian Unity Guy was in Dallas, Texas - outside of Canada, and so it wasn't something I advertised. In my mind I toyed with the idea of sending the producers of "This Hour Has 22 Minutes" a postcard from Dallas saying I'd made a wrong turn, but ruled it out thinking loose lips sink ships. I did feel guilty, but this weekend wasn't for Canada, it was for Carol and I knew this hiatus to the sun after a long winter would be a fun-filled blessing.

I had to cycle to the outskirts of Brantford so that I would be close by for my scheduled arrival on Monday morning. After handing in my certificate at the Town Office, with no fanfare, I said goodbye to Paris. Cycling along Highway 2 in the snow, I passed the Conklin Operations Yard. This is the company that runs the carnival rides, booths that sell cotton candy and games of chance at most festivals in Ontario. It was interesting to see the trailers for the different rides parked in the snow waiting for the warm summer when they would bring smiles to the faces of boys and girls. I arrived at the meeting point at the parking lot of a large Carpet Store where the 403 highway intersects Highway 2. Carol was enroute, driving from Hamilton to Brantford to pick me up. I used the time to untie my gear which was strapped to my bike and disconnect my trailer from my bike. When Carol arrived, my supplies would be ready to throw in the trunk to allow me to mount the bike on my car rack. I had to take my hands out of my cycling mittens to untie the straps and so they quickly got cold. After waiting a half-hour outside, I popped into the store. They were kind enough to let me warm up. Carol soon arrived and I gave her a big birthday hug and kiss. We quickly packed the gear in the car and were off for Hamilton. There, we picked up James at his school and finally were off for Pearson International Airport. We flew nonstop from Toronto to Dallas. It was 80° in Dallas and we checked into the Hilton Hotel. I had started the day in one of the most humble rooms of my life, but tonight I was going to bed in one of the most luxurious.

Monday, March 24, 1997

Carol's birthday weekend had been a wonderful success. Unfortunately, a late evening Air Canada flight delay combined with a very early morning start afforded me only 4 hours of sleep. Carol dropped me off at the same parking lot on Highway 2 and then she quickly got back on the 403 highway so she could get to work on time. I rode into Brantford and met with Mayor Chris Friel. Mayor Friel was a young, enthusiastic individual who made me feel as if I had been invited into his home. We talked about Brantford and what was happening. One challenge for the Mayor, was a beautiful building that was sitting empty yet costing taxpayers to maintain. The building was built for a communication science centre which never opened after a private sector supporter backed out at the last moment. The building was erected at a cost of $22 million dollars but the City would now sell this state-of-the-art facility for $4 million. Brantford is the home of some famous inventors including Alexander Graham Bell who gave us the telephone, Sir James Hiller who gave us the electron microscope and even the Zamboni family who gave us the Zamboni, an ice cleaning machine which was an institution along with our Canadian game of hockey. Canada has given the world many other famous discoveries including insulin, Imax movie technology and the Canadarm on the space shuttle. I wondered why there couldn't be a Canadian Innovation Centre in Brantford. Canadians need to develop enthusiasm for everything Canadian. We need Canadian corporations that will step forward and embrace institutions that celebrate Canada! Why did a large Canadian company back down and leave Brantford hanging in the lurch? Why wasn't there a line of Canadian companies waiting to step in and be the key sponsor of a Canadian discovery centre? Children in Canada should grow up learning about Canadian discoveries so they develop a strong sense of national pride. Do our children feel this is just a place where they live, or is Canada a country they are proud to call home!!!

After doing several media interviews, I was off to the Mayor's alma mater, St. John's College, to address the student body. Following my talk, they presented me with a St. John's College "Eagles" sweatshirt.

In the middle of the afternoon I grabbed a bite at Fast Eddies which is a Brantford based drive-thru fast food chain. Continuing my journey on Highway 2, the busiest highway I had cycled on yet, traffic was whizzing by me. Truck drivers were great and gave me a wide berth but the school busses went shooting by, just missing me by inches. Late in the day, I rode to Duff's Corners on the outskirts of Ancaster. Carol came by to pick me up. I had cycled just under 300 kilometres so far in the *To The Top Canada* expedition. Fortunately for Carol and myself, I was about twenty minutes away from home by car. I looked forward to a long good night's sleep in my own bed tonight.

Tuesday, March 25, 1997

Starting at Duff's Corners, I faced a day of solid rain. I had my full rain suit on which is a bright lime green. Looking like the Jolly Green Giant on a bicycle, I rode into Ancaster, a beautiful small town with many tall trees. When I was a baby my family lived in Ancaster on Fiddler's Green Road. My only memory of Ancaster is a story about my older sister Cathy who had been invited for supper at a friend's house across the street. It was a nice sit-down dinner. Cathy, who was only six, had been told to be on her best behavior. Mrs. Ritchie asked Cathy how she was enjoying her pork chop. Her reply was one that would haunt her the rest of her life. "It's wonderful! It's just the way I like it - tough..."

Ancaster is a bicycle friendly community. It has designated "Bike Lanes". These are paved lanes at the side of the road just for bicycles. Large painted bicycle logos over the word "ONLY" on the road every hundred metres make it clear to motorists that the far right lane is only for cyclists. This was my kind of community.

I stopped at St. John's Anglican Church in Ancaster. As this is the church I had been baptized in, it was a special moment for me. The church was so close to my home, yet my life had been too busy to experience this return visit to my baptism church until now. In my heart, I knew this was not right. In the church office I spoke with Sherry, the church secretary. She told me her niece was a skipping enthusiast who was a member of the Hamilton Hoppers, an all star skipping demonstration team. Sherry shared the story about the Hamilton Hoppers when they made a trip to Quebec. The Hamilton Hoppers could speak only English and the young children in Quebec spoke only French. Despite the fact that they didn't speak the same language, the Hamilton Hoppers taught the Quebec children how to skip. They became friends and a special bond developed. When these children in Quebec grow up, hopefully they will remember these English Canadians as their friends and not as enemies as the separatists would like to have them believe. I learned we need more initiatives that promote interaction, understanding and trust to be a truly united Canada...

After my visit to St. John's Church, it was time to visit Town Hall. There I met Mayor Bob Wade, the nicest Mayor in Canada. Mayor Wade had all the town staff at my reception to hear me speak. There was a large selection of donuts which I enjoyed, as well! After my speech, I was interviewed by the media and I posed for photos on the front steps. Bob took me for lunch as his guest at the Ancaster Old Mill Restaurant, a converted mill overlooking a stream in a pretty ravine setting. The prime rib was delicious. Afterwards, Mayor Wade personally chauffeured me to two speaking engagements where I was the Keynote Speaker. The first was Redeemer College, a post secondary Christian College, and the second was Ancaster High School. Mayor Wade later returned me to my bicycle which was locked up safely at Town Hall. I dove into my gear and handed him a Friend of Canada certificate to show my appreciation for spending the day with me, and for really going above and beyond the call of duty. Thanking him for his kindness and for being such a proud Canadian, I then cycled to my house on the west Hamilton mountain. What a treat, to be so close!

Wednesday, March 26, 1997

I packed my bike up at my house and rode on Mohawk Road back to Ancaster where I'd left off. It was fun to ride down the Niagara escarpment on the Ancaster Hill. With a designated Bike Lane, I glided comfortably down the "mountain". It's not really a mountain but that is what everyone in the area calls it. Then it was out to Dundas for a presentation to Mayor Addison, with cable TV recording our exchange. Afterwards I did an interview at the local Dundas paper. My afternoon was free, so I went in to visit the children at McMaster Children's Hospital. One boy named Nathan was the same age as my son James. I told him about my bike and how it had a one wheel trailer. Nathan wanted to see my bike. I promised I would bring it out so he could see it from his hospital room window. I pulled my bike out onto Main Street facing the university hospital. There were so many windows on the side of the building I wasn't sure which one was his. I jumped up and down and waved my arms. Then I noticed Nathan in his room waving his arms to answer me. I knew I had made his day and Nathan had made mine.

Thursday, March 27, 1997

Hamilton is not just the community I live in, it is also the city where I was born on July 25, 1955 in the Henderson Hospital. I was proud the *To The Top Canada* expedition would go through Hamilton. Today was a professional development day for the teachers so my son James had time off school. We left the house early and cycled down the mountain, stopping for breakfast. James and I laughed because we were thirsty and we bought and consumed so many orange juices that the cups covered the table.

We were off to Radio Station CHML where we did an interview in the parking lot. Here we were joined by cyclists including the Race Canada cycling team. The Race Canada Team is a group of cyclists that race across Canada, sometimes going east, sometimes going west, to show their pride in Canada. They had no desire to ever go north as their tour bikes were no match for the terrain which my mountain bike would eventually face. Together, we cycled downtown to City Hall. I don't know whether it was the presence of the Race Canada team, but with the wind at our backs and a sunny warm day, we quickly arrived. An army of children from St. Joseph's School, waving Canadian flags, cheered as we walked through their receiving line. I tried to give each person a high five as I entered City Hall. Mayor Bob Morrow invited the media, the cyclists, the children, the adults and myself to a room where they had a reception planned. As James and I entered the room, our eyes fell upon several large trays of orange juice. We looked at each other and smiled. Mayor Morrow made an eloquent welcome speech. Then he asked me to sign the city Guest Book. The Guest Book had a large full colour map of Canada and my route fully outlined. It also had my *To The Top Canada* logo. Signing the book, I wrote "God Bless Canada". Mayor Morrow pointed out that many famous people had signed the Guest Book including Prince Charles, who had recently visited the city. The city's Canadian Club made a presentation noting that Hamilton had been home to the first Canadian Club in Canada. The office of Deputy Prime Minister Sheila Copps presented me with Canadian Flag pins to distribute across Canada. Then, the children sang O Canada in both English and French. Now my turn to speak, I did my *To The Top Canada* presentation. I explained the key to answering my question, "What will you do before the year 2000 to make Canada a better country than when you found it?", was to give ourselves permission to get excited about Canada. The reception over, I drew the crowd around my large Canadian flag and had everyone cheer, "I am Canadian!"

After greeting everyone present, James and I headed out, as we had about forty minutes to get to Mohawk College. We cycled to the Jolly Cut access to go up to the top of the mountain but were slowed down by construction. Upon our arrival, we were met by a representative of Mohawk College who had invited me to come and speak. I was escorted to the Mohawk College Pub. The crowd looked like they had been drinking all afternoon. I asked the crowd: "How many here are Canadians?", and only three hands out of two hundred went up. I politely cut my remarks short. Just as we were leaving, ONTV television showed up. Matt Hayes, the friendly weather man, is even nicer in person than on air. We did a long interview, including some riding scenes. We returned to Mohawk College to say goodbye to retiring President, Keith McIntyre, on his last day. James and I rode home and we went to a western-themed restaurant, with our cowboy gear on (from Dallas!) to celebrate my official arrival in Hamilton. Tomorrow was Good Friday and I planned to stay home and spend the Easter weekend with my family.

Monday, March 31, 1997

My destination today was Burlington. My son James was again with me, off school as it was Easter Monday. All weekend, I was as sick as a dog with a nasty cold. This morning, I was on medication so my head didn't explode. I was so plugged up. We rode out of Hamilton, past Dundurn Castle which overlooks the bay. Passing the Crematorium out near the Royal Botanical Gardens where my father's ashes are placed, I said a silent prayer for my Dad and my Mom. I felt the presence of both my parents, as though they were watching over me like guardian angels.

It was Easter Monday. Burlington City Hall was closed but Mayor Walter Mulkewich was there to meet me. As bad as I felt, I knew I would get better. Walter had been recently diagnosed with cancer. A man with cancer coming in to see me on a holiday, Walter epitomized public service. A reporter had us pose for pictures for the Burlington paper.

Afterwards I rode towards the Burlington - Oakville border. I lived in Burlington growing up. Every street brought back memories. I rode by the old Odeon theatre on Lakeshore Boulevard. I remembered going to see my first movie there, Walt Disney's "Snow White". My family reminded me for the rest of my life that I had said to Mom, "I think it's time to go home now", when the evil witch appeared.

Heavy snow flurries were making the last day of March like a lion, as we rode to the city limits of Oakville. We stopped at Burloak drive, at the Pig and Whistle Inn. Right on cue, Carol came to rescue us in the car. Carol works very hard. I felt guilty imposing on her after a busy day but she didn't complain. Carol knew that all too soon I would be gone and she'd be wishing I was home again to impose on her...

Wednesday, April 2, 1997

The sun was shining and it was a glorious day. At the Pig and Whistle Inn, I could see two police officers on bicycles from the Halton Regional Police there to give me a full escort to the Oakville city hall. The Mayor was away on holidays, but she had left instructions to give Chris Robertson the royal treatment. I knew her vacation was well deserved. To me, she seemed like the hardest working mayor. When I was making calls to different Canadian cities before the expedition, she was the only mayor in Canada who answered her own phone. I remembered asking for Mayor Ann Mulvale and she indicated it was her speaking. I was startled because I was used to being screened by an army of receptionists, secretaries, public relation officers and executive assistants. This level of direct access to a major politician made me want to vote for this woman.

I quickly hooked up my trailer and packed my gear for the day. We rode along the lakeshore in one of Canada's most affluent communities. The houses on Lakeshore Road were spectacular. I was rubbernecking to see the incredible gardens, gated entrances and huge living rooms - bigger than my house. It was interesting to cycle by them and wonder, what were the people like who lived in them? These were people who likely never had to worry about money. I wondered if they ever used their resources to make Canada an even better country?

We were making great time. I was leading as the officers rode behind me. Just as we came to the Third Line intersection, the light suddenly turned from green to yellow. My hands squeezed my brakes as hard as they could and my tires skidded to a stop. The officers were caught off guard by how fast my bike stopped. They had to stop their bikes and swerve so they wouldn't run into me. I looked at them and apologized: "Sorry, but there is no way I'm going to ride through a red light with two police officers beside me..." We all laughed!

At one point, we were riding along and came upon an elderly man walking his small dog. Now, at this exact moment his dog was doing his business on the sidewalk. The elderly man was surprised by us. He must have thought the three of us looked like Pooper Scooper Police because he pulled his handkerchief out of his pocket and began cleaning the sidewalk feverishly. We just cycled by and I'm sure the elderly man breathed a sigh of relief.

Being ahead of schedule, we dropped by radio station CHWO and then Oakville Trafalgar Hospital where I visited the patients and nurses. Cycling over the overpass of the Queen Elizabeth Highway, the Oakville City Hall came into view. There were 300 people waiting to greet me with fire trucks sounding their sirens as I came into view. I pulled up to the front of Oakville City Hall. Everyone was singing "O Canada". Flying my Canadian flag, I got off my bike and stood at attention to listen to our national anthem with pride in my heart. When the crowd finished singing, I delivered an enthusiastic speech ending with the cheer "I am Canadian". Invited to step inside city hall and deliver my speech, I cheerfully replied "Of course". I was thinking, "I thought I just delivered my speech"! My mind immediately jumped into action to compose Speech "B". Inside, I was greeted by a giant Canadian flag made out of red and white balloons that covered an entire wall. It was the backdrop for my next presentation.

Before I began, there were official remarks by the city representatives, the Oakville organization Speak Out Canada, and students. Members of the Royal Canadian Legion were present in force, proudly wearing their medals.
I approached the podium to speak.

I spoke from the heart. I told the story of how I experience deja vu when I think of Canada's current situation. It reminds me of the time my Mother was in the emergency ward. I had regrets because I did not push hard enough for treatment to happen faster and my Mother died at the hospital. I miss my Mother, and although everything was being done for her, it was being done too slowly and her life was lost. I didn't want to sit around this time while the future of Canada was on the line. I told the audience that I didn't want to have to say to my grandchildren one day, "We had the very best country in the world and we let it slip away..." I wanted to be able to look in the mirror and know I gave my personal best for Canada. I asked the audience to imagine that they were in the future and they had lost their country of Canada. What would they do or what price would they pay, to get their beloved Canada back. I closed by urging them not to wait for Canada to break up, "to do what you need to do now, to love your country, protect it and keep it strong, not for us, but for generations to come."

The audience gave me a rousing five minute standing ovation. We moved to another room where I was asked to cut a huge Canada flag cake. Children swarmed me, asking me to sign their hand held Canadian flags. I stayed and signed every child's flag. Gobbling down a sandwich and a piece of cake, I stepped into the lobby to answer reporters' questions and do a cable TV interview.

Oakville was the most enthusiastic, proud Canadian community I had encountered so far. It had been a wonderful day. I packed my bike up and finished by riding from North Oakville back down towards the lake to Appleby College where I went to high school. I was scheduled to speak there first thing in the morning. At Appleby, I sat on the steps of the administration building waiting for Carol to pick me up. I spoke with one of the students who was waiting for a ride as well, telling him what I was doing. His reaction was "Wow... It's going to change you, man..."

Thursday, April 3, 1997

Appleby College was my alma mater. I graduated at the top of my class in Grade 12. When I was a student, it was an all boys boarding school. I developed a work ethic at this school because they expected us to work much harder than at university. We dressed in suits, had early morning room inspection, went to chapel every morning, had classes on Saturday, marched as cadets, practiced hours of competitive team sports and completed two hours of supervised homework every night. University was a holiday compared to Appleby. The school had since become co- educational. I'm proud to say that my niece, Joanna Court, was in the first class of girls to enter the school. She would be in the audience of the chapel today, listening to her Uncle Chris speak to the entire school.

Although I had delivered my *To The Top Canada* keynote speech several times, this time felt different. I had been in this chapel hundreds of times as a boy but I had never been at the front before. The students listened to me intently because they knew I had been one of them. I gave them a chance to cheer for Canada and they responded with a roar that echoed to the chapel roof. The sound was so loud it even surprised me! At the end of the service, the physical education master, Don Stewart, came up and kidded me, saying "Chris, I thought you'd be more enthusiastic!"

It was time to cycle down Lakeshore Road towards Toronto. I followed the signs marked "Waterfront Trail". I'd grown up by the shores of Lake Ontario and being by the water made me feel comfortable as I was riding.

In Mississauga, the Waterfront Trail detoured around a giant Petro Canada oil refinery. I was glad to put the fumes behind me. After holding my breath as long as I could while pedaling a bicycle, I soon was on a part of the Lakeshore where I could see the lake again. This was super suburbia. Almost a half million people live in Mississauga and commute into Canada's largest metropolis, Toronto. When I came to the bottom of Highway 10 I had to head north. Tomorrow was my official arrival in Mississauga, but I had to find a place to stay so I thought I'd start my search close to Mississauga City Hall. City Hall was close to Square One which is a Godzilla size mall - one of the top three shopping centres in Canada in terms of size.

Also across from Square One was the Novotel Hotel. I decided to start my search there. I went to the front desk and asked if they would be interested in providing a room for me. They asked me to wait a moment and they would have a person in the Sales Department come out and help me. A polite young gentleman in a dark suit came out to see me. I told him my story and after only a brief pause he indicated they would definitely donate my room this evening. Not only that, but with my permission he would like to contact the other Novotel Hotels in the Toronto area to look after me as I went through Toronto. It took me less than a second to say "yes". The young man went to the front desk and got me my room key. I thanked him very much. This young man and the Novotel Hotel were stepping forward to do everything in their power to help the *To The Top Canada* expedition and Canada with their patriotism. That made me proud!

I started carrying my gear into this attractively appointed hotel - two giant trailer bags, my back pack, my saddle bags, my gear straps and my Canadian flag. At one point, a front desk staff person asked me in a puzzled voice, "Is that a trailer?" I had my BOB trailer hoisted up on my shoulder, carrying it through the lobby full of business people. I said "yes" politely and quickly kept walking towards the elevator, in order to get my trailer up to my room as fast as possible. There was just one last item - my bicycle. I picked it up so my tires would not touch the shining floors and ducked up to my room. When everything was stowed away I said, "Thank you Lord!" My hotel room looked like a storage area, but all my expedition gear was safe and sound. I flopped on the bed to rest after my relay laps bringing everything in. I fell asleep quickly. After several hours, I went downstairs to enjoy the luxury of a hot whirlpool. I thought if this isn't heaven, it's right next door.

Friday, April 4, 1997

Being so near to City Hall, I was not in a rush this morning. At a relaxed pace, I did the relay again, taking everything from my room to the front of the hotel. It took more time to do all the straps up tight and insure all the gear was balanced correctly so I could cycle. Back inside, I shook hands with everyone at the front desk. I leisurely cycled around the block and arrived at City Hall. There was a cement patio the size of a basketball court in front and a small crowd awaiting my arrival. I noticed one of the people in the crowd was the young man from the Novotel Hotels. I asked him to steady my bike, as there was nothing to lean the bike against and the weight was just too heavy to be supported on my kickstand. This strategy ensured he was in all the newspaper pictures and television coverage as my bicycle was the backdrop for the presentations.

There was a television reporter from Rogers Cable who could not pronounce "Tuktoyaktuk". I told her to break it down into the smaller syllables of Tuk-toy-yak-tuk and then just put them together. This didn't work. The reporter, a young aspiring journalist, felt frustrated that she could not pronounce Tuktoyaktuk. She was relieved when I told her she could just call it "Tuk", which is what people in the Arctic most commonly say.

At the end of my presentation and media interviews the Novotel Sales representative informed me that all the other hotels were on board to host me in Toronto.

At lunchtime, I was scheduled to do a community presentation at the library in the City Hall complex. After my presentation, I met Carol at City Hall, ready to spend one of my last weekends at home during the expedition. I had three precious days to savour the company of my family.

Tuesday, April 8, 1997

I had originally planned to spend Monday evening in the Etobicoke Novotel Hotel but it was full. Instead, Carol dropped me off Monday night directly at the Novotel Hotel in Mississauga. I woke up next morning and noticed I had left my wristwatch at home. This was no problem. I pulled my expedition pager out of my gear and decided I would use it to tell the time from the digital display. I was early. It was just before nine o'clock in the morning and my media conference was scheduled for 10:30 AM at Etobicoke City Hall. I estimated it would take me 45 minutes at a comfortable pace to cycle to Etobicoke. With my spare time, I decided to cycle over to Mississauga City Hall. I had been taking GPS readings of my location at each City Hall but I had forgotten to take a reading for Mississauga. It was a beautiful day. I cycled over, pulled out my GPS and turned it on. The GPS immediately went into search mode looking for the satellites to confirm my exact location on the planet. While it was searching, I glanced up at the clock tower of Mississauga City Hall. The time was ten minutes after ten o'clock. This weekend, the clocks had jumped ahead by one hour and my pager time had not been updated! This meant I had only twenty minutes to get to my own media conference in another city!!!

Immediately, I got on my bike heading east on Dundas Street. This was my first media conference in metropolitan Toronto and the media turnout would be heavy. I had learned from playing college football how to push my body past the point of pain. I bit my lower lip and pedaled even faster. At 10:30 AM exactly, I cycled into Etobicoke City Hall. I smiled and bounced off my bike as if I'd only driven around the corner. Inside, I felt ready to drop. Without missing a beat, I launched into my presentation.

Afterwards there were several media interviews. The Etobicoke Guardian newspaper reporter wanted me to lift up my bike and get up on the Council Chamber table. No problem, I thought, it's not like I'm tired or anything... I had to remove my gear from the trailer, disconnect my trailer and then carry my bike inside. I climbed up on the Council Chamber table and we took the picture. The Mayor had to get back to work so I thanked him for his time.

In the pouring rain, I cycled north to the Novotel Hotel directly beside Pearson International Airport. For the rest of the day, I sat in the whirlpool resting every muscle which I had pulled cycling to Etobicoke City Hall.

Wednesday, April 9, 1997

I woke up and put on the Weather Channel. The weatherman reported that the temperature was 30 below zero at Pearson International Airport. I couldn't have been closer, if I had put my tent on the edge of a runway. Listening to the "Apollo 13" movie music soundtrack, I rode downtown. It was sunny and the CN tower looked like a rocket on the launch pad. I cycled through the city core, proudly flying my Canadian flag. Cars, busses and trucks honked their horns in support.

Tucked into the west side of the Eaton's Centre, a huge shopping complex in downtown Toronto, is Holy Trinity Anglican Church. After riding into Toronto and seeing homeless poor, cocaine addicts and the prostitutes in the street, I gave all the cash I had in my wallet, to the collection plate as my offering. Most churches in Canada know they should be involved in outreach activities to make the world a better place, but they struggle to find and decide on an outreach activity which is worthy. I knew this was not the case at Holy Trinity. Outreach was needed on their doorstep.

On Bloor Street, the Second Cup treated me to a hot chocolate. Bicycle couriers were everywhere in the city. They all knew me from an article in *Pedal* magazine. My bicycle trailer, the first of its kind in Toronto, was a hit. I was invited to the "Biker Bar", the Stand By Cafe on Temperance Street. This is where all the cycling couriers go to meet and rap after work. Punk haircuts and earrings seemed to be the common denominator. With new wave music blaring in the background, everyone gathered around and seemed glad to meet the unity guy they had all heard about. I felt like a Dad crashing a teenage party. One third of the courier cyclists did not wear helmets. They were playing with death, especially in Toronto. There were even some cyclists drinking beer out of their cycling bottles. One offered me a "brew", but I had a Pepsi instead. As different as we were, we shared the bond of being dedicated two wheelers. I appreciated their very different hospitality.

I had dinner in the downtown Toronto Novotel Hotel where I was treated like a VIP. In my t-shirt and cycle shorts, I contrasted sharply with the upscale French decor. Still, I was glad to be inside, out of the cold of a winter that would not let go.

Thursday, April 10, 1997

Up early, I rode my bike with flag flying through the financial district. The "suits" took double takes. The Cabbies all honked their horns in support. At City Hall, Councillor Mario (who I called Super Mario), came out to officially welcome me on behalf of the city. Mayor Barbara Hall was busy inside, most likely trying to prepare for battle in the Megacity War. The Province of Ontario was amalgamating all the small cities that made up Metropolitan Toronto to remove duplication and save taxpayers' money. I'm sure Barbara Hall did not relish going up against Mayor Mel Lastman in North York. Mel had won more terms as Mayor than any Mayor in the world. If Barbara lost her fight, she would be forced to go head to head with a legend. The reporters from CFTO TV, City TV, Toronto Sun and CHUM Radio were on hand to cover my arrival at City Hall. I was recognized with a special Proclamation and given a Toronto ball cap. I rode my bike around the City as far as North York, where Toronto's Talk640 radio was located. I was supplying copies of my media release, for those who had been unable to send a staff person to my Toronto media conference. Past corporate experience had taught me that the media would give you coverage, even if they couldn't make your conference, if you went the extra mile and dropped your materials off to them immediately after the event. Wanting my message of Canadian unity spread everywhere, I became a bicycle courier myself, delivering my media release and doing interviews directly at other media outlets for the rest of the day. After visiting Global television, a Swiss Chalet on Don Mills Road provided my lunch. I concentrated my efforts on the media in Toronto because I knew they had the power to take the message of the *To The Top Canada* expedition not just to thousands, but to millions, of Canadians.

My main competitor for coverage was the Bre-X scandal. This fiasco involved investors sinking millions into a Canadian developed gold mine that turned out to be a hoax. At times, it seemed the media was more concerned with protecting the profit of multinational investment groups, rather than protecting Canada. I toyed with the thought of calling the expedition "To The Top Bre-X" to get better media coverage...

That evening I had a swim in the indoor pool of the hotel and then went out for a light supper at a local restaurant.

Friday, April 11, 1997

While cycling to Queen's Park I ran into Barry Shainbaum, the photographer who had covered me leaving Point Pelee. Barry saw me on University Avenue and immediately pulled his car over. On a timetable, I had to excuse myself, after talking for awhile, so I could make it to Queen's Park as scheduled. It was a good thing for Barry because his car was parked in a no stopping zone. Toronto has a notorious reputation for towing your car away if you leave it in the wrong place for even a minute. I rode up the front walkway of Queen's Park. The Security Guard had seen me on TV so he knew I was not a protester. I was escorted up to the Premier's Office. Mike Harris was not in because of voting on the Megacity bill. Just as I was leaving, I heard a woman heading to the Premier's Office yell out, "I'm the Queen's grand-daughter. You can't stop me." Security blocked her advance and as I glanced over, it struck me that she looked more like the Queen Mother.

While enjoying some lunch in the CBC Building, I was recruited for the TV program, Jonovision, during a live taping. The TV host sponsored a kilometre of the expedition. Later, I cycled to the European Bound store for outdoor types, and bought freeze dried camping food. Finally, I headed over to the Skydome where Carol planned to pick me up, so I could spend the weekend at home. I wasn't looking forward to this weekend as much because I knew my income taxes were waiting to be prepared and filed.

Monday, April 14, 1997

Early in the morning, as I was hustling to finish my income taxes two weeks before the deadline, I received a call from the Dini Petty Show. The producer of this national CTV network talk show wanted me on the program "today". I packed up everything and drove to their studio, in east Toronto. Dini was a warm and friendly person. She wanted me to ride my bike and trailer with all my gear onto the set once I was introduced. I had to start by riding down a long narrow hallway and avoid hitting the wall. If I hit the wall it might come down and crush the people in Dini's studio audience. No pressure here.

Once I was on the set, I had to execute a turn almost too sharp for my bike with its trailer and then come to an immediate stop. If I didn't stop, one of three things would happen: a) I could ride through the thin fake wall set thereby destroying the image of a nice living room; b) I could destroy a camera worth thousands of dollars; or c) I could run over Dini, the program host, thereby forcing me to demonstrate to all of Canada what I remembered of my St. John's Ambulance first aid skills. I was now starting to feel some stress! I received the go signal and cycled into bright lights that blinded me just when I had to negotiate my crucial turn. It was a miracle but my bike stopped just where it was supposed to. The audience gave me a wonderful welcome. On the show, I detailed the ways in which Canada is better than other countries. Then I discovered that the audience included the wives of ambassadors from the various consulates in the city! Fortunately for me, the vast majority of the audience was comprised of proud Canadians and they loved my message. Dini also became very passionate talking about Canada. She spoke about her visits to third world areas and how she came home wanting to kiss the ground once she was back in Canada. After my segment, while in the make up room taking off my television makeup, the members of the hit Canadian group Leahy who were on the show before me, came over and commended me and told me they thought what I was doing was fantastic.

After the show, I was off to a CAPS meeting (Canadian Association of Professional Speakers) where I was presenting on the same program with NSA President

(National Speakers Association of the United States), Patricia Ball. I was a little nervous but I put on my game day face. Every person in this audience was not simply listening but rather gauging me as a speaker - watching every gesture, story construction, tone of voice and the rest of my platform skills. The audience was even larger because of a Speakers School Seminar held earlier in the day. After an introduction by current President, and my friend, David Sweet, I broke the tension immediately. In front of this audience dressed in their very best business power suits, I appeared in my *To The Top of Canada* T-shirt and sweat pants.

"Good evening, and welcome to the CAPS Speaking School session on how to dress for Fortune 500 companies." Roars of laughter loosened up the audience and myself. With passion and power I told the audience the *To The Top Canada* story. I finished my speech with the words, "God Bless Canada"! I was honoured with a rousing standing ovation that went on and on and on. I don't know if this was the best speech of my life but it made me feel the greatest. After five minutes of applause I walked off the stage and thought, Patricia Ball, top that! Going head to head with the best, I'd finished the day on top. After the program I was swamped for autographs. Even if they take me to prison for not doing my income taxes, it would still be a great day!

Tuesday, April 15, 1997

The Venture Inn, which hosted the CAPS meeting, had put me up overnight. Enroute to North York, my left elbow and right knee went gimpy with pain. I toughed it out. On Finch Avenue I passed a movie crew producing the feature film "One Tough Cop", starring Stephen Baldwin.

I received a call from an organization called Unityfest that said I was on target with my message encouraging Canadians to go out and make Canada even better.

I was invited to speak that evening at the Thornhill Toastmasters. The talks before mine were entitled "Eat Like a Monkey" and "Nasal Maintenance". I knew the audience would love my speech. It clearly demonstrated the difference between a professional speaker and a public speaker.

Cycling on the way to the North York Novotel Hotel, I was passed by a fire truck going up Yonge Street. I used to be a volunteer fire fighter for the Onslow Belmont Fire Brigade when I lived in Nova Scotia. I have never seen a fire truck travelling so fast. The horn was blaring a mile back to clear the intersections. I can only conclude that it was the driver's house on fire.

Wednesday, April 16, 1997

I took my bike to Cyclepath and had the brakes replaced. The trailer puts additional strain on the brakes. While there, I bought some extra bicycle parts to be ready in the event of a breakdown in the north.

I then met with the organizers of Unityfest. They laid out their plan to celebrate Canada in an outdoor concert festival that would take place north of Barrie, Ontario. The Unityfest organizers wanted me to deliver my keynote speech at the opening ceremonies and they suggested the "Queen" may be there. I indicated that on the proposed date of Unityfest, I would be much further west. They offered to arrange a flight so I could be there. I conveyed my willingness to support their Canada unity effort.

Thursday, April 17, 1997

I woke up after my last night in a Novotel Hotel. This chain had been a good friend to me. I sent off Letters to the Editor at the Globe, Star and Sun newspapers to thank Toronto. The weather had turned cold again. Winter wasn't ready to release its grip of sub zero temperatures. I rode into Mel Lastman Square in North York where I met Mayor Mel Lastman, the political legend. He's in the Guiness Book of Records for longest term as Mayor. Not only is the square named after him, there is also a giant portrait of him hanging in the City Hall. This was my first time meeting him and I would describe him as incredible. During my life I've met Prime Ministers, movie stars and media personalities yet I would have to say Mel had the most positive charisma I've ever encountered. The man oozes magnetic warmth. He came out of his office with this giant shopping bag and kept pulling out shirts and hats for me. I was on City TV while this was happening and I commented it's "Christmas in North York". Mel made the camera man laugh so hard he was shaking. Mel said, "I hope he has a good supply of Bengay sore muscle cream".

It was a long cycle trek back across Toronto to the Airport hotel to pick up my car. Tomorrow, I was speaking at the Race Canada dinner back in Hamilton. Very soon, I would not see my family for long periods and I was thankful to spend a three day weekend with them. I had left the car at the Venture Inn parking lot (for free, but not with permission). I was happy to see it had not been towed away.

Friday, April 18, 1997

The Race Canada dinner was at Carmen's, a large popular banquet hall in Hamilton, where the food is terrific. Famous people ranging from former U.S. President George Bush to Elizabeth Taylor had come to Steeltown to speak at Carmen's. It was my second time to visit, and Carol's first. As the evening's Keynote Speaker, I always bring a back up introduction for the meeting's leader. The evening's Master of Ceremonies was new to events of this kind. I told him I'd left a copy of my introduction on the podium, to which he replied "I promise not to touch it!" Diplomatically I explained it was for him, so that he could introduce me.

It felt strange to be in a suit again after living in sweats for a month and a half. Carmen's served their usual delicious fare. I tried to nibble, so that my meal would not interfere with my speech later. This feast tested my self control to the limit.

This was the first time since Point Pelee that Carol had heard my *To The Top Canada* speech. I had moulded it over 20 cities. I let my passion loose and told the audience how I feel about Canada. I received a standing ovation. It felt special to share this moment with Carol. She now truly understood why I had to go to the top, why I had to ride to Tuktoyaktuk, loving me and supporting me 100%.

Sunday, April 20, 1997

My family drove with me to North York because this week they really needed to have a car. We had a pizza supper, hugged and then I headed out. Carol in the car and I on my bike, we approached Yonge Street and stopped for a red light. A guy flew by the car going downhill at 70 kph on roller blades. Carol looked at me in disbelief. On my bike with safety flashers, I looked like Elmer the Safety Elephant compared to the roller blader. Carol went home thinking I wasn't Toronto's greatest daredevil after all.

Monday, April 21, 1997

I had checked into the Sheraton in Richmond Hill, near Markham. With Richmond Hill City Hall on the east side of Highway 7 and Markham City Hall on the west side of Highway 7, I decided to visit both City Halls on the same morning. I went to Markham for a presentation at 9:00 am. After being taken into the Markham Mayor's office, I was introduced to two ladies who were planning to walk, run and cycle across Canada. They were protesting a bill related to the regulation of drugs. I knew the government might be calling an election soon and I wondered what would happen to their trek if the government changed, effectively killing the bill they were protesting. Despite my questions, these were kindred spirits, because anyone who commits themselves to crossing Canada has set a goal of immense proportions as they cross our vast country. They would be starting in British Columbia in May which meant we would cross paths in the Prairies. We wished each other well before we left. I then rode back to Richmond Hill where I addressed the staff of City Hall. During the question period, to a query about where I slept, I explained that I camp when there is no bed. I told them the Richmond Hill Sheraton donated my room last evening but was charging me tonight. The Mayor came up and announced that Richmond Hill would pick up my room tab and buy my supper that evening! The City was also planning to take me for lunch that day.

The Communications Officer was a former Centennial College Journalism student. He had arranged for me to speak to the journalism students at his alma mater. The room had a "60 Minutes" feel. The panel of three journalism students, in a class full of students, sat down in front of a video camera, ready to tape every word. I was ready, because I had been interviewed about the *To The Top Canada* expedition over 100 times and rarely got a fresh question. The first interviewer talked more than he asked questions. The second interviewer asked what I carried on my bike. One of the items I mentioned was a supply of water. Her next question was, " Why do you need water?" With a straight face I replied, "You tend to die if you don't drink water." The room broke up into roars of laughter. The next young interviewer was different. Her questions were probing and intelligent. Throughout the *To The Top Canada* expedition, I had answered the same questions so many times I had polished my answers with a level of poise that would make a spin doctor proud. This third journalism student elicited an emotional response rather than my usual official response. She wrapped up by saying, "Now, for my final question, tell me what you fear most?"

I started to answer, feeling in control.

"Despite the safety precautions I've taken and the fact that safety is the top factor in all *To The Top Canada* expedition decisions, I fear being killed in an accident that is no fault of my own. In preparation for this risk I have ensured that the proper life insurance was in place to look after my family if there is an act of God."

To this point my voice was pragmatic and normal, but then my heart took over. My voice cracked and I barely finished my next sentence.

"Knowing this danger exists, I made sure that this last year my family had the best possible Christmas . . ." The thought of my final Christmas with my family was what I feared most.

This third young journalist had accomplished what Canada's best had not done. She touched my soul. Her career should be very promising.

The course instructor then asked the students to answer the question I posed to Canadians: "What will you do before the year 2000 to make Canada a better county than when you found it?" For a moment there were no answers forthcoming from the class.

I thought, not as good at answering the questions as you are at asking them. Then one student answered by saying "When I try to be a good journalist, I make Canada better." I challenged the answer. Making Canada better is not maintaining the status quo. I told the student that in the past there have been "good journalists" so he has not challenged himself to make Canada better. To make Canada better you have to have the vision to give Canada something that it has never had before. As an example, I suggested that if he went into a community which had never had a newspaper serving it, and started the first paper, worked hard to sustain it, only then will he have made Canada better. The students looked at me with respect. They knew they would have to work hard to meet the standard I had set for them.

Tuesday, April 22, 1997

My next stop was Aurora. Leaving the Sheraton I learned why they call it Richmond Hill. It is a steady incline. People in cars don't recognize when they are going up hills because the car is doing the work. I'd driven up this stretch of Yonge Street many times in my career but never thought of it as a hill. Carrying 200 pounds of equipment, I had no choice but to use a lower gear. This meant more pedaling and more time. I was scheduled to be at Aurora Town Hall at 10:30 am. At 10:25 am I called Aurora and told them I was at Oak Ridges, a community south of them. I was late but they knew I was enroute and going as quickly as I could. When I arrived, the Mayor presented me with a letter of congratulations and a pin from Aurora. After the ceremony, I headed to the house of Walter and Jeannette Blonski. They were hosting me for the evening. Jeannette is another person who, like myself, decided she had to do something to make Canada stronger. She started a home based business called "Canadian Pride", selling clothing and premium items that showcase pride in Canada. She is a great Canadian because she not only shows her love for Canada with words but with her wallet. It is challenging enough to start any new business today but one having the goal of promoting Canada, before promoting profit, is a spiritual quest.

Wednesday, April 23, 1997

A beautiful sunny day greeted me as I headed up to Newmarket. We had a system for getting media coverage. I had written a strong media release on my computer in my home office. The name of each city had to be changed in the headline and body copy. The arrival time also had to be changed. The media release for Newmarket looked like this:

NEWS RELEASE

To The Top Canada expedition going 6520 kilometres arrives in Newmarket and challenges Canadians to answer the "question"!

For immediate release

NEWMARKET - Imagine telling your family you're going to leave home for almost a year to make Canada a better country, you're cashing in $36,928.69 in RRSP's to make it happen and you hope to be the first person in history to travel from the very bottom of mainland Canada to the top under your own power? That is exactly what Chris Robertson is doing as he left from Point Pelee Ontario, the most southern point of mainland Canada, on March 1, 1997. Chris' "To The Top Canada" expedition has him cycling 6520 kilometres from Point Pelee to Tuktoyaktuk. Enroute he will be giving speeches in 51 Canadian communities where he wants to get Canadians' attention to have them answer the question: "What will you do before the year 2000 to make Canada a better country than when you found it?"

On Wednesday, April 23, 1997 the *To The Top Canada* expedition officially arrives in Newmarket with a presentation scheduled at City Hall at 10:30 AM.

Chris believes every Canadian has a special gift and that we have a duty as Canadian citizens to make our country a better place. Chris imagines how many wonderful changes there would be if 30 million Canadians each did one important act to make Canada a better place. Chris believes it is up to every individual Canadian to decide how they can best enhance our country.

One year ago Chris Robertson was at the Montreal Rally with his 11 year old son James to try like many Canadians to save Canada from the separatist forces before the Quebec referendum. Before the Montreal Rally, Canada was losing in the polls by several points. The Montreal Rally made the difference and Canada won the referendum even if only by a razor thin margin. Chris Robertson knows that the Quebec government will soon be putting Canada on the line again in the not to distant future. A last minute Rally will not be the difference in the next moment of judgement. Therefore, Chris believes it is what we do now that will bring us success or failure at the next hurdle in Canada's future. As an individual Chris Robertson won't be able to look himself in the mirror if he does not do everything in his power to keep Canada together. For this reason he is taking 1997 off from work to lead a Canadian cycling-speaking expedition called "*To The Top Canada*"!

Chris believes we should live our life not as it, but as it should be: "Canadians need to give themselves permission to get excited about Canada. We need Canadians who have the courage to show pride, passion and patriotism for Canada. The United Nations Human Development Report has ranked Canada the number one country to live in on the planet, three times in a row, in terms of health care, education and income. How do we respond as Canadian citizens to being the most privileged individuals in the world? Can you look in the mirror and honestly say that you took on one project during your lifetime with the specific intent of making our country of Canada a better place? If the answer is no, then now is the time to act. Canada needs you more now than anytime in its history. Rise up and, on the occasion of following your personal quest for your country, stand tall and let the world know you do it proudly for the glory of Canada!"

Chris' journey from Point Pelee has him travelling the most direct Canadian route which is like riding a large "S". From Point Pelee, Chris is riding east to Toronto and then heads north over the Great Lakes. Chris then rides west passing Manitoba, Saskatchewan, Alberta and then when he reaches British Columbia he heads north for the Yukon Territory. Chris heading north passes into the Northwest Territories before he arrives at Tuktoyaktuk overlooking the Arctic Ocean.

-30-

Chris Robertson may be contacted by calling the national pager number (905) 540-2732 but if the return call is long distance he must be left a 1-800/888 number or a number he can call collect. In the case of a collect call, please indicate your understanding of this policy by leaving him your area code and phone number with a "0" as your first number. Thank you for your understanding as the phone company was unable to provide long distance sponsorship for the "To The Top Canada" expedition due to CRTC regulations.

Carol would go through a Bowdens Media Directory and fax the release directly to the editorial departments and newsrooms.

In Newmarket the only media is the Evening Banner newspaper. Arriving in Newmarket, I was greeted by members of council but no newspaper representatives. I knew Carol had faxed the release. My wife is the ultimate systems person. Her ability to master any challenge made her the only person I ever met that was Valedictorian of her Public School, High School and University class. I knew they had the release, so why didn't they come? A councillor made the comment, "I'm sorry the newspaper wasn't present to hear you speak." With no media interview, I headed on to my next destination of Bradford, where I was scheduled to arrive at 2:00 pm. I made it just past noon, so after eating lunch I used my extra time to call the media. Bradford had their own paper, The Times. Bradford was also covered by the Evening Banner. The Times were on board. I called The Evening Banner to see if they'd cover me in Bradford. The editor mentioned that their sister paper, The Liberal, had passed their photo and story on when I arrived in Richmond Hill. I subsequently learned The Evening Banner ran a colour photo of me along with a major story, on page one. The moral of today was that it never pays to worry.

In Bradford, the Times Reporter photographed me as I arrived at Town Hall. Just as she started interviewing me, a secretary from Town Hall ran out and said the Mayor was on his way and would be there in five minutes. I heard the screeching of tires as an old Cadillac wheeled into the Town Hall parking lot - it was the Mayor. I laughed to myself because the car reminded me of John Candy's car in the movie "Uncle Buck"! The Mayor, in his plaid shirt and work pants, was touched when he read my Canada's Prayer, which is on the certificate I present to every town and city.

Canada's Prayer

I'm dreaming of Canada tonight.
A country where mountains and hopes touch the sky
A country where an ocean of kindness fills all hearts
A country where ideas are a forest of wisdom
Oh God, let me wake up in Canada!

50

I'm dreaming of Canada tonight.
A country where compassion is as tall as a douglas fir
A country where understanding is as deep as a great lake
A country where confidence grows like grain
Oh God, let me wake up in Canada!

I'm dreaming of Canada tonight.
A country where happiness flows like the water of a river
A country where love is a breath of fresh air
A country where peace covers the land like snow
Oh God, please let me wake up in Canada, tonight...

Chris Robertson

The Mayor promised he would read my prayer to the citizens of Bradford on Canada Day.

I headed north again as I was planning to meet my family on the southern border of Barrie. Back in the countryside, the suburbia surrounding Toronto in the distance behind me, I continued riding up Highway 11, passing farm after farm.

I cycled through the community of Innisfill which looked as though it had a church, a donut store and an arena. The small Town Hall was closed but I left a note for the Mayor and a certificate in the mail box. It was a beautiful evening as I cycled by children fishing in a river. Some other children were operating a remote control boat. If they ever got together, they might try trolling with a net behind the boat.

I arrived in Barrie and dialled Carol's cellular phone number. She and James were just 15 minutes away on Highway 400. This was an early start to the weekend but it would be my last one home for some time so I wanted it to be a long one. While waiting, I asked for the General Manager's card at the Holiday Inn so I could contact him about a room on Sunday evening.

Monday, April 28, 1997

The Holiday Inn came through for me and for Canada! As I cycled away, I was greeted by CKVR television news - "the New VR". I showed my appreciation for the Holiday Inn by calling out, "Another great night at the Holiday Inn" as they taped me coming into town.

Prime Minister Jean Chrétien had just yesterday called a federal election for June 2nd, 1997. When I pulled up to Barrie City Hall, a media swarm was there to greet me. After answering a few brief questions I realized a representative from the City was not there. I walked into Barrie City Hall with TV, radio and newspapers following me. Just inside was an NDP Campaign Kickoff but they had no media. The candidate immediately ran over to me to shake my hand. Suddenly, I found myself addressing the NDP supporters. Now you have to appreciate that my personal political leanings are to the right. I am a strong advocate of the free enterprise system. The candidate declared she was going to make Canada better by working to give us an NDP Federal Government. I thought about quoting Voltaire by saying, "I disagree with what you say but I will defend to the death your right to say it". I knew that would have stepped across the line and no longer would the *To The Top Canada* expedition be nonpartisan. Biting my tongue as the TV camera rolled, I actually said, "You are to be commended for involving yourself in the political process". Before I choked, I excused myself to look for the Mayor.

I met the Barrie Mayor as she came down the steps looking for me. She presented me with a medallion and city pin. As I exited city hall with media following me, the NDP candidate tried to get my attention again. I told her that I had to make a phone call, which was true.

It was a day of heavy rain as I cycled north to Burl's Creek. There, I stayed at the home of Don Haney, the owner of the park where Unityfest would be held. The organizers of Unityfest had not paid their deposit yet, but he was giving them some flexibility because he loves Canada and wanted to see them succeed. Don had a pet goat in the house named Matilda, or Mat for short. He also had a collection of birds including pheasants, ducks, geese and chickens. That evening in his basement he passed me 30 chicks that had just hatched and I placed them gently in the warmer.

Tuesday, April 29, 1997

As I got up from the breakfast table to get a spoon, Matilda the goat jumped on my chair and started eating my cereal. After the goat was pushed away, she started to eat my jacket. This was a contingency I had not planned for. I put my pack on my jacket. Matilda started butting it but without success. I thanked Don for his hospitality and headed out. At the Oro Municipal Office, I met with the Mayor. Later, enroute to Orillia, many cars honked and waved as I headed north. This evening, I was scheduled to stay at the home of Ross, the owner of the Orillia Pizzaville store. I located the Pizzaville store where my bike would stay overnight. Ross lived several kilometres out of town. He had to work until 7:30 pm that evening to ensure the dinner rush went well. I met customers coming in for their take-out pizza. While the pizzas cooked, I told them the *To The Top Canada* story.

Wednesday, April 30, 1997

Ross and his partner rented a $300,000 home overlooking a million dollar view of a lake, for just $1,200 per month. After our breakfast, we headed out. Beside Orillia's City Hall is the Opera House, a great building constructed in the 1800's. I compared the vision of those citizens in the 1800's, with the vision of the 1990's, by asking what our legacy will be in the 21st Century. During an Orillia radio interview at City Hall, I was asked by a reporter if the *To The Top Canada* expedition was planned as part of the federal election? I was in a playful mood so I answered: "Yes, Prime Minister Jean Chretien called me 6 months ago and said: (I went into my best Jean Chretien voice) Chris I want you to get on your bike and ride to the top of Canada. Just before you get to Orillia, I'm going to call a federal election. Orillia is the most important liberal seat in the country". The reporter laughed and realized that the *To The Top Canada* expedition was not about partisan party politics.

The City of Orillia gave me a CD disc of an Orillia jazz group, Jazzmatazz, who I understand was formed at the local high school. As I cycled toward Gravenhurst listening to my CD player, I discovered that this group is great! At 4:00 pm I stopped to do a 15 minute on-air interview with Bob Bratina on Talk 640 Radio in Toronto.

Thursday, May 1, 1997

I learned in Gravenhurst that the Howard Johnson that donated my room the previous night was the same hotel Terry Fox had stayed at during his Marathon of Hope. When he passed through Gravenhurst, the town celebrated his birthday with a giant cake. This was Terry Fox's last birthday. Gravenhurst is also the birthplace of Dr. Norman Bethune, the Canadian who is revered in China for his heroic medical efforts during the revolution. The ceremony at the Gravenhurst Town Office was short, which suited me just fine because a bad storm was approaching. The weather office had issued a high wind warning with gusts expected to exceed 100 kph. I watched this storm on CNN when it went through Chicago and the weather office had issued tornado warnings for this same weather front. Fortunately I only had about 15 kilometres of cycling this day. I shot down the highway at a fast clip as light rain started to fall. The first hotel I approached in Bracebridge, the Riverside Inn, provided a room for me. God does a great job looking out for me! I came back out of the hotel to start unloading my gear. The storm had started and the rain was blowing sideways. I bunkered down in my room and ordered a pizza with a Pizzaville gift certificate, using the opportunity to bring my journal completely up to date for the week.

Friday, May 2, 1997

The storm had passed and the sun was shining in Bracebridge when I awoke. Enroute to Bracebridge, I was passed by photographer Barry Shainbaum who wanted to cover yet another official stop of the *To The Top Canada* expedition. He photographed me crossing the bridge into downtown where there is a spectacular waterfall. We stopped for a hot chocolate and coffee before I proceeded to Town Hall. Riding up to the Town Hall, I saw a television crew just arriving. It was a CTV national news crew with Susan Ormiston. I asked if they wanted me to circle so they could tape me arriving with my flag flying high. This time I was greeted by a clean cut man, neatly and casually dressed. He said, "Welcome Chris, I'm Lew Mackenzie". I realized instantly who this was and exclaimed "General!". Four years of Appleby College Cadet Corp training immediately kicked in as, sitting on my bicycle, my body went to attention. This was Canada's General Lewis Mackenzie who heroically commanded United Nations forces in Bosnia. His efforts slowed the hardship of war including ethnic cleansing, starvation and general terror. He was now entering the political arena and running for the P.C.'s in Bracebridge. Although I had never met the man before in person, I was very familiar with his accomplishments and his strong leadership style. In my eyes he was a genuine living Canadian hero. As television taped us I said "General, Canadians appreciate your service to our country and your sincerity when discussing issues." He then presented me with his personal military coin.

He explained that when you show the coin to other officers they have to buy your drinks, unless someone has the same coin which they show you, in which case you have to buy them all their drinks. I thought my cousin Captain Peter Harbert would be a good person to try this procedure on. I also discovered we both had something in common, which was, we had lived in Truro, N.S. I then proceeded to make my official presentation to Town Officials who stood in the background until the General was finished. I guess it makes sense not to mess with the General.

I then went to Bracebridge's High School where an assembly of 300 students was organized. Next week was Unity week at the high school and students were planning to "dress up" to show their pride for Canada. They asked me how they could make an impact on Canada when they can't vote. I told them to simultaneously have every student write and mail a letter about the steps needed to secure Canadian unity, to be sent to the editor of the Globe and Mail, Canada's National Newspaper. If all the letters arrived at once there would be an editorial impact that the national politicians running for office would feel obligated to respond to. When I left it was clear that before students could celebrate Unity week they would have to decide on a personal project answering my question: "What will you do before the year 2000 to make Canada a better country than when you found it?"

Visiting at the local hospital, I made patients laugh by telling them that they would be out of the hospital long before I got to Tuktoyaktuk. Before I went in to see one young man, the Nurse Manager pulled me aside. She told me not to kid this next patient about getting out of the hospital. He was terminally ill and would never leave. We just talked and I think he enjoyed my company. I told him I was riding for all Canadians, especially for him. He told me he would watch my progress on TV. Before leaving, I also visited an elderly couple who were together in the hospital. She was 87 and her husband was 94. She immediately recognized me and said I was much bigger in real life than I am on television. I replied, "I hope so since on TV I'm six inches tall." Her husband shook my hand so hard he sprained my wrist. He said his eyesight was poor and his hearing was going. I told him there was nothing wrong with his hand.

After the hospital I headed down to the local Esso station on the east side of town.

Then I called Carol on her cellular to see where she was. James answered the phone and told me they were in Toronto just getting on Highway 400.

After this weekend, our next family visit would be several weeks away. Our game plan today was for Carol and James to pick me up in Bracebridge and then we would drive to meet my sister Cathy at her beautiful cottage nearby on Kennisis Lake. I purchased a Globe and Mail at the Esso station and read the paper cover to cover.

Taking all four bags off my bike, I disconnected the trailer to be ready for transport. I tied up all my straps, put my warning lights in my jacket and saw Carol's car flash by. I raised my arms to signal with my bright yellow jacket, and Carol hit the brakes, turning into the last exit of the Esso station. With all the weight, the rear bumper of our car was just inches from the ground. We drove off to enjoy our weekend.

Sunday, May 4, 1997

Carol and James dropped me off mid Sunday afternoon in Bracebridge and then drove home to Hamilton. I rode west on Highway 118, heading for Port Carling. Although it was a sunny day, I faced the dual challenge of steep hills and strong head winds. I thought there must be some very expensive cottages on the lakes I was passing because I counted five Jaguars on the road. I remember living in Nova Scotia for seven years and I never saw one Jaguar. Going up one hill, a pickup truck pulled over with a family of four in it, and asked me where I was going. I told them, Tuktoyaktuk. The next question was, "Were you the guy on TV?" They then asked me how far I was going today. I said, "Port Carling". They wanted to know where in Port Carling I would be staying and I explained that I didn't have a place to stay. I planned to look for a place when I got there. "You can stay with us. We're just on the left when you enter Port Carling. Ford is our name and you'll see the truck in the driveway. We'll see you later", and off they drove up the hill.

I continued pedaling up hill but felt better because I now knew I had a place to stay. I'll never forget it was the people in the pickup truck that thought to help me and not the people in the Jaguars . . .

It was 7:00 pm when I rode into Port Carling. I found the Ford house and knocked on their door. The Fords had a spaghetti dinner waiting for me. After a shower, Nigel Ford and I took a walk through Port Carling. Nestled between two lakes connected by two locks, I found this beautiful small town that had become a playground for the rich. Nigel's wife worked at an LCBO government liquor store. You could drive your boat up and park at this store. Some of the "who's who" in the area cottages included the financial elite such as the Seagrams, sports stars such as Eric Lindros (Wayne Gretzky had a place currently under construction) and Hollywood stars, Kurt Russell and Goldie Hawn. Nigel's wife was in the perfect place to star-watch and get autographs because it didn't matter how famous you were, if you wanted liquor, you had to get by Nigel's wife. That night, we ate popcorn and watched the hit TV series The X-Files, produced in Vancouver, Canada.

Monday, May 5, 1997

After cereal and toast, I posed for pictures in front of the house with the Ford family, and headed down the highway. At 9:00 am I pulled into a roadside restaurant and called Air Miles. I tried to use my Air Miles to fly Carol and James to Sault Ste. Marie to meet me on Saturday, May 17, 1997. Even though I had the required Air Miles, they would not accept my request because of time restrictions. You have to wait on hold for over a half hour, so rather than phone back I booked a trip for myself from Thunder Bay to Toronto on June 2, 1997, so I could return home on election day to vote and have a visit with my family. I then called Carol and told her to book flights to Sault Ste. Marie using our Air Canada Aeroplan points. I participate in seven frequent flyer programs to maximize benefits whenever I fly. Arriving in Parry Sound at 1:30 pm, I went into a Harvey's that donated my lunch. It was starting to rain and I knew thunder showers were expected tonight so I tried to get a room donated. After 5 local motels said no, I ended up at the Brunswick Hotel located downtown. They said "Yes" right away. In my eyes, they were the kindest people and the proudest Canadians in Parry Sound's hospitality industry.

The room was humble, but it was dry and I was glad to have it. When night fell, I pulled the curtains tight to block out the bar's flashing strobe light. As I stared up into the black darkness, I decided the room now looked the same as any five star Marriott or Hilton.

Tuesday, May 6, 1997

After a breakfast of two Nutribars and two tetripack orange juices from my supplies, I packed up my bike for another day. I visited the hospital just down the street from the Brunswick Hotel. One patient I was asked to visit had an itchy spot near her eye. She couldn't raise her hands to scratch it. I scratched it as lightly as I could and she said harder. I rubbed it harder but was cautious because I didn't want to hurt her. I don't think I'd make a very good nurse, because if I had to help patients all the time, I would accidentally break more bones than I would help mend. After I finished at the hospital I went back to my bike. I rode under a high train trestle that towers over downtown. I took a few moments to enjoy the waterfront and cycled out to the end of a pier. There was a large tourist boat that gave tours of the 30,000 islands in the area. I thought, this boat was big enough to load up all of the separatist politicians, take them for a tour of the 30,000 islands and let them spend a year on each island.

Parry Sounds' most famous export is still considered Bobby Orr, the greatest NHL defenceman of all time. I wouldn't describe the town of Parry Sound as a world class sports training ground. The town was so small they didn't even have their own police force, using the services of a local Ontario Provincial Police detachment instead. Bobby Orr's success was the product of his own vision and determination. Canada needed that same vision and determination to rise above the status quo and achieve our most positive future, characterized by greatness.

Later at Town Hall, I met a lovely lady who was the Mayor. In my remarks I made my usual statement about Canada being the best country in the world. I brought to everyone's attention that the United Nation's Human Development Report had ranked Canada #1 in the world in terms of education, health care and income, not once but three years in a row. The Mayor chirped in "Well yes, but we spoil it, if we talk about it." That was the wrong thing to say to a passionate Canadian who had cycled several hundred kilometres to showcase Canada's strengths. I immediately responded with a smile, "This is exactly what to say. If Canadians can't be passionate about Canada, who will?" The mayor was silent. She realized by my expression that she had made a mistake.

After the ceremony I started riding north on Highway #69. Up to this point, Highway #69 offered a nice road shoulder to ride on. After Parry Sound, the shoulder disappeared. Now I was riding in the driving lane, although I was completely to the right, just 3 to 4 inches from the edge of the pavement. My life was in the hands of the drivers behind me. I realized a momentary slip of driver alertness could result in my death. I knew my destiny, as it always had been, was in God's hands. I camped overnight in Point Au Baril Station. I saw the sun set and the temperature dropped like a rock. In just a minute I could see my breath steaming. When I took my shoes off my feet were steaming. Camping with a rock cliff behind me and the Trans Canada highway just 100 feet away, it sounded as if I was at the Indy 500 raceway. I did not sleep soundly.

Wednesday, May 7, 1997

My running shoes were still soaking from setting up my base camp the night before. I saw no point in wearing socks that day as they would soon be wet. I walked from my tent to the Haven Restaurant. This is where the local hockey fans meet. The large TV was either on TSN or CBC during a game. The owner said my breakfast was on the house. His wife told me they both ran the restaurant seven days a week. They were locked to their business and certainly could not take the leisure time to start any community project for Canada. Buying my breakfast was their way of saying, "I love Canada". It was up to me to carry their love of this great country. I knew I was riding for them and I would not let them down.

After cycling all day, I arrived in Britt, a small river inlet that had a population of 500. Oil tankers came up the river to bring diesel fuel to a CP fuel station that had a capacity of 58 million litres. I met Jerry, the terminal manager, in the lounge of the Britt Inn where I stayed that evening. Jerry was trained by his dad who was the terminal manager before him. The Britt Inn offered me supper on the house in the lounge. Jerry had created excitement because he had just shaved off his ZZ Top beard. Jerry had been working seven days a week due to the Manitoba floods. The province of Manitoba was experiencing the "Flood of the Century" and had been declared a disaster area. The western C.P. Operations east of Winnipeg had their fuel cut off from the west and their operations threatened to grind to a halt if they didn't get fuel. Jerry wouldn't let that happen. Shaving his beard was his way of going to war and pushing his fuel terminal to the limit. He wasn't going to let his fellow CP employees, and fellow Canadians that depended on CP, down at this time of crisis.

Thursday, May 8, 1997

Awaking sick with a sore throat and headache, I felt the pain of my sprained right wrist and both quads more acutely. Despite the pain, I pushed forward. My first stop was Britt School where I was scheduled to talk to Grades 5 and 6. As I walked in I noticed a stone was inscribed "1967" when the school opened. That was Canada's centennial year, our 100th birthday as a nation. I was twelve years old that year, almost the same age as my son James is now. I remember participating in centennial celebrations in school. My community opened a library, a pool and a park as centennial projects. Our family went to Montreal's Expo 67, our national showcase of Canadian celebration. In 1997, the Britt School was the best building and community facility serving Britt. The positive vision of the Canadians in Britt leading up to and including Canada's centennial year created a legacy that still serves the community. We need to recapture that centennial spirit. We need to get passionate about Canada and enthusiastically love our country, not just with words but with deeds that make Canada better for our children's children!

I pedaled toward French River where I was planning to camp that evening. I read a plaque that spoke of the significance of the French River as a major transportation route for the fur industry. The plaque also noted that French River was the home of the Massassauga rattlesnake. I feel the same way about snakes as Indiana Jones does so I got on my bike and went another 20 km up the Trans Canada highway. I stopped at Loose Wheel Rodeo Motel and Family Restaurant. It is run by Denis and Nicole Brisson in Alban. When Denis heard my story, he gave me a free room for the evening. He also wouldn't let me pay for my meals. I enjoyed good food with large portions. I think of Denis and Nicole as the angels of Highway #69.

Friday, May 9, 1997

Facing a day of showers and fog, I donned my wet gear. On my way to Sudbury, I passed a very large yellow sign that said "MILITARY ZONE SLOW MOVING VEHICLES AND TROOPS". Now, I was wearing a black bicycle helmet and was cloaked shoulders to ankles in a fluorescent lime green rain suit with Canadian flags sewn on it. I'm sure cars passed me thinking, the government has really cut back too far in the Defence Department. Here is a single soldier on patrol and he only has a bicycle to get around on.

I pulled in to the outskirts of Sudbury where I paid for a room at the Comfort Inn.

The manager, after hearing my passionate explanation of my Canadian unity mission, agreed to knock a portion off of their corporate rate for me. I was wet but ahead of schedule. I was still feeling squeamish from a bad cold. Only once in my lifetime have I had pneumonia. When I was diagnosed, I remember the doctor ordered me to bed for several weeks. I didn't want my cold to deteriorate into pneumonia. I needed to get in where it was warm because northern Ontario was experiencing unseasonable lows, with the temperature close to zero celsius.

Saturday, May 10, 1997

My presentation in Sudbury was not scheduled until Monday morning. I needed a place to stay for two nights. I spoke by phone to the Holiday Inn manager who was drained and exhausted from a Head Office inspection that had just taken place. He wasn't in a position to say whether he could donate a room to me. I knew from my professional sales experience that it is easier for someone to say "no" on the telephone than it is in person. So I packed everything up and headed to the Holiday Inn downtown. I had done an economic impact study in Sudbury during the eighties and lived at the Sudbury Holiday Inn for a week. So you can imagine my surprise when I pulled up at the Holiday Inn to see a sign that said Ramada Inn.

I went into the hotel and checked the yellow pages at the pay phone. The Holiday Inn was at 50 Brady Street. I looked at my watch which read 10:55 am. The Holiday Inn General Manager asked me to call him just after 11:00 am. Fortunately Brady Street was only two city blocks away. I shot over to discover a beautiful new Holiday Inn had been built. After waiting patiently behind an elderly couple who were talking to the General Manager about every detail of their daughter's wedding reception, I spoke to him. He found me a room for two nights which they supplied at no charge. After taking my gear down to my room I relaxed, knowing I had a day and a half of rest before I headed into action. This was my first weekend without seeing my family and I missed them terribly. I had supper in this large Holiday Inn restaurant and I was their only customer. Even the music system in the hotel made me feel lonely as they played the sad instrumental music track from the movie "Home Alone", which I recognized because I had watched the video with my son several times.

Sunday, May 11, 1997

I called home early in the morning and wished my wife Carol a happy Mother's Day. She told me that James was making her breakfast. At the last minute, he had grabbed a decorated letterhead that featured a scroll and wrote the following poem.

Dear Mom,

I'd like you to read this poem,
even though I forgot,

so I took some eggs and bacon,
and put them in a pot.
And while I'm carrying the food,
and the coffee is on brew,
I'd just like to say
Happy Mother's Day to you.

Love, James

I went to the downtown Anglican Church of The Epiphany. There, I met Dr. Tom Gerry who taught Canadian literature at Laurentian University. He invited me to join his family for dinner that evening. We agreed he would pick me up at the Holiday Inn at 5:00 pm.

When I was riding my bicycle from church back to the Holiday Inn, I looked to the side of the road where I saw something that shocked me. Elephants! Now, I'm the first to admit that I am a novice outdoorsman who was not fully prepared for dealing with the wildlife of Canada's north. This was not the wildlife I was expecting. I rode my bicycle over to the elephants and discovered they were in town with the circus.

That evening I enjoyed being in Tom's home. We had a lot in common. We both had lived in Nova Scotia and returned to Ontario. We both had tried to have books, we had written, published in Canada. When that didn't happen, we both had them published in the U.S. My book, *Exceeding Expectations: The Strategy of Personal & Organizational Excellence*, was published by Kendall Hunt in Iowa.

Tom discussed why the Canadian publishing industry was weak compared to their large U.S. counterpart. The discussion was enlightening because I suddenly realized an important reason why my industry, the Canadian professional speaking industry, was dominated by Americans. Seventy percent of all speaking engagements in Canada go to Americans, not Canadians. Many of these American speakers are also American authors, whose books have become popular in Canada. A weak Canadian publishing industry was putting Canadian professional speakers at a disadvantage because their profile as authors, in many cases, was nonexistent.

Because it was Mother's Day, Tom cooked supper for his wife Linda. He did a wonderful job. It was great to eat a home cooked meal. While eating I also had my laundry on the go, taking advantage of their offer to use the washer and dryer. After supper I folded my clothes and it was time to go.

Monday, May 12, 1997

A phone call from home woke me up. My son James was scheduled to leave for a school excursion which was a three day camping trip. He had been excited and waiting for this trip for weeks. James had been sick in the night and Carol didn't know how to break the news to him that he should stay home. I told her to tell him that even though he would miss going on this trip, to look forward to the weekend when he would fly to Sault Ste. Marie to spend the holiday weekend with me. After the call I felt down because I felt sorry for my boy.

My Canadian flag flying proudly, I rode through the downtown streets of Sudbury. I stopped at a war memorial and said a prayer for those Canadians who gave their lives during the wars. The memorial bore the message not to fear death but only fear itself.

At Sudbury City Hall, I met cyclists, politicians, staff and media. After completing a newspaper and television interview the cyclists and I rode to CBC where I was a guest on Radio Noon. This CBC program aired from near Thunder Bay in the west, to the Ottawa River in the east and from Parry Sound in the south, to James Bay in the north. Sandra, the program host, loved my passion for Canada. Our interview ended with a song from Stompin' Tom Connors. A police escort waited outside the station to lead me west to the city limits. As we rode out of Sudbury, we passed the giant "big nickel", high on a hill. One of the cyclists with me laughed when he told me the big nickel is, in fact, made out of wood.

I rode west to Whitefish and got a motel room for half price. Speaking to Carol that evening, I learned that she had changed her mind and let James go to camp. The moral of the story, once again, is that it never pays to worry.

Tuesday, May 13, 1997

That morning I talked to the children of R.H. Murray School in Whitefish. I went from classroom to classroom speaking to children about being passionate for Canada. Just before I was ready to leave, the entire school came out to say goodbye. When one of the teachers asked how far I would ride today, I replied, "To Espanola". One of the kindergarten children exclaimed, "Espanola! It stinks there!" The whole school roared with laughter. The young student, surprised by the reaction, defended his statement by saying, "It stinks because they make paper there!" I knew what he meant. I remember visiting Saint John, New Brunswick which had a paper mill, where the air was so bad that if you weren't used to it you would choke. The children cheered me on, and I rode in the rain to Espanola. I appreciated the kindness of Leo Joki of the Alta Vista Motel, who gave me a free room for the evening.

Wednesday, May 14, 1997

Bringing my journal up to date, I thought about the rest of the week. I was 240 kilometres out of Sault Ste. Marie. On Saturday at 10:00 am, Carol and James would fly into the Soo. I warned Carol I may not arrive at the Sault Ste. Marie Holiday Inn until Saturday night, but when I was finished in Espanola I would try to exceed my maximum daily kilometres to be with my family sooner. It would be tough because the Trans Canada highway in northern Ontario was the poorest highway I'd been on. Time would tell if I could make it happen.

Trying to get ahead of schedule, I arrived at Espanola Town Hall one half hour early at 10:00 am. The Mayor and the local reporter were ready for me. The Mayor commented that when people started calling Toronto "cosmopolitan" because of its new found ethnic diversity, she thought to herself, Espanola's been cosmopolitan for years. Not just French and English, but many different ethnic origins including herself. She was Lebanese. I spoke to the reporter about having a grand vision of Canada's future. As an example, I mentioned one idea for Espanola may be building a 21st Century economy around ecotourism, a future growth industry. I then was presented with a pin of Espanola, and an Espanola sweat shirt. Leaving Espanola, the self-declared home of Ringette, I cycled until sundown. I passed three separate signs indicating 55 kilometres to Blind River, each 20 minutes apart! Pulling into the Spragge Bible Church, I asked the elders for permission to camp on their church ground overnight. They asked me if I was the Unity Guy who had been on Dini Petty's show. I said yes, and they granted me permission to stay.

Thursday, May 15, 1997

I went into pack-up mode immediately on waking at 7:30 am. With all supplies on board I rode down to Rocky's Restaurant to have breakfast. Just west of Blind River, I met a convoy of trucks from Canada's military. These were the thousands of troops who had helped save the city of Winnipeg from the worst flood of this century. Before leaving Winnipeg, the convoy was honoured with a parade. We saw each other at the same time. They honked their horns and flashed their lights. I saluted them by circling my fist high in the air while I cycled. I felt solidarity with the troops because our mission was the same - to protect Canada!

In Blind River, the local Mr. Submarine donated my lunch. Cycling until late afternoon, I stopped at a motel restaurant overlooking a lake in Thessalon. I had supper at the restaurant, paying for my meal and asked if they would donate a room. They said no, so I headed west on #17 thinking I would cycle until sunset and camp at the side of the road. I was startled by a large fox that darted in front of my bike as it ran across the highway. Coming into Bruce Mines, a beautiful small community on the water, I treated myself to a $30 a night motel room as a reward for cycling so far.

Friday, May 16, 1997

In spite of the sunshine, the day was very cool so I donned my mittens for the ride. During one of my rest breaks, I was sipping a drink under a tree when a Swiss couple pulled up on their bicycles. The husband had a BOB, the same trailer I had. This was the first time I had ever seen anyone else with my trailer. He told me that they were avid cyclists and had left Vancouver on April 1, 1997, heading east. They had decided on an easier route and had cut into the U.S. in Minnesota and crossed back into Canada at Sault Ste. Marie. (I should note that Switzerland is a country where the military really does use bicycles). I questioned them about their set up of equipment and supplies and discovered they were doing many things similar to myself. I felt good that I was doing just as well as these "super cyclists". I presented them with a Friend of Canada certificate. The wife, after reading the Canadian Prayer, said she would be dreaming of Canada when she returned to Switzerland. She commented on the beauty of the Rockies. I returned the sentiment, recalling the magnificent Alps. She insisted the Alps were not as majestic as the Rockies and were too crowded. We exchanged business cards and headed off in opposite directions.

Arriving in Sault Ste. Marie successfully, ahead of schedule, I went to bed early at the Holiday Inn, happy knowing I would be able to spend every minute with my family this holiday weekend.

Saturday, May 17, 1997

The Holiday Inn van ferried me to the Sault Ste. Marie airport. With permission to go outside and stand on top of the control tower to await my family's flight, I took a picture of the Air Ontario Canadian-built "Dash" commuter plane as it was on final approach. Clothed in my bright fluorescent yellow jacket, I waved both arms at the plane as it landed.

I'm sure the other passengers were thinking, "Wow! Sault Ste. Marie really goes out of their way to make tourists feel welcome". As the plane taxied in, I ran down to the arrival gate. When James and Carol saw me they ran to me and gave me big hugs. We headed back to the hotel for our Victoria holiday weekend together.

Tuesday, May 20, 1997

Today was the beginning of a race. I had until June 2nd to travel 700 kilometres over what would be one of the toughest terrains of the whole expedition, north of Superior, through the heart of the Canadian Shield. My Air Miles flight to fly home from Thunder Bay to vote on election day was not interchangeable. I could not miss that flight. I now had to peddle every day with no time to rest.

At Sault St. Marie City Hall, I met with the Mayor. We talked about the waterfront development at length. Sault Ste. Marie has done a wonderful job of making their waterfront a people place. After a BBS television interview, I headed north.

Immediately I was greeted by the hills of the Lake Superior region. After working up a good appetite, I pulled into a roadside restaurant in Heyden. It was filled with local residents and travellers. It was also filled with smoke. I had noticed that in northern Ontario, it seemed as though three quarters of the people smoked, versus the thirty percent who smoked in the south. I had a choice: not to eat or inhale second hand smoke into my lungs. I like to eat, so I ordered the trucker's special.

As I cycled by a ranch, all the horses stopped what they were doing, their heads slowly pivoted in unison, and their eyes locked on me. I don't know what the horses were thinking. Maybe they thought, finally, a machine that will allow us to retire, or maybe they were worried about being replaced.

That afternoon I pulled into Batchawana Bay. There were two motels to pick from, side by side. I went into the first motel and told them about my Canadian unity expedition and asked if they could give me a discount. They offered me 10%. I thanked them but said I needed to do better. Next door, the motel gave me 50% off so I stayed there. More tired than hungry, as soon as my gear was stored away, I fell asleep.

Wednesday, May 21, 1997

Today I would face the toughest hill of the Lake Superior trip, at Montreal River. As I approached Montreal River, I saw it dead ahead. The road suddenly went vertical. It looked like a rocket launching pad as I approached. I built my speed up so my momentum would help carry me up. I hit the hill at top speed and geared through my 21 speeds to my lowest gear. On my speedometer I watched my speed drop below 4 kph. I was only a quarter of the way up the hill and my feet were pedaling feverishly but the drag of my trailer and 250 pounds of gear was winning. I decided not to fight physics and walked up the hill, pushing my bike at a speed of approximately 4 kph which is walking (pushing) speed. At the top of the hill I came to a combination restaurant, grocery and liquor store. I had a spectacular view of Montreal Island in the Agawa Bay.

This northern Ontario community store resembled American stores in that it sells liquor. No government owned and regulated outlets to be seen. The waitress told me that they receive no local television or radio signals. So much for keeping up with current events. I noticed the waitress wrapping butter tarts and putting price tags on them. I wasn't sure I should eat a butter tart old enough that it needs a price tag, but I like to eat so I threw caution to the wind and had one.

After lunch I called home and left a message on the voice mail telling Carol that I had conquered the Montreal River hill.

Cycling down the other side of the hill, I made a dreadful discovery. The hill I had just conquered was only a warm-up. The real Montreal River Hill lay ahead and rose three times as high. I buckled down and went to work again. It took the rest of the afternoon. Once on top, I shot down the other side at warp speed. I entered Lake Superior Provincial Park which covers approximately 80 km of Highway 17. Just inside the park, I stopped at a restaurant for a beverage break. I asked the owner where I could camp overnight, at no charge. He described a clearing ahead on a road, leading to the water. It sounded great. Then he added that it was owned by "the judge". I pictured the judge turning me in for trespassing and convicting me. I opted for the provincial campground. There was no attendant and it operated on the honour system. The smallest I had was a $20.00 bill which was more than I needed to pay. I put $20.00 in the envelope with my business card. I would hope someone in the government would send me my change. I'm not holding my breath.

I set my tent up on the beach and watched a spectacular sunset. It was like being in Maui. Well, it was like being in Maui if the temperature ever drops down to zero. I looked at my watch before I dropped off to sleep. It was 9:30 pm. I was exhausted from the most challenging day so far in the *To The Top Canada* expedition.

Thursday, May 22, 1997

Lying in my sleeping bag, at 7:30 am, I ate my breakfast - a blueberry Nutribar, a granola bar and an orange juice box. I shaved and washed up and then packed my gear. It was 9:15 am when I hit the road. I cycled 50 Km and did not see any restaurants. At Rabbit Blanket Lake I came to my first pay phone all day. It was 4:45 pm and I called home. My son had been worried about me because he knew that I was camping. In the promotions for the Jurassic Park movie "The Lost World", the clip shows a T-Rex dining on campers. I told James that except for red squirrels, I had not seen any wildlife.

Crossing the Michipicoten River meant two things. I was on schedule to arrive on time in Thunder Bay and I was past the 1,300 kilometre mark of the *To The Top Canada* expedition. The first restaurant after 70 km was the Cedarhof. This was not a truck stop but a wonderful restaurant featuring fine European cooking. I enjoyed one of the best meals of my life.

My legs were sore and I checked into a motel next door just 10 km south of Wawa. The kind lady offered me a half price room. I was looking forward to soaking my legs in a hot tub.

Friday, May 23, 1997

The early morning hours past quickly as I brought my diary up to date. I packed my bike up and before I even had breakfast, it was 10:30 am. After riding only a kilometre, I paused for a bite at a truck stop. The waitress forgot my order and after waiting patiently I reminded her. She brought the food but no utensils. It was now after 11:00 am and I noticed my tires were on the flat side. I put air in them and then had a problem with the service station air pump as the valve jammed open and air was escaping. I managed to fix the problem before their compressor had mechanical difficulty. I rode out, only to discover that the seat clamp on my bike had come loose which made my seat fall to the lowest position so my knees were in my face when I pedaled. I turned around and returned to the service station. It was like a Twilight Zone episode where I could never leave the service station. I wondered, was this the 23rd or Friday the 13th? I fixed the seat problem with some service station pliers and then headed out in a downpour of rain. A sign ahead announced, "Wawa. Are you ready for goosebumps?" I thought, "What next?" Then I saw a giant goose as I cycled passed the highway that went east to Wawa. After cycling 20 kilometres, I pulled into a roadside restaurant for a hot chocolate to warm me up. On the table was a brochure for a truck rodeo taking place in Notre-Dame-du-Nord. Like most people in southern Ontario who live close to Toronto, I have a geographic perspective of Quebec being many kilometres to the east. This Truck Rodeo brochure readjusted my geographic perspective because Notre-Dame-du-Nord, Quebec was 500 kilometres due north of Toronto.

Back out into the rain, headed further north on Highway 17. Two campaign busses, carrying Jean Charest and his supporters, passed me heading south. I waved to them and in return the busses splashed me. Soaking wet, I pedaled on. Riding past a ravine, I looked over the guard rail and spotted a large moose with huge antlers just 30 feet away. After living seven years in Nova Scotia, I had learned respect for encounters with a moose. I knew if a moose hits a car, the car loses. Suddenly the moose bolted, galloping south. I was cycling north and my legs picked up speed. I didn't look back but I just knew my well being depended on my putting maximum distance between the moose and me quickly. After cycling many kilometres, I stopped in the pouring rain and had my lunch - a Pepsi and power bar. Cars passing by honked their support. They knew that a person wearing a Canadian flag, riding a bike, in the pouring rain, many kilometres north of Wawa must be on a mission from God. As I rode, I noticed trucks pulling boats and quad tracks both going north and south. These were sportsmen heading out for the weekend. I know the sportsmen and I had passed many small lakes and rivers but these sportsmen continued on, looking for that "magical location". I was riding to the top of Canada on a national mission, but these people were going incredible distances to fish. I thought, if I drove this far to fish, the fish better jump right in the boat. I passed the intersection of Highway 519 and Highway 17, which was the destination I had decided to ride to that day. There were no motels or even buildings of any shape or form. Just an intersection with fir trees on all sides. I continued cycling along Highway 17. The time was after 5 o'clock and my body started to chill from being wet head to toe. The temperature was dropping. I knew there was a provincial park up ahead and I would camp there or pull into a motel, which ever came first.

After many minutes of cycling I saw the first motel since Wawa. As I walked into the office, the manager said, "Mr. Robertson, we got a call you were coming." I was taken aback by this response and then I figured out what was happening here. In Sudbury a parishioner at the Anglican Church said she knew of an Anglican who rented out cabins just past White River. That same Sunday, the parishioner slipped away from me to the Church office. She came back and said that they would be happy to donate a cabin for free but they needed advance notice to reserve the cabin because they fill up quickly. She gave me a piece of paper with a name and number on it. On Wednesday night of this week, I noticed I didn't have the piece of paper with the contact information. I thought I must have given it to Carol in the Soo, to take home with other receipts from the expedition. On the phone call home, Carol checked and she had the paper. At that time I didn't have a pen with me so I asked Carol to call them on my behalf. I told them I would arrive at their place just past White River on Saturday night. On Thursday I spoke with Carol and she said she had called on my behalf, but that they hadn't heard about me. A woman told Carol that Saturday was Memorial Day weekend in the States and they expected to be full and would not have a cabin for me, but would let me camp on their property. I sensed frustration in Carol's voice as she relayed this conversation. I knew I would adapt to whatever the circumstances were.

Now, here was the cabin! It was this side of White River, and not the other side! Today was Friday and not Saturday! Despite these contradictions, I now realized where this manager knew me from. He gave me a key for the complimentary cabin and I gave him a Friend of Canada certificate. I had brought the certificate in, ready to give my Canadian Unity speech and to request a discount, but after I figured out what was happening, I just presented the certificate as if it had been my plan all along.

In my cabin, I was warm and dry. What had started as an awful day had a wonderful surprise ending.

Saturday, May 24, 1997

It was cloudy, but no rain so far. The highways were full of Michigan hunters enjoying the Memorial Day Weekend in Canada. Halfway between Wawa and White River, I stopped in a restaurant for a hot chocolate to warm up. One Michigan man who saw me said, "You must be tougher than the average bear!" In the coffee shop, I gave them my speech and these guys from Michigan were ready to go out and do one thing to make Canada better.

Early in the afternoon I pulled into White River where the claim to fame is being the birthplace of "Winnie The Pooh". A handout at a rail car tourist booth, that is also a small Winnie The Pooh museum, tell this story of Winnie.

Winnie, a little bear that crossed the ocean.

Once upon a time Winnie-the-Pooh lived all alone in the forest near White River, Ontario. She wasn't quite Pooh yet but this is how her story goes.

Winnie was the surviving cub of twins and her mother had been killed by a hunter. A kindly trapper brought the little black bear cub into the town of White River, which was a common thing to do in 1913. Many families have photos showing pet bears, leashed and posing for the camera.

White River is on the mainline of the Canadian Pacific Railroad and it was at the *station platform that a young army soldier admired and bought this cub during a stopover. An entry in the man's diary reads: "August 24, 1914. Left Port Arthur 7A. In train all day. Bought bear. $20.".*

The soldier was Harry Colebourn, a Canadian Expeditionary Force veterinarian, aboard a troop train bound for Val Cartier, Quebec, and active duty in World War I. He named his bear Winnipeg, after his hometown in Manitoba, and she became known as Winnie for short. The little bear was very tame and became a loving and loyal pet to all the soldiers but chose to sleep under her master's cot at Salisbury Plains, England.

In December, Colebourn had to find a place to leave Winnie for safekeeping because his troop, the 2nd Canadian Infantry Brigade, had been called to service in France. He placed her with the London Zoo where she was one of five bears left by Canadian regiments, but she was different.

Reports of the day tell how people could knock on the door of her enclosure and she would open it herself and come out. She would allow children to ride her back and would eat from their hands.

This little bear from Canada captured the hearts of many people, among them British author A.A. Milne and his son Christopher Robin Milne, who were frequent visitors. Before long, the loveable bear had become the inspiration for Winnie-the-Pooh, a character known the world over in children's books about the adventures of a little boy and his stuffed animals. Milne wrote about the zoo bear in an introduction to the 1926 edition of Winnie-the-Pooh. An inscription on Winnie's record card with the Zoological Society of London identifies her as coming from White River and being, "Winnie, from whom Winnie-the-Pooh got her name."

I enjoyed a tasty meal in White River donated by the A&W restaurant. The teenaged boy at the information centre tried his best to find me a place to stay but with the U.S. holiday, every room was gone. I went up the Trans Canada for a total of 75 km that day and camped at the White Lake Provincial Park. I've decided that provincial parks are cruel to cyclists. Imagine cycling into a provincial park after 70 km and finding the entrance gate is 3.5 km away, and then the campground by the closest shower is another 3.0 km past the gate. Tired, I set up camp, showered and slept well that night.

Sunday, May 25, 1997

There were no churches close by so I celebrated my faith in God by listening to the "March For Jesus 1997" music track. I encountered the first part of a small section of Highway #17 undergoing repaving. I have a CD that plays all the inspirational theme songs from the "Rocky" movies. In one song, sung by James Brown, I listened to the words about America that say, "Super highways coast to coast!" The Trans

Canada Highway north of Superior is a national disgrace. This two lane road had pavement that was cracked and crumbling in the driving lanes and the road was also full of pot holes. This small bit of construction was like a doctor giving a bandaid to a man with his right arm ripped off. Too little, too late.

All Canadians should take their children to all parts of Canada. The knowledge and understanding that would result from seeing and meeting Canadians coast to coast would make our nation stronger and more united. To make this vision happen in Canada we need a super Trans Canada highway coast to coast!

Arriving in Marathon, I was grabbed by a breathtaking view of Lake Superior from the hill that leads downtown.

The Zero-100 motel donated a room for the evening. I enjoyed watching the TV news and the sparks flying between political parties with just one week to the election.

Monday, May 26, 1997

Up early, I read the first ten chapters of Matthew in my Good News Bible. It was a sunny day and not a cloud in the sky, but still cool. I went to Holy Saints School to see if they wanted to have me speak. I took in my Friend of Canada certificate, national media release and my business card which shows I am the past president of the Canadian Association of Professional Speakers. The Principal was away and the official designate decided not to take any chances by having me speak. The secretary came back and said that because there was no advance written notice, they could not allow me to speak. I thanked them and asked them to pass my material on to the principal when he returned. I wondered if Terry Fox, Prime Minister Jean Chrètien or the Queen would need advance written notice to speak at the school. At the Marathon Town Hall, John, the Town Clerk, received the *To The Top Canada* certificate. I then rode out to the Marathon Mercury which was a community newspaper, printer and office supply store. The editor said he was printing the paper today but couldn't take my picture because his camera was at home. I thought, I sure hope nothing earth shattering happens in Marathon today, because there won't be any photo coverage. I then proceeded to the local laundromat where I met Carol, the manager, who was the nicest person I met in Marathon. I washed my clothes to be ready for my journey to Thunder Bay.

Later on in the day I was stopped at the top of a high hill taking a water break when a cyclist pulled up. His name was Steven Staples. He was a Queens University student who was cycling from Halifax to Vancouver. He stopped and we talked for half an hour. This trip was a personal challenge for Steven. His parents advised him not to do it and he had left his girlfriend in Kingston. Steven needed this incredible challenge of crossing Canada under his own power to show everyone he had the determination to do it, but most importantly, to show himself.
We decided to camp together after I covered my required daily kilometres. We

picked a spot by a lake in a valley. There was a telephone booth by the only motel for kilometres. I called Carol. We actually connected after a few days of her being out or on the phone when I called and leaving voice mail updates. We were enjoying talking, when something strange started happening. Remember Alfred Hitchcock's terrifying thriller, "The Birds"? I was just beginning to have a similar experience but with one difference - in my case, it wasn't birds, but mosquitoes. Carol was telling me about my niece's 18th birthday when I suddenly interrupted, "There are mosquitoes in the phone booth, I have to go! Bye!" I'm sure Carol was surprised by my sudden exit. Steven said he was going to make a call. I warned him not to go into the phone booth. He did. All I could hear was the sound of his hand hitting the phone booth walls. Wham . . . Wham. . . Wham ...! His call was less then 30 seconds.

We went across to the place where we'd decided to camp and the mosquitoes chased us. I pulled the Muskol insect repellent out of my bag and smeared by body. There were thousands of mosquitoes but none would land on my body because of the Muskol. Hey! This stuff really works. I remembered the TV commercial where a man sticks his arm in a container with hundreds of mosquitoes and at the time I'd thought, you couldn't pay me to do that. Right now I was surrounded by more mosquitoes than that TV commercial. Steven and I quickly gulped down supper from my supplies. Even though the mosquitoes were not biting us, their buzzing as they flew around our heads drove us nuts. During supper I choked on two mosquitoes which had flown inside my mouth, the one place I hadn't sprayed Muskol. We both retired to the safety of our separate tents that were mosquito free. We couldn't see each other but we talked to each other, tent to tent. I needed to answer nature's call that evening but I held it because there was no way I was going out to face that mob.

Tuesday, May 27, 1997

I awoke next morning to feel my bladder was about to burst. I dressed, ready to open my tent. I was greeted by the morning sunshine and no mosquitoes. On my way back to the tent a single mosquito buzzed me. A sentry! Whack! I got him before he could report back to base. Taking no chances I immediately started packing up. Another sentry! Whack! I redoubled my efforts. Shortly a battalion of mosquitoes showed up. I guess they were sent out when the sentries I'd killed didn't show up and report in. Steven came out of his tent to be greeted by the friendly welcome committee. Seeking relief, I told Steven I would head down the highway and we both knew his lighter load would allow him to quickly pass me. I headed out, glad to leave the dreaded mosquito valley behind. I breathed a sigh of relief, feeling as if I had just been a character in a Stephen King novel.

As I rested on top of a hill, Steven caught up with me and I sang the theme to Rocky as he pedaled up the hill to my position. We talked for a while and then headed out. Last evening Steven had shared thoughts of quitting with me. I gave him a pep talk (tent to tent) that reaffirmed his desire to finish. As he headed out, like a high school football coach, I yelled at him. "The Pacific, Steven! The Pacific!" Steven sped ahead as he had no winter gear, no office supplies (presentation certificates or journal), or even long term food. I later caught him at a large hill where he was just at the top and I had come to the bottom. To let him know I caught him, I shouted to him, "The Pacific!" . I thought, he'll want to get to the Pacific just to get away from this guy shouting "To the Pacific!"

I passed a second large moose who saw me and bolted into the woods in fear. Then a Mack truck passed me from behind, which must of been the cause of the Moose's fear. As I rode that day I was concerned about the environment. Riding through the Canadian Shield forest, suddenly I'd see a large barren square, completely flat, where the forest had been raped and all trees removed. It appeared as though a bomb had been dropped, flattening everything. There were also two types of creeks and rivers. One type was a beautiful blue, plucked from a scenic postcard. The second type were rivers that had a sick green colour that had been poisoned by pollutants being poured into the rivers. Just by Terrace Bay I passed a stream that had been covered by galvanized steel shield and I wondered what was happening here, that it had to be covered up. I was disgusted by this abuse of the environment and I decided I would be joining Greenpeace when I finished the *To The Top Canada* expedition.

That day, Steven and I passed each other. When I caught him, I yelled "The Pacific!". When he caught me he yelled "The Arctic"!

Close to sundown, I pulled up to Steven and we camped on a cliff in a scenic lookout at the side of the road. Thankfully, there were no mosquitoes. The view was spectacular. Steven told me that after speaking to me he had decided he wanted to enter medical school. We slept well after cycling approximately 100 kilometres.

Wednesday, May 28, 1997

I awoke early and wanted to get down the highway. Before I left, I pulled out a tetripack O.J. and a fruit Nutribar for Steven and left it by his bike as I knew his food was low. On Monday night I had given him some of my supplies, as he was almost down to zero. He would start the day with a small breakfast when he awoke. I was planning to ride to Nipigon, which was 20 kilometres away. There I would get a motel where I would rest my body. I was now two days ahead of schedule for my arrival in Thunder Bay. My body could use the rest.

All the way from Sault Ste. Marie, I had passed huge rock cliffs where people had proclaimed their love with spray paint in many languages. Every now and then I would pass a rock that had a square spray paint block over the message, a sign that the relationship had broken up and one party wanted to leave no sign of the previous relationship. After reading the hundreds of messages, noting the times indexed with the year of travel, I determined that a message could last 19 years before the weather would erode the message. So, if you wrote a message 20 years ago, it's time to return to north of Lake Superior.

Two crows picked at the ribcage of a dead moose at the side of the road. The skeleton was in clear view. You could take your standard household refrigerator and put it inside the rib cage of that moose. I was amazed at the size of this animal.

In Nipigon, every motel was full, as road construction workers had taken every room. I cycled another 50 km before I arrived in Dorion where I got a room in a two storey hotel. The whole building shook when a train went by. When it first happened it startled me from my sleep and I thought it was an earthquake. My California training kicked in and I jumped up and stood under the doorway of the bathroom for safety. Then as my room, furniture and I shook, I listened to the deep rhythmic sound and the long lonesome whistle. Deciding it was a train, I went back to sleep.

Thursday, May 29, 1997

Not needing to ride far today, I determined to rest in the morning and then ride 30 to 40 kilometres. For the very first time this year, I saw leaves on trees. Up to this point unseasonably low temperatures had kept the branches bare. I'm not complaining because these same low temperatures had kept the black flies away. If you can believe it, black flies would have been worse than my mosquito encounter. The leaves were like banners celebrating my *To The Top Canada* expedition, conquering the challenge of Highway 17, north of Superior. Others had told me this would be the toughest part of my journey. Learning from my Montreal River experience I thought, we'll see. . .

While riding, I got a sharp pain in my right knee, for no apparent reason. I was going downhill at the time and pedaling gently. The pain scared me. I knew that pain from tearing my cartilage in my left knee during a college football game. I played receiver for the University of Guelph Gryphons and I was clipped by a defensive back who played for the McMaster Marauders. I immediately stopped and gave my knee a rest. For the rest of the day I rode gingerly with no problem.

As I got closer to Thunder Bay, I noticed that every store along the highway sold amethyst, a beautiful rock only found in Thunder Bay. Homes sprang up in greater numbers, eliminating my chance of camping by the side of the road. After riding 40 kilometres I stopped at a restaurant for a drink. The local people recommended that I turn on the Lakeshore Drive just ahead, to ride into Thunder Bay. I followed their advice and enjoyed the view of Lake Superior as I rode towards Thunder Bay. It was a quiet road where I could ride in the middle of the lane instead of on the shoulder, which was my usual Trans Canada protocol.

I stayed at the Old Country Motel on the north side of town, where they gave me a half price room for the night. I finished off my food supplies that night for supper. I was in Thunder Bay in 9 1/2 days and had averaged 73.6 kilometres per day over the challenging terrain of many difficult hills. I had pushed myself to maintain that pace and had now proved the critics wrong, those who said I couldn't pedal my 500 pounds of total weight that punishing route in 14 days!

Friday, May 30, 1997

Today, I began a three day process of killing time. I was not scheduled to arrive at City Hall until Monday, June 2nd. Carol had already notified the city media of my June 2nd arrival. This was a day of beginnings and endings. It was the end of the dreaded North of Superior stretch. It was the beginning of me focusing on the stretch of my journey that would have me leaving Ontario and entering another province.

I watched CBC Newsworld coverage of the opening of the 13 kilometre Confederation Bridge between New Brunswick and Prince Edward Island. Two thousand people were in a road race across the bridge. The ferry service between Cape Tormentine, N.B. and Borden, P.E.I. would now be cancelled. My experience of running a large Atlantic Canada food service chain had brought me to the Island many times on the ferry. I had been on every ferry - the Abbegweit, the John Grey, the Vacationland and the Holiday Island. These ferries were now to be sold off. I wondered how the island would change in the years to come because of the Confederation Bridge.

Today was also Peter Gzowski's last show on CBC's Radio Morningside. Peter Gzowski facilitated a national dialogue about Canada. He was a friend to me for many years, even though we have never met. I enjoyed his show that probed, showcased and celebrated everything Canadian. There was a church in Thunder Bay playing the final show, where you could sign a farewell card to Peter Gzowski. I listened to the show on my walkman as I cycled over to my first order of business which was to visit Cyclepath for a full check up. The Cyclepath store had Morningside, the finale, playing in the store and in the maintenance room where my bike was being tuned up. When Morningside was over they went to their punk rock youth music in the Cyclepath store. My bike was done and ready for the next leg of the *To The Top Canada* expedition.

I called a professional speaker friend who invited me to stay with her when I got to town, only to discover she was just leaving town for the weekend. It was 1 o'clock and I went to Swiss Chalet for lunch. The General Manager, Tony Mengual, donated my lunch and joined me. He was inspired by my Canadian unity effort and he tried to find two nights of complementary accommodations. After calling several hotels and motels he came back and told me he had no luck. It was grad weekend in Thunder Bay and every room seemed full. I thanked Tony for all his efforts. I rode towards downtown looking for the Anglican Church. No one I stopped, even at other churches, knew where the Thunder Bay Anglican Church was located. Now late afternoon, I knew my options were disappearing fast. I made a deal with the Shoreland Motor Hotel to give me one night free, if I paid for one night. The room had a shower and a very small single bed, but I was grateful. I unpacked my gear and called Carol to let her know where I was that night.

Saturday, May 31, 1997

I slept in and made a vow to myself not to ride my bike this day so my cycling legs could rest. I looked in the phone book to find out where City Hall and the Anglican Church were located. The closest church was St. John's on Pearl Street. I walked several blocks over to the church. The church had stood for over 100 years and was the oldest church to serve Thunder Bay that was still in use. I then walked to a very attractive modern office complex I passed on the way to Cyclepath. I discovered that it was the Province of Ontario building. I meandered over to the waterfront where final touches were being put on the Anchorage, a Royal Canadian Navy memorial scheduled to be dedicated June 1, 1997.

Sunday, June 1, 1997

I cycled to St. John's Church where the minister gave a sermon about knowing when to be the master and when to be the student. I knew, especially in northern Canada, that I would have to be the student and listen to the Canadians who live in Canada's north and know how to stay safe and survive. I knew God meant this sermon for me.

I rode to the home of Glen and Delaine Karam. Glen is the brother of Vivian Brown who works at Idlewyld Manor in Hamilton with my wife Carol. I arrived to a warm welcome. Glen had invited the whole family to his house to meet me as we all enjoyed a spaghetti dinner. The highlight of the afternoon was watching Donovan Bailey prove once and for all that he is the fastest man in the world. I ran track and field in school. As soon as I saw Donovan overcome the staggered start and pass Michael Johnson early in the curve I knew Donovan would win. This one man, the Canadian, had overcome the American media hype that dominated the event. For the time being, Americans could not claim to have the world's fastest man. Everyone at the party in Thunder Bay enjoyed the passion of Canadian Donovan Bailey. Glen relished Donovan rubbing salt in the wound by calling the mighty representative from the USA a "chicken" on CBC and then a "coward" on CBS. Johnson had pulled up in the race after Donovan had passed him. (Donovan Bailey later apologized for these remarks made immediately after the heat of the battle.)

Later that evening, Glen drove me out to the Terry Fox memorial on Highway #17. My shortcut along Lakeshore Road caused me to miss this monument to the greatest Canadian of this century.

The giant statue of Terry Fox towers over its admirers. Terry Fox was a hero and personal inspiration to me. I saw Terry Fox in Toronto as he ran towards Toronto City Hall. It was the hottest day of the summer when Terry ran into Toronto. As I stood on University Avenue, I remember baking on the sidewalk with the incredible heat, and sweat pouring off me on this sweltering summer day. I thought to myself, what a terrible day to run. Then I saw Terry Fox running and I saw the excruciating pain in his face, a vision I will never forget. He was late for Toronto City Hall where thousands waited for him including celebrities such as Maple Leaf Captain, Daryl Sittler. At the point Terry Fox was right in front of me, I saw him pick up the pace and run faster, despite the pain and despite the heat!

Terry Fox epitomized determination. Terry ran from the east coast of Canada, to Thunder Bay where he had to stop his Marathon of Hope because his cancer was spreading. I remember being stopped at a traffic light, while driving my car in Toronto, when the music on the radio was interrupted with the news that Terry Fox had died of cancer. I cried and then looked to the car beside me where a woman was wiping her eyes. We both knew we were crying for the same reason. A great Canadian had been taken from us. To this day, when I talk to the media about being passionate about our country, I encourage them to hold up symbols of Canadian greatness. When the media ask me "Aren't we already doing that?", I remind them that no Canadian music artist has ever written a song about Terry Fox, that has received national recognition, to the point where all Canadians can sing a song in tribute to Terry Fox.

Monday, June 2, 1997

I rode my bike to City Hall for my official welcome into Thunder Bay. I was met by my friend Maggie Milne. Maggie is an international professional speaker who lives in Thunder Bay. Maggie speaks on "Guts, Drive and Perseverance". Her warm support meant a lot to me. After my presentation at City Hall, Maggie helped me find the Thunder Bay CBC building. I was a guest on the noon program of CBC radio.

Afterwards I was off to Agnew H. Johnson school where I spoke to the students. We couldn't use the gym, as it was in use today as a voting station for today's federal election. We used a large open classroom area. The students in the school crowded around my bike, trailer and gear. They told me it was the coolest bike they had ever seen. I knew they thought my bike was awesome but I kidded them. "My bike has faced cool weather so far in the *To The Top Canada* expedition, but there is even colder weather waiting for me in the Arctic!" The teachers laughed. A reporter named Kirsti MacDonald from the Thunder Bay Post interviewed me at the school during my visit. With a reporter snapping pictures, the children cheered "I am Canadian!" so loudly I'm sure everyone in Thunder Bay heard them.

It was time to fly home using my free Air Miles flight on Canadian Airlines. Glen and Delaine were wonderful to let me keep my bike and gear at their house while I went home to vote and have a short visit with my family. From the Toronto airport we drove straight to Hamilton and to our local polling station. I was proud to do my duty as a Canadian and vote in Canada's federal election.

Monday, June 9, 1997

In one week, there were a lot of changes. A federal election re-elected the Liberal Government with a smaller majority. The Reform Party was now Canada's Official Opposition, bouncing out the Bloc Québécois. The Progressive Conservatives and New Democrats rebounded to regain official party status. Back in Thunder Bay, the election signs that had been planted on every corner were now gone. Weather-wise, it was as if Thunder Bay had jumped from winter to summer in one week. The temperature was in the high eighties and green leaves were budding everywhere.

My first stop was a courier office, where I mailed my one-man tent to my son. I had purchased a new three-man tent. My small tent was like a can of sardines, when I squeezed in with my gear. I found that after a long day of cycling, I was very stiff and I would have to bring my foot up to my face while lying on my back to take a sock off. It was like playing Twister. Unfortunately, I was getting terrible leg cramps from this twisting which for me is the worst pain on earth. Sometimes I was getting multiple cramps all at once in the night. The small tent was so small I called it the "body bag". The new tent would end the pretzel aerobics. When I got a leg cramp now in the night, I could stand up and stop the pain by putting weight on my foot and stretching the muscles. It meant even more weight to pedal for, but I gladly accepted it, to stop the excruciating pain of leg cramps in the night. James would enjoy using the small tent for summer camp outs in the back yard.

I cycled and stopped west of Thunder Bay to see Kakabeka Falls which is referred to as Niagara of the North. I found these falls very impressive but not large enough to merit a Provincial Casino like the one in Niagara Falls. I was impressed by the story of an Indian princess named Greenmantle. Greenmantle was the daughter of the Ojibway Chief. Greenmantle was captured by the Sioux, the enemies of the Ojibway. The Sioux hoped to question Greenmantle and discover secrets that would help them conquer the Ojibway. Greenmantle convinced the Sioux that she was their friend and she would help them defeat the Ojibway. She volunteered to personally lead the Sioux warriors and show them which rivers were the best way to sneak up on the Ojibway. Greenmantle was paddling the lead canoe herself down river, leading the Sioux warriors in their attack. As Greenmantle approached Kakabeka Falls, which the Sioux warriors did not know was ahead of them, she paddled faster and faster pulling away from the warriors. The warriors paddled even faster than Greenmantle to close the gap. Almost at the top of Kakabeka Falls, Greenmantle suddenly swung her canoe to the left. She jumped out and successfully swam to shore just before she would be swept over the brink of the falls. The Sioux warriors were perplexed by Greenmantle's sudden turn but did not realize the Kakabeka Falls were coming. All the Sioux warriors were swept over the falls to their deaths. Greenmantle had risked her life so her Ojibway tribe would live. As I faced the dangers of the *To The Top Canada* expedition I hoped to do so with the bravery of Greenmantle.

Near Raith, I saw a sign marking the beginning of the new Arctic Watershed. Behind me, all rivers flowed to the Great Lakes and eventually to the Atlantic Ocean. In front of me, all rivers would flow to the Arctic Ocean. After cycling 85 kilometres, I camped in a park where the Central Time Zone crossed Highway #17. The sign declared that this spot was 90° longitude and the beginning of the Central Time Zone. My GPS indicated this location was 90° 01. Sir Sanford Fleming, a Canadian, designed a system of world wide time zones. Today the whole world benefits from the Time Zone system and Canadian ingenuity.

I set my new tent up and it was wonderful. I could move around and stand up. I was in heaven.

Tuesday, June 10, 1997

As I prepared for the day, I noticed a sign forbidding overnight camping and warning of a severe fine for violations. This sign was at the north entrance and I had come in the south entrance where there was no sign. I hustled to take my tent down. At the same time, nearby, a fox was opening garbage can doors with his paws and sticking his long snout in for breakfast while he balanced on his hind feet. I moved faster as I did not want to be the fox's next entree on his breakfast menu.

Two kilometres down the road, I was riding northwest when a United Van Lines truck pulled out to pass a U-Haul truck. I was wearing a reflective construction vest that glows bright in the morning sunshine but this United van Lines driver ignored it. He forced me off the road and my bike crashed, forcing my face into the gravel. Lying on the ground, I opened one eye and saw that the United Van Lines truck didn't even slow down. That driver saw me crash and he didn't stop or even slow down. I could have been critically injured or dead but that driver didn't care. I don't plan to use United Van Lines personally or corporately ever again.

I was angry and I thought of contacting my lawyer, one of Canada's best, and suing the driver to teach him a lesson. After counting to ten, I remembered Jesus' message to turn the other cheek and worked to put the matter out of my mind. Up the road in Lac Des Mille Lacs, I pulled into a restaurant in an Esso station. The change of state helped me relax. Cathy, the waitress, read about me in the Thunder Bay Chronicle Journal and said she wanted to pick up my check. Her kindness melted any bitterness left in my heart. I cycled on and as I went by the forest I was chased by deer flies or, as I like to call them, stalker flies. It was a very hot sunny day. I needed to apply UV skin block on a regular basis to my legs, arms, neck and face. The sweet smell was like a dinner gong to stalker flies. I was riding at a speed of 17 kph, and these stalker flies were chasing me. I saw a down hill incline up ahead and thought I'd lose them. In my top gear and 500 pounds of total weight, I quickly accelerated. My bicycle speedometer clocked me at 58 kph down hill. I glanced over at my shadow to the right and at the black dots behind my back. The stalker flies were staying with me. I hit the brakes hoping the stalker flies would zoom by me. No luck. I rode for 50 kilometres hoping they would tire. No luck. Arriving in English River after cycling

77 kilometres that day, I ran into the Country Kitchen restaurant and for the first time, I lost the stalker flies. Don, the owner of the English River Motel, donated a room for the evening. I looked forward to a bath and a long sleep. I called Carol and then did an interview on Winnipeg Radio, CJOB, with James Lowen, on his program Interactive Radio.

In my room, after a shower and just before bed, as I was writing in my daily journal I felt a sharp needle like pain in my back - Stalker Fly!!!

Wednesday, June 11, 1997

Looking in the mirror this morning I noticed my arms were deeply tanned but my hands were still white because of my cycle gloves. It occurred to me that when I'm finished, I can have a career in mime theatre.

The day of cycling to Ignace was gruelling, as the road was entirely torn up for construction. There was a silver lining - the Stalker Flies didn't like the dust. I'll take choking on dust over bites from Stalker Flies any day. In Ignace, the Majestic Motel donated my room for the evening.

Thursday, June 12, 1997

At the Ignace School, to speak to students and teachers I sensed two things. They identify more with western Canada than eastern Canada and they feel Quebec had been over privileged in Canada. Just the word, Quebec, was a sore subject. I made a mental note of this as I was now heading into western Canada. I rode wet through heavy road construction. At one point I saw a mother moose and baby moose just enter the woods after crossing the highway. When I arrived at my 70 kilometre destination there was nothing at the corner except a phone booth. I called home and left a voice mail message on my progress. I decided to ride to the 100 kilometre mark, putting me in Dryden. I arrived at 8:30 pm and promptly devoured a fast food supper. After eating, I learned every motel in town was full because of a motorcycle rally in Dryden. I went to the Northwestern Tent & Trailer Park where Walter, Eliana, Stephanie and Christopher were the Swiss family who ran the campground. I spoke with Eliana who agreed to donate my campsite that night. She also worked at Pharmasave and was saving up to apply for Canadian citizenship. The application fee is $600 per person. The grounds were impeccably clean and decorated with flowers that had been nurtured with loving care. I set up my tent and called it a night.

Friday, June 13, 1997

Dropping by the Dryden High School, I introduced myself to the acting principal and offered to speak to the students about the *To The Top Canada* expedition. He said he would try to set things up with some history classes and asked me to meet him in the office at 12:30.

At the Anglican Church, I said my daily prayers and gratefully accepted lunch at the Central Hotel restaurant. A nearby store donated a large caution flag (the strong winds had blown my trailer flag away the previous day). It was now 12:30.

Returning to Dryden High School, I waited an hour in the school office but it became clear that the acting principal had left the school and nothing had been set up for me to speak. This meant the opportunity was lost for me to address the students about the responsibility of Canadian citizenship. In the office, there is a plaque on the wall commemorating Dryden High School students who put their lives on the line fighting in wars for Canada. Sixteen students are named, in alphabetical order, from Adrian to Vost, who had made the ultimate sacrifice and given their lives for Canada. I wondered what the spirits of these 16 students would think of this acting principal who had disappeared, rather than be there to celebrate Canada.

Visiting the Dryden Hospital, I spent some time with a young boy named Rob. He told me he could speak three languages - English, French and Ojibway. I told him that was a special gift because I could only speak one. Rob had been alone in his dark hospital room with the curtains drawn. I could tell he enjoyed the company. I let him talk and I listened. When he was talked out I left, but we were now friends.

At the Home Hardware store, I bought some clamps to attach my new flag to the trailer pole. With the flag secure, it was time to head to the Town Hall. Leaving my trailer and gear at the campsite, I felt like Superman without the extra weight, biking through town. Even going over an overpass, I was in top gear as I went uphill. At the Town Hall at 3:30 pm, I was presented with a glass plaque by the Town of Dryden. Afterwards I went to the Post Office, wrapped the plaque in bubble paper and mailed it home where it would be safe. My supper was donated by KFC. I then went to a special Centennial Service for the First United Church. It was a Hymn Sing and the beginning of a weekend of festivities to celebrate their 100th birthday.

Back at the campsite, sleep came easily.

Saturday, June 14, 1997

I awoke to discover Eliana had left a lunch of food and juices in my trailer that morning. I packed up and then stopped by the house to give my thanks and say goodbye. I headed out of Dryden to see that, even on a Saturday, the pulp and paper plant which employs 1,000 in this community of 6,500, was working and chucking out smoke.

My chain broke at Vermilion Bay and it took me an hour to fix it. My hands were black from the grease. Riding for 85 kilometres, I pulled off the road, just into the forest. Experience had taught me that I would be facing a major bug situation, so I donned my white "Don't Bug Me Shirt". It covers my head and has a bug screen where the face opening is located - I looked like a NASA astronaut. That was a good move, as in minutes there were thousands of mosquitoes around me. Once safely in the sanctuary of my tent, I listened to the deafening sounds of the night forest. The crinkle and crunch of footsteps, as animals scurried across the large ground sheet around my tent, made for a restless night.

Sunday, June 15, 1997

At 5:00 am, I packed up. The sky was blue and the mosquitoes were waiting for me. I wore my bug shirt until I made it out of the forest.

It was Father's Day and I remembered my own father who had passed away. I had a unusual relationship with my father. I remember my dad giving me a special gift at 15, by taking me to the Joe Namath Football Camp in Dudley, Massachusetts. As a young football player and a Canadian, I competed against the best football players in the USA in my age category. At the end of the camp my father announced abruptly that we were leaving, just before the farewell award ceremony. I asked my dad to check with Camp Officials before we left because I had an outstanding camp and might be receiving an award from Superbowl Champion Quarterback, Joe Namath. My dad went inside the camp office and then came out and told me I hadn't won an award. We left on our nine hour drive back home to Canada. Two weeks later my Joe Namath trophy arrived in the mail. I had been chosen as the "Outstanding Receiver".

Then I thought that here it was Father's Day and I wasn't with my son. Alone on the highway, early Sunday morning, I cried as I pedaled, thinking I wasn't much better. But in my heart, I knew that the results of the *To The Top Canada* expedition would change my son forever. He would learn that either "anything is possible" or that "quitting is easy". I was determined that James would have a father that would not quit, not now, not ever!

I pedaled through road construction but this was not just paving. An accident had occurred in the eighties that was an environmental catastrophe, whereby a truck leaked PCB's all over the highway. Here it was 1997 and they were just cleaning it up. I pedaled faster when I read the fluorescent orange words sprayed on the highway, "PCB'S CLEAN". The words on the highway implied that I was cycling directly over the area that needed to be cleaned from hazardous PCB chemicals.

After three hours of early morning cycling I arrived in Kenora to be greeted by a hail storm. I tilted my head forward so the hail wouldn't hurt my face. It sounded like someone was dropping gravel on my helmet. I arrived in town in time to attend the church service. I mentioned to a few people at the coffee hour that I needed a place to stay. There were no takers. After the service it was pouring rain and I looked like a drowned rat. I tried an independent motel for a donated room. They said no. I tried

Days Inn. They said no. I called home to talk to my family and my son read his Father's Day card to me over the phone.

Carol encouraged me to treat myself to a nice meal for Father's Day. I went to a local restaurant and enjoyed the luxury of table service.

I then went to the Kenora Comfort Inn. They said yes to donating a room. It was just early afternoon but I was tired and once my gear was in my room I took a long hot shower and went to bed.

Monday, June 16, 1997

It was sunny when I woke up. Kenora is beautiful in the sunshine as it sits on a beautiful lake. I met the Mayor and the media at my 9:30 am ceremony. After a late breakfast, I headed out on 17, west towards the Manitoba-Ontario border. By noon hour, I was starving again and stopped at a roadside restaurant for dinner. At 3:20 pm central time I crossed the border into Manitoba. It felt great to finally enter a new province!

Stopping at the Visitor Centre, I made some phone calls and sought direction from two friendly receptionists. Following their advice, I rode another 14 kilometres to Falcon Lake Provincial Park. In the centre was a small shopping area with a grocery store, doctor's office, video store and what's this . . . a restaurant! On this day where I couldn't stop eating, the owner gave me my hot turkey sandwich and pie for half price. I felt like a glutton eating three restaurant meals in one day. But today was a special day. Not only had I crossed my first border, but I had arrived at the 2,300 km mark of the *To The Top Canada* expedition.

Tuesday, June 17, 1997

In the rain, at 6:30 am, I raced the mosquitoes to the shower cabin. Just as I returned to my tent after cleaning up, it started raining very hard. I wrote in my journal until almost noon, waiting for the rain to stop. A puddle seemed to have formed in my tent but my mattress was an island, where I was dry, so I just kept writing until I was up-to-date.

I headed out in the rain and cycled 50 kilometres. The construction and rain slowed me down. Near the end of the day I pulled over to set up camp at a small rest stop located in the Provincial Forest Reserve. In Ontario, there is no camping allowed at roadside rest stops. I saw no "camping prohibited" signs but, to be cautious, I set my camp up behind an information display sign that completely hid my tent. My gear was still wet from the night before but I was tired and went straight to sleep.

Wednesday, June 18, 1997

At 1:00 am, I was awakened by the sound of a bear opening steel garbage cans. The bear's jaws sounded like a can opener on an aluminum beer can. I grabbed my survival knife and my safety flare from my bag and lay perfectly still in my tent. My heart was pounding so loud I thought the bear would hear it. He was getting closer. I got out of my sleeping bag - if we were going to fight, I wanted to be mobile. I was ready to fight for my life. The only time I could remember being this scared was scuba diving in my twenties in the Caribbean by a coral reef. A shark the size of a Lincoln Continental Town Car came out of the haze and swam overhead. I stopped breathing so there would be no bubbles to alert the shark, and froze. Fortunately, this same strategy, and the hidden location of my camp, worked for me again. The bear passed by. I didn't fall asleep for two hours. Early that morning the sun greeted me. I went into the rest room facility. There, I took up one of the most dangerous of extreme sports - shaving and swatting mosquitoes.

The ground was littered with garbage from last night's bear visit. I wore my bug shirt as I packed up camp. With good weather I made it to Winnipeg. At the City Limits I stopped to take a picture of the city sign. At that time I noticed my BOB trailer tire was flat. I put a new tube in and went down the highway and the new tube ruptured. I checked the tube and found it was defective. The problem was compounded by my BOB trailer tire being almost worn out. Arriving in Winnipeg meant I had travelled 2,450 kilometres. At a local store, I purchased a new tire. By the time I completed the installation it was 9:30 pm. It was close to the summer solstice so it was still light out. The Holiday Inn South on Pembina Highway was going to put me up for three nights in Winnipeg but they weren't expecting me until Thursday afternoon. I decided to continue riding from the east end of Winnipeg, downtown, where I would scout out City Hall and the provincial Legislative Building to find the entrance and the best location to park my bike when I arrived.

I ended up at a community landmark called "The Forks". This is where human settlement began in the west, 6,000 years ago, where the Red and Assiniboine Rivers meet. Today it is a combination park and shopping complex. I sat on a park bench and put my feet up on a special foot rest built in front of every bench and watched the water flow by.

There was a full moon and great music was playing at a nearby patio restaurant. I enjoyed resting and feeling the breeze. I spoke with a fellow named Eric and he told me a story about the 1997 Flood of the Century. Sandbag dykes were built and patrolled by the Canadian Armed Forces. During the flood rescue efforts, Eric and two workers took a cigarette break late one night by the dyke. Suddenly, they were surrounded by soldiers with rifles who came flying over a wall. After explaining what they were doing, they were asked to move away from the dyke. An overhead armed forces helicopter, in the black of night, had detected their heat signatures on infrared sensors. A special emergency response team was immediately dispatched to contain the targets. The stakes were high, as even a small leak in the dykes could quickly turn into a giant leak that could wipe out the City of Winnipeg.

As The Forks closed up late in the wee hours of the morning, I headed to the south end of Winnipeg, to the Holiday Inn. At 2:00 am, I arrived and was greeted by Sheldon at the front desk. Sheldon knew that I was a "VIP", but he had no rooms. I suggested we put my gear in the baggage room and I would sit in a lounge chair until morning when a room would be available. Sheldon agreed and indicated that he would ensure housekeeping staff were notified next morning and I would have the first room available.

I sat down in a comfortable chair and thought, "This is a business class seat". As a seasoned frequent flyer, I have the ability to effectively kill airline flying time by sleeping through any flight, regardless of the distance. This chair reminded me of a first class airline seat. I turned toward the wall so the hotel didn't look as if they had provided a stopover for some vagabond wanderer. True to form, I immediately fell asleep.

Thursday, June 19, 1997

I woke up at 6:00 am, still tired. In the hotel washroom, I splashed cold water on my face. People would be checking out and didn't need to listen to my snoring. At 6:30 am the hotel restaurant opened, giving me a chance to order some breakfast. At 8:30 am, I was assigned room 813. Up in the room, I got an additional three hours of sleep. Around noon, I tidied myself up and headed out on my bike with no gear. At the CBC, I did a short in-studio interview. Then I was off to radio station CJOB, where I took part in an hour long phone-in show with host James Loewen. James was a great guy, down-to-earth, and very likeable. It was good to discuss the real importance of the *To The Top Canada* expedition with the people of Winnipeg. One regular caller named "Cowboy Bob" wrote a poem for me which he read on the air.

James had never expected me to ride my bike to the station - he had taxi vouchers prepared for me. That evening the radio station news room was covering the weather which had turned bad. Thunder storms and a twister had touched down near Winnipeg. I took up James' offer and my bike and I went back to the Holiday Inn in a taxi van. The Holiday Inn had arranged for a $30 a day food credit in their restaurant. That evening, I enjoyed their prime rib and salad bar. It seemed as if I'd died and gone to heaven. I went right to bed as I faced an early start next morning.

Friday, June 20, 1997

I loaded all my gear so television could capture the full picture of the *To The Top Canada* expedition, even though I would be coming back to the hotel that night.

At City Hall, I was presented with a book about Winnipeg, a large chocolate coat of arms of the City of Winnipeg and a T-Shirt depicting the Great Flood. Councillor Pat took great care of me with cold refreshments. At one point I started calling her "Mom". Knowing my giant chocolate bar of the coat of arms would melt in my bag, I ate it all after the media interviews and washed it down with a drink. Right after my reception, the Ambassador of Mexico arrived for an official visit. All I can say is, I hope the Government of Mexico has a dental plan!

That afternoon I headed to the Legislature, where I was greeted by MPP Merv Whittle who represents the constituency of Turtle Mountain. Later, I needed to find a phone for a drive time interview with radio station CFRA in Ottawa, that would be re-broadcast throughout the CHUM national radio network. At a pay phone in the vestibule of a Zellers department store, I strained to hear the interviewer's questions over the sound of shopping carts crashing into doors.

Back at the Holiday Inn, I called it a day.

Saturday, June 21, 1997

With my supply of clean clothes exhausted, I caught up my laundry in the hotel facilities and later mailed my gifts from Kenora and Winnipeg, home to Carol. It was important to keep my travel weight down to a minimum.

Today was my son's first football practice and as I talked to him on the phone I knew he was ready for it with a vengeance. Last year, he was a captain of his football team and after only a couple of games he was injured with a broken collar bone, not in football, but in gym class at school.

He was coming into this season knowing that even tough football practices are a privilege that should be cherished while your body "allows you" to play the great game of football. I felt the same way at age 41. My body was performing well, but as injuries had taught me, at anytime your ability to do physical activity can be taken from you with the break of a bone or snap of a ligament. I cherished every day that I could pedal during the *To The Top Canada* expedition.

I used the remaining time to update my daily journal. Finally, I enjoyed some leisure time in the hotel whirlpool, warming my muscles that now experienced perpetual soreness.

Sunday, June 22, 1997

I delivered a thank you card to the Holiday Inn Hotel which had been one of Canada's kindest hotels on my expedition. Now I was off on a 70 kilometre ride to Portage La Prairie. The sun was shining and it was a great day to ride. I stopped at a restaurant for lunch in Elie, Manitoba. The restaurant was full and everyone spoke

French. People in southern Ontario tend to think that most French Canadians live in Quebec, with very few French Canadians outside Quebec. I have found that there is a geographical band of French Canadians, outside Quebec, in Sudbury, Sault Ste. Marie, Thunder Bay, Winnipeg and now Elie. The French culture is alive and well in a part of Canada that had been labeled "English Canada"! I wondered if Quebecers also have the same misconception about French culture outside of Quebec. If Quebecers only knew how much French culture there was outside Quebec they might reject the isolationist strategy of separatists.

My clean white T-shirt was covered with little black dots. On closer inspection I saw that they were miniature flies which I dubbed "nanoflies". The Flood of the Century had covered most of southern Manitoba with water. This created superb conditions for insect development. This would be the worst summer in history in southern Manitoba for pesky insects.

Arriving in Portage La Prairie, I discovered most motels had no vacancy. CN workers were laying down a special fiberoptic cable and had taken all the motel rooms. I did get the very last room at the Sunset Motel, hidden on the west side of town. The owner gave me $7.00 off the $45.00 rate to help Canada.

Turning on the TV, I caught the news and discovered evening thunderstorms were in the forecast so it was a good move to be in a motel that night. The next day I had an in-studio appearance on MTN TV, so I wanted to be cleanly shaven.

On TV I noticed that there were only seven channels. One channel was HBO which was the U.S. Network Home Box Office, usually not available in Canada. Another channel was the Trinity Broadcasting Network. It reminded me that in Canada the Crossroad Ministries, which professionally produces 100 Huntley Street and purchases air time on Canadian stations, had applied for permission from the CRTC (Canadian Radio and Television Commission) to start a Canadian Christian network and was turned down. This government regulatory body had forgotten that "God" is in Canada's national anthem. I said a prayer that God would help the members of the CRTC change its mind. I took pleasure in knowing that Trinity Broadcasting Network (TBN) was on the air in Manitoba. I took a GPS reading which revealed I had cycled 85 kilometres that day from southeast Winnipeg. I settled in and enjoyed watching both TBN and HBO that evening.

Monday, June 23, 1997

Being in Portage La Prairie had special significance. It meant I had travelled 2,520 kilometres and had an even 4,000 to go. In the morning I visited the newspaper, radio station and City Hall. At City Hall, I was approached by a girl behind the counter. With some sense of urgency she said she had received a call from Scott Jenzi, the host for Pulse News on MTN TV. He wanted to be notified immediately when I arrived in town. With that said, she picked up the phone and called Scott. I motioned for her to put me on but she kept the phone. It soon became apparent to me that she was talking with the handsome news anchor, Scott Jenzi, and she wasn't going to give up the phone. After saying "please let me speak" a dozen times she finally released the phone, although reluctantly. I confirmed with Scott that I would be available for our interview at noon, ahead of schedule. Enroute to the station, I was met by a Pulse News truck. A camera man directed me to Island Park. This was a beautiful landscaped park surrounded by a circular lake called "Crescent Lake". In the Island Park, he videotaped me riding my bike for footage as part of my Pulse News segment. At MTN studios, Scott was very friendly and we filmed our interview outside to allow me to head down the highway sooner.

Just outside of Portage La Prairie I turned onto Highway #16, known as the Yellowhead Highway. This road would take me the 1,280 kilometres to Edmonton. The Yellowhead Highway got its name from an Iroquois trapper in the early 1800's. His name was Pierre Bostonais and he had a tinge of blonde in his hair. I rode 60 kilometres and camped just off the road between Gladstone and Neepawa. It was a hot muggy night. I poured water on a t-shirt to dampen it and pat my body, to cool off.

Tuesday, June 24, 1997

Surprisingly, not a single mosquito greeted me from the opposite side of my tent netting. Every morning up until this point, I had felt like a U.S. marine stationed at Guantanimo Bay in Cuba. Hundreds of mosquitoes would be on my tent netting waiting for me to emerge. This morning I enjoyed the truce from the war against the insects.

Neepawa proudly wears the mantle of being Manitoba's most beautiful town. Every home's landscaping is manicured with precision. After meeting the staff at the two newspapers in town, I went to the Hazel M. Kellington School, called HMK for short. At ten to twelve I met Principal Nelson and after presenting myself to him, we agreed I would address students at the closing ceremonies being held at 1:00 pm that day at the Roxy Theatre. I shaved in the staff washroom at the school. A local restaurant up the street from the Roxy Theatre donated my lunch. The Roxy was a great venue, because I had not only all the students, but all the parents in town as a captive audience. I kept my program short and high energy to keep the attention of the students. As I finished I left the stage to their cheers and high fives.

Enroute to the next community, Minnedosa, I was buffeted by the powerful prairie winds, slowing me down. On my arrival in Minnedosa, the local pizza parlour (which is also an inn), donated supper. Riding through town that evening I met a nice couple who were drawing water out of the river to soak the hanging flowers downtown. Jim and Kelly Bennett owned the local flower shop. They invited me to come to their house for the night, situated a couple of miles outside of town. On my way there I ran into two problems. My trailer fender came off, jamming into the wheel and bringing me to a noisy stop. As I completed a temporary repair, my saddle bag fell apart, something I had been expecting. I had been holding it together with black electrical tape from Radio Shack in Winnipeg. Tying my saddle bag and fender to the trailer, I continued on to the Bennett home. Just as I was arriving, a bad storm was heading in with black clouds and high winds.

I apologized for arriving late and explained about my technical difficulty. The Bennetts happened to have a new pair of good quality saddle bags. They offered to sell them to me for their cost of $85.00. I agreed and we made the plan that I would pay by Visa at their flower shop tomorrow. I slept well, glad to be in out of the rain.

Wednesday, June 25, 1997

After breakfast with the Bennetts, I headed into town and met with the Minnedosa Tribune. Afterward I went to the Minnedoso Flower and Gift Shop and paid for my saddle bags. The night before I had told the Bennetts about the chocolate coat of arms from Winnipeg. Kelly said she didn't want to be outdone by Winnipeg and presented me with a chocolate Manitoba Buffalo. After goodbyes, I headed over to the Tansley Crossing School to offer my services to speak to the students on their last day of the term. The secretary came back after speaking to the Vice Principal and told me that they couldn't fit me in. It was interesting to compare responses over the last two days. It seemed that I had encountered teachers and processors. Teachers, like Principal Nelson at HMK and the high school teacher in Bracebridge who put a high school assembly together in ten minutes were leaders, willing to do whatever it took to put student learning first. On the other hand, I had encountered processors who treated students like numbers, or cattle, and just moved them from program to program. Heaven forbid someone should ask to change the order in their schedule. For the rest of my life I would be watching to ensure my son got a teacher to teach him and not a processor.

I pedaled out of town to where the bypass highway met the road through the town. Calling home from a telephone at the corner, I spoke with Carol and James who had just come from his Grade 5 graduation ceremony at Holbrook School. James got straight A's in all subjects and had won seven awards at the special ceremony. I was heart broken that I had not been there to share this moment with him. My voice cracked as I told him how proud of him I was. As I rode off down the highway into a heavy downpour of rain, I yelled to the heavens, "You're going to have to throw more than a storm at me to stop me. I'm the proud father of an award winning student!"

The train tracks were directly parallel to the Yellowhead highway and a CP train engineer gave me the thumbs up and sounded his horn as he passed. I cycled 53 kilometres into Shoal Lake. As I walked through the door of Linda's Restaurant, the owner asked me what I wanted. After ordering a hot chocolate and toast, I went to the washed up and looked forward to relaxing after a busy day. When I came out of the washroom, I found my toast in foil and my hot chocolate in a styrofoam cup. The woman said she was closing the restaurant. I commented that I thought the restaurant closed at 9 pm, because that is what I read on the hours of operation sign at the front.

It was now 7:00 pm. She said she had a staff member arriving on the Gray Goose Bus in Brandon and she had to go to pick her up. I paid for my food and ate it on a bench outside the restaurant. I wondered if the Ambassador of Mexico had ever been to Shoal Lake.

At a local campsite run by the Lions Club, I chose a campsite beside a couple who were travelling in their Volkswagen Rabbit. I set up my tent, stowed my gear inside, read half of the Gospel of Mark in the Bible and then walked to the washroom. I noticed the couple with the Rabbit were still setting up their tent. It dawned on me that I had finally become extremely proficient with this camping routine. Practice does make perfect!

Thursday, June 26, 1997

I was one day ahead of schedule on a plan that would put me in Yorkton, Saskatchewan, on Canada Day. I decided to make Shoal Lake a rest and maintenance stop.

First, I visited the Shoal Lake newspaper called "The Star", then the office of The Village of Shoal Lake. I met Mayor Mary Fiel who worked running the community for only $3,200 a year. She presented me with a pin of Shoal Lake which had a duck on the insignia. This was appropriate, as the wildlife organization Ducks Unlimited had a maintenance compound here. At the hardware store, I picked up some nuts, washers and bolts to fix my disabled trailer fender.

I had some breakfast which was donated by Allen Choy's Restaurant. On the restaurant TV, CNN reported that the MIR space station had sprung a leak after a collision. And I thought I had a bad day yesterday!

After making some phone calls in replying to requests for media interviews, I went back to my camp to relax. Reading the local paper, I came across a story about an uproar caused by bureaucrats in love with Manitoba mosquitoes. It seems a local store was selling a tiny battery operated device called the Mosquito Hawk. This device replicates the wing-beat frequency of the dragon fly, the number one predator of the biting mosquito. A local government inspector ordered the store to "Get it down!" from the shelf. The device's label declared it a "Mosquito Repeller", which was in violation of the Canada Pesticide Act. Manitobans unanimously hate the mosquito as much as I do, and they were outraged that they now could not buy this device that worked so well. They were also outraged that the government has staff being paid salaries with nothing better to do than hassle people who are trying to kill mosquitoes. This story has a happy ending. The federal government has agreed to let the device go on sale as soon as the label says "The Mosquito Hawk replicates the wing beat frequency of the dragon fly, the Number One predator of mosquitoes." I wondered if the label would also have to carry this message in French.

Near my camp was a re-created barracks constructed of logs, a North West Mounted

Police base used in the early 1800's. I'm not sure how authentic it was, because I couldn't see a Tim Horton's made of logs near by.

I was bold that evening and went back to Linda's Restaurant. It was full of seniors who were enjoying the senior's special, a full turkey dinner and ice cream sundae for under $7.00. The owner, Linda Rose, donated my supper, the seniors' special with huge portions. I sat with two elderly ladies I'd befriended, named Avis and Margaret. They were dear friends, both widows, and both with a sense of humour. Avis said she was looking for a single rich man with one foot on a banana peel and the other in a grave. Margaret was Irish and too busy for a social life because she said she was "running the Canadian chapter of the IRA". I enjoyed the company of these spirited Shoal Lake citizens. After supper, I sprayed lubricant on my bike chain as the one day holiday was over and tomorrow I had some serious cycling to do.

Friday, June 27, 1997

Heading out early, I was faced with a 30 kph head wind. My only choice was to drop down several gears, keep pedaling and move slower. The wind felt like horizontal gravity. I went through a beautiful valley where horses and young colts were galloping in the fields. Except for an early morning Nutribar, I had not eaten today. In Foxwarren there was a restaurant at the Esso station. They had a special of all-you-could-eat stew and mashed potatoes. I had three helpings and then two helpings of jello for dessert.

I arrived in Russell, my destination, just around 4:30 pm. I arrived at the Russell Banner just before they closed. The reporter mentioned to me that Russell doesn't celebrate Canada Day. The look of shock on my face was quite evident. The reporter further stated, "I was surprised too, when I first came here and heard that!"

I wasn't in a position to look into the matter further, but I pondered the circumstances where apathy for our country would be strong enough that there would be no Canada Day celebrations in a whole town. Riding through Russell, I did see Canada's flags flying but to me, Canada Day means more. I had been through some very poor little towns in Manitoba but even there I saw tremendous Canadian pride. In these small towns, there would be canisters labeled Canada Day next to cash registers, where locals collected loose change for a Canada Day fireworks display.

On Canada Day, there should be fireworks, a parade, a concert and a community picnic, at least. The essence of the *To The Top Canada* expedition is to create an environment where Canadians celebrate Canada every day with action and deeds of merit, not only on Canada Day. Maybe I had arrived in Russell with my Canada pride message, just in time, before the spark of spirit went out.

Saturday, June 28, 1997

Up early, I went over to the local laundromat before heading down the road. This was the last day of the *To The Top Canada* expedition in Manitoba. When I crossed the border, I entered a new time zone called Central Standard time. This put me two hours behind my home in Hamilton.

I wanted to phone home to tell them I was in Saskatchewan but there was no phone or visitor centre at the border. The first public phone was at Gopherville, Saskatchewan. James laughed when he heard I was in Gopherville. This is a small tourist trap featuring the world's longest bicycle which is 85 feet long. The restaurant plays lively polka music and small shops sell knick knacks. After lunch I headed into Langenburg and, just after visiting the first Saskatchewan visitor centre, my chain snapped again. You would think it would be easier, but it seemed tougher to fix the second time around. After cleaning up in the small engine store, I met with the editor of the local paper. I was lucky to catch editor Bill Johnson on a Saturday. Late in the afternoon, my supper was donated by Kevin who owns the local Chinese restaurant.

As it was sunny out, I decided to ride on to Churchbridge. In Churchbridge, I was greeted by a giant loonie that commemorates Canada's 125th anniversary. The artwork for this coin was created by Ruth Swanson, a local artist, and features a family in front of Canada's parliament building.

I found the local campground, but I wasn't sure if I had to pay or if it was complementary for the public like the one I'd stayed at the night before in Russell. Later that evening a camp collector came by. The camp collector asked about my bike and I told him about my *To The Top Canada* expedition. He asked me how it was going and I told him great, that local hotels and campgrounds were donating their facilities. He made it clear Churchbridge was not donating and he wanted $10.00. I pulled out my VISA and he said he only takes cash. I looked in my wallet and confirmed I didn't have cash. To look after him, I rode into town and used Interac at the local bar to obtain the money, as there was no ATM bank machine in town. It was late and when the camp collector came back I gave him $10.00. Before he left, he told me not to be startled if I heard gunshots at 4:30 am that morning, it would just be him killing crows, (or camp people who had not paid their $10.00, I suspect).

Sunday, June 29, 1997

I must have slept through the crow shooting because I woke up at 7:00 am, or 9:00 am eastern time. I read ten chapters of the Book of John in the Bible. Then I packed up and headed off to the local Anglican church. While waiting outside the church which was locked, some local people came over and told me that on the fifth Sunday of the month the church had their service at another church in the region. With no church today, I decided to move on. Before leaving town, I took some pictures of beautiful murals painted on the front of a building commemorating historic community life. One mural was dedicated to an old town doctor who had delivered over 3,000 babies.

I popped into Bredenbury for lunch. There is only one restaurant in town. They don't take American Express, they don't take Visa, they don't take Mastercard and they don't take Interac. If I had not learned my lesson yesterday that you have to carry large sums of cash in Saskatchewan, I was about to. Upon confirming that they only take cash, I asked if there was a bank machine in town, to which the answer was "no". I got up to leave the restaurant but the owner said he would take a cheque. I told him I had no cheque with me. He said I looked very hungry. He asked me to sit down, have lunch and send him the money when I had a chance. I was hungry, so I agreed. It felt terrible to eat and have an I.O.U. hanging over my head. The first ATM I could find would not be too soon for me.

I cycled on to Saltcoats. Jack Dawes did the Agriculture report on radio GX94 in Yorkton. He also ran the local campground. When I met him he was working in the canteen and doing a brisk business as a local team was playing baseball. His son Kyle made a double burger and fries for my supper. It looked like rain so they asked me to stay at their house for the evening instead of camping.

Monday, June 30, 1997

I was off to Yorkton where I would be today and tomorrow, which was Canada Day. It was raining when I cycled off. Jack left in his car at the same time. Jack, drawing on his own experience cycling into town, told the Tourist Bureau staff that the earliest I would arrive would be 11:30 am. I actually arrived at 9:45 am. I was just in time to meet the media who were there for a conference announcing that the Chamber of Commerce were committing $10,000 to the Weinmaster Centre, a community fitness facility that was proposed for the future.

It was an excellent opportunity to introduce myself to the area's reporters. Afterwards, I used the Chamber's phone to contact several media outlets that had asked me to check in with them to let them know where I was from time to time. It was a special time to let them know that, on Canada Day, I was celebrating in Yorkton, Saskatchewan.

I tried some local motels to see if they could donate a room. With the holiday and the Yorkton Regional Fair opening that week, everything was gone. KFC donated my lunch. Using a phone to check my voice mail box, I learned that the national radio network Broadcast News was trying to get in touch with me. I called them in Toronto and gave an interview. Later, at radio station GX94 Jack Dawes gave me a tour.

I did a long interview with Blaise, the afternoon program host, slipping in a plug for a volunteer to put me up for two nights, especially considering it was raining hard.

After the interview, Jack gave me a copy of my story that had just come over the wire service from Broadcast News. The station got a call from Bev Craig who volunteered to take me in. I spoke with Bev and made arrangements for her husband Jim to rendezvous with me in their pickup truck. Jim drove towards his home in the country, just outside Yorkton. The pickup truck was travelling very fast. I glanced over and saw our speed was 100 kph on a wet dirt road. I was worried that my bike would flip out of the back. Also, I was glad I was still wearing my bike helmet. I hadn't been in a car since June 2nd, almost a month, and perceptually my senses now related to bike speed. This was too fast for a bike and the sensation was frightening. I remember once having the same sensation on an Air Canada flight when the pilot invited me into the cockpit, to sit on a fold down chair during landing into Toronto. We broke through the clouds and there was the runway. We were travelling much faster in relation to the ground than any speed I had ever done on the 401 highway. My right foot instinctively pushed forward, to brake. This was a speed I was not used to experiencing! We soon arrived at their country house and I carried in the gear that needed protection from the rain. I met Bev and her young grandson, Brian. We sat down to supper right away. Afterward, I did a phone interview with CJOB in Winnipeg. I called it an early evening because tomorrow was Canada Day!

Tuesday, July, 1, 1997

Despite my best efforts to move about quietly, it seemed every floor board creaked in the early morning silence. After a delicious breakfast, I loaded all my gear in order to be ready for a TV interview that morning with the BBS affiliate.

In the studio, I talked at length with video journalist Robert Brown about every aspect of the *To The Top Canada* expedition. We then went out for a morning of videotaping. First I unloaded all my gear from my bike, so he could film me loading up. Then Robert had me approach numerous people at McDonald's and speak to them about my question, "What will you do before the year 2000 to make Canada a better country than when you found it?" In front of McDonald's, Robert interviewed me at length on camera. Finally I rode my bike up and down Broadway, which is the main street, so he could videotape me riding.

After that session, Robert said he would catch me again at 2:00 pm, where he would tape my Canada Day remarks.

At St. Mary's Catholic Church in Yorkton, I was astounded to find North America's greatest religious painting. The painted interior dome of St. Mary's features Jesus, in heaven, with over 100 angels. Yorkton achieved celebrity status when a question about St. Mary's was asked on the television programme Jeopardy! I took some quiet time, before marvelling at this work, saying my personal prayers to God. I then admired the ceiling for its beauty, but more for the dedication it took to complete this masterpiece. I needed to have that same strength of purpose to complete the *To The Top Canada* expedition.

Then it was off to Yorkton's Western Development Museum where the Canada Day celebrations would take place.

I spoke with many people who wanted to meet me after hearing me on the radio. Many of these people were farmers, who had a special personal bond with their land. A person like me, who would leave home and travel a vast distance across Canada away from their land, was a foreign concept to them, but they sensed that there was strong importance to my mission and respected me for it. Then the official ceremony began, as the Yorkton Regional High School Marching Band came parading in. As they played O' Canada, I took my *To The Top Canada* cap off and covered my heart. Ben, the Mayor, and Clay, the new provincial Minister of Health, gave eloquent speeches from behind the microphone stand in the gazebo. Then it was my turn. To this point, the crowd of 500 people had stood quietly and politely, in cool weather of only 9° C, on a cloudy day, listening to the speeches. I took the mike from the stand and left the gazebo, where the official delegates were standing.

I spoke with passion about my love for Canada. I then brought the crowd alive by having them cheer "I am Canadian". After my remarks, Robert from BBS told me that I was great and said he'd received a call from CTV National News and they wanted him to send a clip. I was swarmed by people who came up to express their appreciation for my speech. After meeting many people who were inspired by my remarks, one man interrupted me as I spoke to a farmer and his daughter. He complained, "I didn't hear you say one thing about Western Canada. You easterners are always telling us what to do! We'd be better off if the west broke off from the east!" At this point I jumped in and casually remarked, "Oh, so you're a western separatist. What are you doing at a Canada Day gathering?" The man, embarrassed, said nothing more and slipped away. The farmer gave me a grin that told me he enjoyed me putting the man in his place, and watching him leave like a dog with his tail between his hind legs.

Jim met me for another pickup truck ride, at warp speed, to the country house. Outside their home, it was so cool that a hummingbird could not fly and Jim brought it in the house to warm up. I couldn't help but think how much I had in common with the hummingbird. We were both depending on Jim and Bev for shelter and warmth from the cold. It had been a Canada Day I will never forget!

Wednesday, July 2, 1997

Jim left the house at 4:00 am to get to his job with the Post Office. After breakfast, Bev drove me to the Western Development Museum so I could continue on my journey. At the museum, I showed Bev how to use my GPS. Heading out, I saw the first blue sky in three days, but the winds were gusting at 40 kph out of the north and were quite cool. Many cars and one train honked their horns at me in support. At a beverage room in Theodore, I relished a pork chop meal for lunch. To my surprise a man next to me was a radio GX94 sales representative who had heard me on his station and he picked up my bill. I thanked him and headed on.

At Foam Lake, a campground spot was donated by the tourist information station. According to my GPS, I had pedaled 86 kilometres today. I listened to country music all day on GX94, including a Jack Dawes agriculture report about how a producer of pigs' ears sent a box to Mike Tyson, after he was disqualified this week in a championship fight, for biting Evander Holyfield's ear. I listened to CBC to hear the political fallout as the Somalia report was released. The report was very critical but the government seemed to be dismissing it. Like the reporter covering the story, I was shocked at this response to this very serious matter. Also, I was saddened to hear of the death of Jimmy Stewart today. I was inspired by his portrayal of George Bailey in "It's a Wonderful Life!" The moral of this movie is that one man does make a difference, which George finds out when an angel grants his wish that he never be born. I personally believe that one man does make a difference and that my *To The Top Canada* expedition will change our country for ever...

Thursday, July 3, 1997

At the Foam Lake Campground washroom, I noticed that the shower was coin operated. I didn't have any coins so a shower was not going to happen this morning. I shaved and washed up in the sink. Packing up, I cycled west along a straight, flat road that wound past field after field. On each side of the road, I could see green all the way to the horizon. Occasionally a gopher would run out on the road, try to outrun my bike and then bail back into the tall grass.

I stopped for lunch in Elfros. My waitress had a husband in the armed forces, who was home from maneuvers. He was close to being able to retire with a pension. She watched her husband wake up in the morning, with numbness in his limbs. Even though the Gulf War was over, Gulf War Syndrome was a very real part of his life every day. The other peeve she had with military life was substandard housing for military personnel. She told me that the Canadian military had more housing capacity than they needed so they offered it to Social Services to be used for Canadians on social assistance. After an inspection of the military housing facilities, the Canadian Armed forces offer was rejected because the housing did not meet minimum standards for those on social assistance. Not good enough for social assistance, but good enough for brave Canadians who are ready to put their lives on the line to protect our country. The injustice of this story sickened me. When I went to pay my bill for lunch they wouldn't take any money. I thanked them very much and headed on my way. After just under 50 kilometres, I pulled into my destination of Wynyard, Saskatchewan. I went to the local paper, the Wynyard Advance, and told my story. After checking my voice mail I returned a call to CBC North, which provided service to the territories. I did an interview but it gave me a funny feeling. In some ways, I still can't believe I'm on my way to the top of Canada. The thought of me standing at the edge of the Arctic Ocean gives me goosebumps. Talking to CBC North made

My family and I at the tip of Point Pelee.

Photo: Barry Shainbaum

All the national television networks cover the To The Top Canada expedition.

Photo: Barry Shainbaum

Spreading the gospel of pride in Canada in Bracebridge.

Photo: Barry Shainbaum

The bug shirt saved my life in Northern Ontario.

One of over twenty flat tires, during the To The Top Canada expedition.

Painted landscapes on buildings made Prairie towns delightful to explore.

The Big Sky of Saskatchewan stretches as far as your eyes can see.

Camping by the side of the road thousands of kilometres from home.

Getting directions in Watson Lake's Sign Forest.

Once you're on the Dempster there is only God to help you.

Only your determination will allow you to triumph over hundreds of kilometres of mountains.

The Arctic Circle seemed more like a desert than the tundra.

Mud, ice and snow work to defeat me as the temperature is quickly dropping.

Cracks in the ice are everywhere on the ice trail over the Arctic Ocean.

Dancing with Inuvialuit children made the community cheer at my Tuktoyaktuk welcome celebration.

Welcome home by my family celebrating the success of the To The Top Canada expedition.

me realize that the people of the Arctic have heard of the *To The Top Canada* expedition and are waiting for me. This isn't a dream. I am actually on this incredible history-making journey!

The Southshore Motor Lodge donated a room for the night. I enjoyed a long shower that evening, and supper donated by the local KFC. The staff had seen me on TV so I didn't have to explain my expedition. Riding through downtown Wynyard, I noticed that the community was raising money for Jerome and Audrey, whose home and belongings were destroyed in a fire. Love, kindness and caring was the character of this small town. I knew, because I had experienced it first hand.

Friday, July 4, 1997

Riding along, the scenery looked just like it had the day before until I saw something beside the road that I had not seen in Saskatchewan before. It was a huge lake. Growing up on the shores of Lake Ontario I have always liked being close to the water. This lake was big - in the distance the water met the horizon and I could not see the land on the other side.

I learned that this was Big Quill Lake. Big Quill Lake was an important staging area for millions of migratory birds, including some endangered species. The Yellowhead Highway also wound past several ponds that were formed when a melting glacier had created this natural habitat. I discovered that Ducks Unlimited doesn't need any lessons from McDonald's. I passed several signs all showing the Ducks Unlimited logo and identifying each special duck reserve. This part of the Yellowhead, with its gentle rolling hills, the water and the rural homes, reminded me of PEI and the drive from Borden to Charlottetown.

After cycling 29 km, I came to the first restaurant where I stopped for my first meal of the day. It was located at the spot where the Yellowhead meets Highway 6. On the menu they had a hamburger, a loaded hamburger and a double loaded hamburger. I opted for the clubhouse, because I had this vision of dropping dead 1/2 mile down the road from the cholesterol in the double loaded hamburger.

By mid afternoon, I reached Lanigan which was my goal for that day. I met with the local newspaper. It was a sunny day and I felt good, so I decided to keep riding.

Several kilometres down the road, it turned cloudy. Then it started! The worst thunderstorm of my life. Lightning was flashing all around. Bolts as round as telephone poles and taller than the Toronto CN Tower were striking the ground a stone's throw away from me. I was listening to gospel music on my Walkman as I pedaled through the storm. The violent crashes of thunder would drown out the music even through headphones. I pedaled as hard and as fast as I could to get out of the storm's line of fire. Once again, my life was in God's hands. After what seemed to be a long time, I cleared the storm. After a day of cycling and an hour of sprinting, I was totally exhausted. I slowly cycled into Viscount. There was a beverage room where I thought I'd grab some supper. It was Friday night and the bar was busy. I walked in with my fluorescent green rain jacket, wearing my helmet and gloves. The bar went silent. It was like a science fiction movie, where the alien creature comes in and everyone is too scared to talk. After taking a few steps inside I said, "Looks like we had a little rain today!" With that the space time continuum started again and the bar patrons unfroze. This would be the part in the movie where someone says, "He's friendly and he's not going to kill us!" I asked the bartender if they had a menu but she told me that they didn't serve food. I asked if she could point me towards a restaurant in town. She explained that there was a restaurant in town but it was closed because the owners were on holidays. One of the bar patrons asked if I was that guy on the TV news. I spoke to everyone about the *To The Top Canada* expedition, telling them I wanted Canadians to answer the question, "What will you do before the year 2000 to make Canada a better country than you found it?". One bar patron yelled out with slurred speech, "Get rid of Mulroney!" I replied, "Have you been in a coma? Mulroney has been gone for four years!" The entire bar roared with laughter. At a telephone booth, I called Carol. Drenched, I set up my tent by the local arena in a spot where I would be sheltered from the punishing rain that continued to pound down.

Saturday, July 5, 1997

The ground was soaking wet but the sun was shining. It was 7:00 am as my bike nosed out onto the Yellowhead, 45 kilometres ahead of schedule. I decided Saskatoon was reachable a day early. Cycling by green fields of wheat and bright yellow fields of canola, I passed several large industrial plants with the large letters "PCS" painted on them. These letters stand for Potash Corporation of Saskatchewan. Potash is a major provincial export, a fertilizer rich in potassium content.

Saskatoon is a beautiful city located on the south Saskatchewan River. I soon learned that every hotel room downtown was gone, as the Exhibition Fair was opening today. At the Gordie Howe Campground, I asked if they could donate a campsite or give me a discount for two nights to help me with my Canadian Unity Expedition. They made me pay full price. I wondered if Joni Mitchell, a famous Saskatoon native, had a campground. I guess Gordie has experienced hard times since he left the NHL. From my tent, I could hear the sirens and truck air horn sound effects of the exhibition rides. Despite this noise, I quickly fell asleep.

Sunday, July 6, 1997

My legs were aching with pain from the cumulative effects of cycling. It was as if my legs were saying to my brain, "We're going on strike today!" To which my brain responded, "You don't have to strike dummies! This is a day off." I was too sore to go to church so I lay in my tent and read my Bible all morning. By one o'clock, it had gotten very hot, too hot to stay in my tent. Gingerly, I cycled to a near by community pool, locked up my bike and entered the wonderful facility of Riverside Park. I didn't really swim but enjoyed sitting in the water to soak and cool off all afternoon. On leaving, I discovered that my waterbottle and a $200 battery pack for my Cats Eye night lights had been stolen off my bike. Maybe it was God sending me a message saying, "You can go to a pool, but you can't come to church. . ." God was right. Despite the pain, I should have toughed out the situation and gone to church.

At a local sports store, I bought my son a Saskatchewan Roughrider T-shirt. James plays in the Hamilton Minor Football League and his team is the West Mountain Riders. In their uniforms, they look like the Saskatchewan Roughriders.

That evening there was a severe thunderstorm which dropped over an inch of rain on Saskatoon. All that water seemed to flow straight to my tent. Well, at least I had a mattress to float on...

Monday, July 7, 1997

Commandeering three picnic tables, I used the surfaces to spread out everything I owned to try and dry it all out. Enroute to Saskatoon City Hall, my way was blocked by the Exhibition Parade. I had only one option if I was to get to City Hall on time for my presentation and media conference - join the parade! I ducked in behind the Coop float and just before the Saskatoon Lions Marching Band. People along the route, who recognized me from television, started to applaud me when I cycled by. STV was covering the parade but also planned to be at my media conference. Their crew had also been blocked by the parade. When their reporter saw me, he yelled out "Chris!". He could interview me, get his story and cover the parade. I did the interview as the band behind me played the theme song from the old TV programme "Hogan's Heroes". I arrived at City Hall just in time, as other members of the media were waiting for me.

After my presentation, I headed out of the City. I stopped by Robin's Donuts where their head office had sent some gift certificates to help me. Then, it was off to Fedex where I sent home a package to my family.

West, outside the city, there is an overpass that cuts over the highway so you can get on Highway 16. Cycling up the overpass my chain snapped. At the very top of the overpass I turned my bike around the wrong way facing traffic. It was necessary to lean the bike against the guard rail and have the chain to the outside facing me so I could fix it. Below, the traffic heading into Saskatoon could see me above, my bike facing the wrong way. I thought that someone would call the local radio station news desk and tell them, "The Unity Guy is up on top of the overpass and he looks like he's going to jump!".

After an hour's delay, the chain was repaired and I headed out. When I was 20 kilometres out of town my wheel rim split. This ripped my tire tube causing it to explode. The Kevlar tire went flat and an antiflat, fluorescent green liquid spewed forth from the tube coating everything, including me. I looked like a leprechaun - a big leprechaun. This is what NASA calls total system failure. I was surrounded by fields with too much gear to carry and my split rim wouldn't even allow me to walk my bike for help. There wasn't a building in view. I was surrounded by fields as far as the eye could see. This situation looked so bad I took out my camera and snapped a picture of the whole sorry scenario, my bike effectively dead. After surveying the damage, I decided I would have to become a blacksmith fast and repair the rim. I used my tools and hammered the rim back into shape. I put a new tube in and inflated the tire. This now allowed me to walk my bike, with my gear on it. I didn't dare put my weight on the bike or the rim would re-split. I walked to a local weigh station which was closed, but it had a telephone. I called back to Saskatoon to a bicycle store called the Bicycle Doctor. I prayed that this doctor made housecalls. The owner, Davey Jones, agreed to bring me a new wheel and a new chain. Sitting in the shade of the weigh station, I waited. Davey pulled up in his pickup truck. It was a welcome sight to see this angel from Saskatoon. In a half hour, I was operational again. It was now 7:00 pm. I had to cover as much ground as possible, as I was on a deadline to arrive in North Battleford early Wednesday, 138 kilometres from Saskatoon. I reached Borden at sunset. The bar manager of the Borden Hotel was in charge, so I asked if he would consider donating a room, sharing with him an interesting fact - his hotel was halfway to the top of Canada. He said he had one room left and he would donate it to me. The bar patrons had listened to the whole conversation. The Bar Manager proclaimed to his customers, "Serving you guys, I always thought I was in a Halfway House!"

I carried my gear and bicycle up the stairs to my room. The bar customers looked on in disbelief that so much gear could be on a bicycle. Réal Degagne, the bar manager, made me a bowl of soup and the best clubhouse sandwich I've eaten in my life. The patrons all had questions for me. Real, realizing I was tired of talking, invited me to play darts with him. He taught me a dart game called Cricket, which we played until 3:00 am. Finally in my bed, the last thing I saw before falling asleep was a Charlie's Angels sticker on my bed headboard.

Tuesday, July 8, 1997

At 8 o'clock, I awoke still tired from my unusually late night. After washing up in the sink in my room, I carried my gear downstairs. The bar was already full with people who wanted to meet me. I gave my speech and then I was asked to stop by the village office, before I left.

I had accidentally put sunblock in my right eye and it was stinging, which did not help my cycling. In Raddison, a restaurant donated my lunch. The owner said his daughter saw me at the Borden Hotel Bar the night before. I went to the washroom and bathed my stinging eye in cold water. It had no effect.

I was having an allergic reaction and my eye had swollen shut. I cycled the 80 kilometres to North Battleford with only one eye open. My first stop was a Shoppers Drug Mart where the pharmacist recommended some eye drops that cleared up my problem in 30 minutes.

You may remember that on June 23, 1997, I told you that the Yellowhead was named after Pierre Bostonais. I got this information right off of an information sign in Manitoba. In North Battleford, Saskatchewan the information sign says Pierre Hatsination is the person the Yellowhead highway is named after. Maybe Pierre was in the witness protection programme and changed his name. I haven't been able to solve this mystery.

I met Helène Cloutier of The Battleford's Inn, who donated a room for me where I enjoyed going to bed as early as possible.

Wednesday, July 9, 1997

McDonald's donated my breakfast and I headed off, early, to North Battleford City Hall. The City Council representative spoke sincerely after my presentation. He talked about the community having struggled through tough times recently. People, including himself, had gotten a little selfish. It was good that Chris Robertson had come along to remind everyone that we have to be more giving in our community. I was impressed by this politician who spoke from his heart and not from a spin doctor's script.

A restaurant in Delmas, 29 kilometres out of Battleford, donated a hot turkey sandwich. In Paynton, 25 kilometres on, another restaurant donated my dessert of pie and ice cream. I pedaled 27 more kilometres to reach Maidstone, where a senior citizen volunteer, Daphne, manned the tourist bureau and community owned camp ground.

Daphne was a sweet elderly lady who took her responsibilities very seriously. I asked her about donating a campsite and she indicated she had no authority to make that decision. After I gave her more information she called the Village Administrator at home. She told Daphne it was okay with her, if it was okay with the Council Committee Chairman. When Daphne tried the Chairman, there was no answer. I could see that Daphne was frustrated by the bureaucratic run around! She got off the phone and pulled out a card and said she was going to write "donation" on it. Before I left, Daphne got me three glasses of water. I thanked her very much. I set up my tent close to the washroom pavilion for shelter because I knew a storm was coming tonight.

Thursday, July 10, 1997

Showered and shaved early, I spent most of my morning writing in my journal in my tent. After packing up, I visited the Maidstone Hospital. The pain on the inside of my baby right toe had become severe, caused by the stirrup strap squeezing my foot. The pain wasn't my main concern but I thought it might be an indicator that my toe had become infected. Unfortunately, I couldn't get a clear view because the muscles that gave me the strength to pedal also took away my flexibility. I needed the help of a second pair of eyes. At the hospital, nurse Jackie cleaned the open abrasion on my foot and decided to ask a doctor to see it. The doctor said I had a severe pressure sore but it was not infected, yet. They gave me several gauzes to keep the pressure off my toe. I felt better knowing my foot wasn't infected. As my mother said, "Better safe than sorry". Nurse Jackie told me she had been stationed in Tuktoyaktuk and asked me to say hello for her to the nurses up there, when I arrived. I promised I would.

After the hospital visit, I washed all my clothes at the local laundromat. Flipping through a Canadian Living magazine, the pictures of beautiful food reminded me that I had not eaten for almost 24 hours. At 3:00 pm, after finishing my laundry, I popped into Sonny's Restaurant before leaving town. The owner donated my meal but insisted that I have a hamburger. Grateful, I agreed and found the meal to be delicious.

Enroute everyday I had seen Greyhound buses along the road. We got into the habit of waving at each other. I am sure the drivers had the same routes and looked forward to checking my daily progress. Today I passed three buses. I went into Lashburn and visited the town office. I knew I had a small window to catch Carol after she got off work and before she took James to football practice. I reached her on the phone and had her fax me an important transcript to the Town Office. The Magna Corporation promotes Canada with the annual publication of a book called *As Prime Minister, I Would...* I had been chosen, as a 1997 Distinguished Canadian, to be a co-author. The transcript contained the editorial revisions of my original submitted essay. Reading the edited version, I noticed some changes that needed discussion. It was another project for my "To Do" list later. Riding further west, I encountered another thunder storm. I raced to stay ahead of it but could feel the drops of rain as the storm stayed pace with me. I pulled into Marshall where a room was donated by Gerry and Maxine, the new owners of the Marshall Hotel. Maxine made me a sub which I appreciated. Glad to be out of the rain, I thought about tomorrow, my last day in Saskatchewan. The room was hot, as the temperature was in the nineties, and sleep would not come. I took a shower to cool down and read my Bible.

Friday, July 11, 1997

At the Alberta Tourist Bureau on the Saskatchewan side of the border, I got information about Lloydminster. The city is split in half, with the border going right up the middle. In Alberta, there is no provincial sales tax so the west side of town pays no tax. The Province of Saskatchewan does have sales tax but has exempted Lloydminster so as not to throw the city into retail chaos, with one side of town being abandoned.

My heart went out to Mary and Barb, managers of the Cedar Inn Motel. They donated my room despite the fact that it was the weekend, with a softball tournament and the Colonial exhibition going on today. They would most definitely be full, but they put Canada first before profit. I remember back to London Ontario to the hotel that would not donate a room because they were "almost full" and thought they should learn from Mary and Barb.

Mid morning, I decided to visit patients at the Lloydminster Hospital. At the main reception desk, I checked in with Sandy, explaining about the *To The Top Canada* expedition and my habit of visiting patients in local hospitals. Sandy was going to put me in touch with the appropriate senior hospital staff, but I asked to be excused for a moment. I had to make a phone call to City Hall to confirm that I would be on time to arrive at 2:30 pm. Sandy did not know that I was making a phone call. While I was on the phone, a crazy-looking clown came into the hospital and said, "I'm ready to visit!" Sandy thought I was the clown. I guess the Lloydminster Hospital rarely gets national unity crusaders, or clowns, coming through their front door. Sandy sent the clown up saying, Chris Robertson was on his way. I then reappeared and Sandy exclaimed, "Aren't you the clown?" Sandy's expression turned to extreme distress, realizing that she had sent a clown to meet senior hospital officials. We got the matter sorted out but news of the incident spread through the hospital like wildfire. Every time I walked up to a staff member and said, "I'm Chris Robertson", they would break up laughing. After a few people, I started introducing myself as, "I am the real Chris Robertson!" This reduced staff members to helpless giggles.

At the border, I met with a newspaper reporter who wanted my story and my picture crossing into Alberta. As I waited at the busy corner of the Yellowhead and the border, cars were honking their support and I waved my appreciation back to them. Traffic was very busy and my arm was getting tired of waving. I thought of this vision of the Queen weight training her arm so she could wave for long periods of time.

After meeting the reporter, I went to City Hall and did my program and media conference. At the Superstore on the Alberta side of town, I dropped off a film for development. While waiting, I went to Bonanza Steak House who were kind enough to donate my supper. Back at the Superstore, I asked if they would be interested in donating my film development to conserve my cash flow during the expedition and I would give them a "Friend of Canada" certificate. The clerk wanted to help me but said the store manager would have to approve the plan. The store manager told me donation requests had to be submitted to senior management in Calgary for approval. I explained that I would pay for my order as I was just in town this weekend. As the store manager wished me good luck and walked away, the clerk muttered, "And they call this the Real Canadian Superstore". He just learned the lesson that policy comes before patriotism for some companies.

Back at the motel, I watched the Winnipeg Blue Bombers beat my Hamilton Tiger Cats. I could see the crowd was small and I estimated it at 12,000. Breakeven for a CFL team is about 18,000 attendance. The Tiger Cats had not won either an exhibition or regular season game so far this season. When a team loses, it hurts the attendance gate. Still, I was impressed by the crowd. Ivor Wynne Stadium is right in downtown Hamilton. Today, parts of downtown Hamilton were evacuated because of deadly levels of benzene in the air from a terrible fire at a local plastics factory. Considering fans were risking deadly cancer, I thought it was an excellent turnout. These fans, like me, loved the Tiger-cats. I love Hamilton!

Saturday, July 12, 1997

Mary and Barb, managers of Cedar Inn Motel, gave me a big hug when I left that morning. McDonald's on the Alberta side of Lloydminster donated my breakfast. Just outside Lloydminster is a large "Welcome to Alberta" sign. Behind it was an information sign but, being near sighted, I couldn't quite read it from a distance. I thought it might be an Alberta tourism attraction, or more on the mystery of who the Yellowhead is really named after. When I got close I discovered it was an information sign extolling the virtues of the "Rat Control Program". Earlier in the century, rats were first noticed sneaking across the border. Albertans came down on the rats with vengeance. Rats weren't wanted, dead or alive! The sign encourages you to enjoy Alberta, one of the few rat free places on this planet.

I was feeling tired after cycling 23 kilometres into the second toughest headwinds I had experienced yet. (The winds into Chatham were still the worst). I pulled off the highway and cycled into Kitscoty and stopped at a local restaurant for toast and hot chocolate. I called Carol from the restaurant pay phone. It must have been telepathy because, especially that morning, Carol and James were really missing me and I them. Carol told me she was successful in selling our beautiful family organ, which would help our financial situation. Once I reached Edmonton I had a ticket to fly to Hamilton during my birthday and Carol's holidays, so we could spend some time together before I headed towards the Arctic. It was less than a week until I would see them but it was still too long for me. I missed my family so bad it hurt. I missed Carol, my best friend in the world. I missed playing football with James. I missed lying on my own living room couch with my dog Smooch lying on my chest. I missed breakfast cereal in the morning. I missed going to movies with my family. I missed checking my computer for E-mail. I missed playing Scrabble with the family. I missed driving my car. I missed it all. I kept saying to myself, "Short term pain, for long term gain".

On the way to Vermilion, the flat terrain gave way to large rolling hills. Enroute, I encountered two rain storms separated by one hail storm. It was the hardest rain I had encountered to date. It was as if a bucket of water had been turned over on me, leaving me barely able to see the road. Reaching Vermilion, I had cycled 60 kilometres in tough conditions. It was 4:30 pm when I cycled into a KFC in Vermilion, which donated my supper. This KFC proudly displayed a plaque "Best of the Best", as it was the top service store in all of Canada. This was a tremendous achievement because there are many hundreds of KFC's in Canada.

All motels were full because of one wedding in town. I finally found a room in the

Vermilion Hotel above a rock bar that the locals nicknamed, "The Zoo". After hauling all my gear, my bike and my trailer upstairs, I went to the bar for a coke. Kelly, the bartender, was getting married in two weeks with plans for a small Ukrainian wedding at her parents' house, with 450 invited guests! I have an average size home in suburban Hamilton but I couldn't see 450 people at my house. This would fill up the house, the back lawn and front lawn. Heaven forbid the groom and bride would ever get separated in this huge crowd because the wedding would turn into a "3-D Where's Waldo."

Kelly told me she was paying for the wedding but their parents were paying for the food and liquor for all of the guests. If I was Kelly's father, I would have to rob a few banks in the coming weeks.

I had met members of the bar's rock band, Secret Lives, upstairs. They were the only other guests on my floor. They introduced me to the bar crowd during one of their sets: "Hey! Let's give a hand to Chris Robertson. He's a Terry Fox kind of a guy!" At one point during the evening a bride came into the bar, all alone, and began dancing to the rock music. After about an hour, the groom came in, picked her up over his shoulder and carried her out. This was not something that happened when I got married.

Sunday, July 13, 1997

With 90 kilometres of highway to cover to reach Vegreville, brutal winds from the west, at 60 kph, were forcing me to cycle in my lowest gear. It was a battle to move metres let alone kilometres. I cycled 22 kilometres by toughing it out but took a break in Mannville where I stopped for a break. I was served by an ultra perky waitress. I presented her with a Friend of Canada certificate and asked her to tell everyone I was in the village about my question, "What will you do before the year 2000 to make Canada a better country than you found it?" She was born to fulfill this mission!

After pedaling another very slow 13 kilometres, I stopped into the community of Minburn. I needed to use the washroom. In the Prairies, it wasn't like Ontario, where you could sneak into the woods for privacy and do your business. Traffic was busy on the Yellowhead and there was no place for privacy on the flat prairie. In Minburn there wasn't a single hotel, restaurant, gas station, convenience store or a church for me to use. Riding up a side street I saw some people on their porch. I asked them if they knew where I could find a washroom to use. They offered me their washroom. As I entered the house I could see they were extremely poor. I remember the words of Jesus when he said, "Blessed are the poor for they shall inherit the Kingdom of God".

The inside door handle was gone from the bathroom door and there was a hook and eye screw to hold the door shut. When I went to flush I discovered the handle was broken off the toilet. I had to take the top of the toilet off and flush it manually. When I went to leave, I released the hook but the door did not open. Despite the door knob being gone, the mechanism for closing the door had tripped and now I was trapped in the bathroom. There was only a tiny window above the tub and I could not squeeze through the opening. I didn't want to call for help, because I had visions of the people calling the local fire department. The local paper would cover this story and then I could see a national wire service story with the headlines - "Canada Crusader Trapped in Bathroom!" No, I wasn't going to call out for help. In the medicine cabinet, I found a toothbrush and used it to jimmy the lock. When the door opened, I breathed a sigh of relief. Despite my awkward situation, I knew this family was kind and had the best of intentions so I gave them a Friend of Canada certificate to thank them.

I cycled another 13 tough kilometres and stopped in Innisfree for lunch. For just $5.00 (including GST), I enjoyed soup, a 3-piece chicken dinner with potato and vegetable, and dessert. In Alberta, there is no PST. The low cost and high value of this table service meal amazed me. Your money goes further in Alberta.

I cycled another gruelling 12 kilometres. The sun was hot and the temperature was in the nineties. The harsh wind felt like the air coming out of one of those hand drying machines in washrooms. Exhausted, I pulled into a highway service station and ate my power meal: Pepsi, pie and ice cream. It rejuvenated me enough to go 27 kilometres into Vegreville. In Vegreville, I saw the world's largest Pysanka or Easter egg, which celebrates the Ukrainian heritage of the community.

It seemed like everyone spoke with a Lawrence Welk accent. The Vista Motel donated a room and the Dairy Queen donated my supper. This had been the toughest day so far. My body ached, from fighting the winds that seemed to have a vow to stop me, but I won!

Monday, July 14, 1997

I had slept well after a rough Sunday. With my bike loaded up and some time before my 11:00 o'clock presentation at the city hall, I went to St. Joseph's Hospital in Vegreville and visited patients. People were watching Dini Petty on television that morning. The patients enjoyed my telling them about my earlier appearance on Dini Petty. At City Hall, I discovered Vegreville's Mayor was the incoming President of the Yellowhead Highway Association. I told him about the discrepancy between Pierre Bostonais and Pierre Hatsination, as founder of the Yellowhead. He didn't know who the Yellowhead was named after, but promised to look into it for me.

One reporter asked if I was in favour of the "tough love" approach for Quebec. During the recent French debate prior to the federal election, I had liked the comments of Preston Manning. He said something like, "Yes, means yes. Then there would be no negotiations on what Quebec would get, but simply a discussion on when Quebecers would surrender their Canadian passports". I remember a front page report in the Globe & Mail that ran the week before the last Quebec Referendum. It was a poll that indicated that Quebecers thought they would continue to have a Canadian passport in an independent Quebec. The federalist forces could have, and should have, made the consequences of a Yes Vote crystal clear. Some of these include:

1. No Canadian Passport.
2. Canadian dollar would not be the currency of Quebec with a joint monetary policy.
3. Quebec would not have a seat at the G8.
4. Quebec would not automatically be in NAFTA.
5. Quebec would not be a Pacific Rim country trading with the Asian Tigers.
6. Canada would not hold "paper" on Quebec's 24.8% portion of the national debt.
After my speech at the Vegreville Rotary Club, I received a standing ovation.

Twenty five kilometres outside of Vegreville, enroute to Edmonton, my rear wheel went flat. I unloaded my gear, unhitched my trailer and turned my bicycle upside down so I could pull the wheel off and patch up the tire tube. While I was working on the tube, a large transport truck came by and the wind blew my bike over hard on me. My chain wheel cut into my upper arm like a ninja star. I pulled the bike off of me and continued to work on my tire as blood dripped from my upper arm. I pumped up my tire with my hand pump. The tire was not at the inflation PSI, where I wanted it, but it was good enough to gently continue. Down the road a few kilometres, I met a transport driver out of Winnipeg who was cleaning his windshield. I asked him if it was possible to tap into his airline and inflate my tire. He pulled out an electrical air pump and it did the trick nicely. I told him what I was doing and he asked would if it be alright if he took my picture by his truck. I would have sung the "Twelve Days of Christmas" if it made him happy! He told me he thought my *To The Top Canada* expedition was great. He told me he had a plan in the next referendum to drive coast to coast and collect letters from Canadians, encouraging Quebec to stay in Canada and he would deliver them to the front door of the Quebec Legislature. Almost like the movie, Miracle on 34th Street, where the judge's bench is buried with letters to Santa. I told him to go for it!

I rode until sunset and set up my tent near Elk Island. It was 10:45 pm when I was all settled in for the night. I was camping on a green lawn by an information booth that was closed but had an open washroom. Unsure if I was allowed in there, I made a mental note to wake up early and be on my way in case I was someplace where I shouldn't be.

Tuesday, July 15, 1997

At 4:00 am, I packed up as much as I could inside my tent as the mosquitoes outside were thick. Wearing my "Don't Bug Me Shirt", I packed up my tent and loaded my gear on my bike. I called radio CHED in Edmonton from a pay phone. The morning deejay was surprised that I was calling her before 6:00 am. I did an over-the-phone interview. Eileen said I sounded like a politician and asked if I want to be in politics. I assured her that I did not want to be in politics and kept to myself that I was speaking through the mosquito netting of my "Don't Bug Me Shirt", which might account for me sounding like a politician.

I stopped to look at buffalo that were grazing near the highway. Having journeyed 3,690 kilometres, I arrived in Edmonton. In the east end industrial section, I cycled by a large oil tank that was being sand blasted. The old paint chips rained down on me like snow. Crossing the North Saskatchewan River, that runs through the middle of the city, I faced a circular vertical climb up MacDonalds' hill with my 500 pounds of total weight.

The Crowne Plaza Chateau Lacombe donated a room for the evening. It was early afternoon but I'd been awake since 4:00 am. I grabbed a nap on the most comfortable hotel bed I've ever slept on. After some rest, I called home and spoke with Carol. She indicated a fax had come to me from the senior editor of the *As Prime Minister, I Would...* Book, which she re-routed to me at the hotel. I wrote up my comments and had five pages faxed to Toronto. The hotel front desk staff thought I was a pretty busy person for a guy riding a bicycle.

Wednesday, July 16, 1997

I packed up all my gear and headed to City Hall where I was greeted by Councillor Rose, who was dressed in a Klondike period costume. There was a good media turn out from television, radio and newspapers. I was thankful because I was up against Disney in competing for editorial space, who were a special attraction at this year's Klondike exhibition in Edmonton, starting tomorrow.

Afterwards, I did an early afternoon phone-in talk show with Al Stafford at radio CHED. I loved the talk show format because it gave me a chance to tell my full story to the Province of Alberta.

At the Legislature building, I was received by MLA Mary O'Neil, of the constituency of St. Alberts. The Premier, Ralph Klein, was in New Brunswick for a Premiers' Conference, but Mary took me into his majestic office.

The Alberta Legislature is a magnificent example of early Canadian architecture. The designers and builders of the legislature had a special vision for the future. I hoped that Canadians in the 1900's would capture this spirit and leave an equally inspiring legacy to the 21st century. Mary had pictures of me taken in the Premier's office and asked me to sit in Ralph Klein's chair. Seated, I signed the provincial guest book. It suddenly occurred to me that there was bicycle grease on the back of my sweat pants. With photographers around me, I dared not look down to see if I had left a stain. I could imagine Premier Ralph Klein quoting that line from The Three Bears, "Who's been sitting in my chair?". Mary escorted me outside to see my bike which had fallen over. She offered to help me pick it up. I asked her politely to stand back because it was over 200 pounds and lifting it up required a quick motion, like an Olympic weight lifter. Even if Mary could lift it, I had visions of her ripping a sleeve or splitting the skirt of her business suit.

I appreciated her kindness just the same. Before I left, Mary gave me some money to treat myself to some Alberta beef. I love beef and appreciated her gift.

The bridge behind the legislature, that crosses the North Saskatchewan River, has a pedestrian section with a low guard rail. As I cycled across this high bridge, my heart beat hard as my fear of heights reached a peak. I held the handlebars as hard as I could and didn't dare blink, especially when I had to pass pedestrians on the bridge bringing my body just inches from the guard rail.

It was now rush hour and many cars were on their way home, traffic backing up at every stop light. On my bike, I passed the cars and shot through the congestion with no delay.

I arrived at Edmonton Cycle and Sports, which had been established in the city since 1947. Brad took my bike, my trailer and my gear. I told him of the several things I wanted done to my bike before my return on Monday August 3, to pick it up. I knew that replacing my Cats Eye Arctic light battery pack, that had been stolen, would take some time. I also encouraged Brad to make any modifications or repairs he would want to see if he was riding this bike to the Arctic Ocean.

Keeping one large back pack with me that held my clothes, I called Joan Proulx to pick me up. Joan was my step mother when my father passed away. I was staying with Joan overnight and she was going to drive me to the airport tomorrow. We went for supper at the Outback Steakhouse. Joan offered to show me around West Edmonton Mall, Canada's largest shopping centre. I had walked through once before, when a firm had flown me to Edmonton, to recruit me for their company. I declined the position in favour of a better offer from another firm that was also looking for my services. I was tired and passed on visiting the spectacular mall that night. We went to Joan's condominium. It was my first time there and it gave me a funny feeling because I knew dad had died on the elevator after driving from Burlington, Ontario to Edmonton, Alberta nonstop. Joan had a beautiful apartment that she had decorated immaculately. After reading the paper and watching TV, we called it a night and I retired to the spare bedroom.

Thursday, July 17, 1997

At 5:00 am, I checked the time and slept lightly for another hour. By 6:00 am, I has shaved and showered. After breakfast, Joan and I headed out for the airport. I was flying for the first time in my life on Greyhound Airlines. It had two advantages for me in that they had the lowest rate to fly home from Edmonton and they flew directly into Hamilton, which had an airport fifteen minutes from my house. Check-in was fast and efficient. At the gate, there was open seating and you boarded the plane when your boarding pass letter was called out. I had the letter "Q". Having the letter Q on my boarding pass gave me the same feeling as when you get the letter Q in Scrabble. As a frequent flyer, I am used to a three stage boarding call, 1) business class, 2) the rear section of economy class and 3) the front section of economy class. The letter Q is the seventeenth letter of the alphabet so I had to be attentive to the sixteen before me. I noticed this process was disconcerting for the other passengers, as they all stood around playing "boarding bingo" waiting for their letter to be announced. When Q was finally called, I boarded the plane with no fixed seating. There were three seats on each side of the aircraft. It seemed all window and aisle seats were taken as I walked down the aisle. People could see that I was the size of a Tiger-Cat middle linebacker and they did not want me to take the middle seat, either. They looked at me with a harsh look that said "don't you dare sit here". I found a seat, between two thin people, near the back. The flight attendants had casual uniforms that were similar in style to that of my local pizza delivery boy. Greyhound had lost $38 million on their operations last quarter, playing in the high stakes game of the airline business. I hoped they weren't cutting back on maintenance as Valuejet had done in the States, or that they might even go bankrupt before my return flight. On a positive note for the airline, the flight today was completely full. I arrived in Hamilton and was almost knocked down by my son James who ran to hug me. Carol soon caught up and kissed me. My father-in-law Eric gave me a big handshake. Although I had just landed in Hamilton, I had a surprise in store, as Carol started driving to Toronto. I had arrived early enough to get to the Skydome to see my Tiger-Cats play the Argonauts. It felt great to be home.

Monday, August 4, 1997

I had flown in last night to Edmonton, from my brief birthday - family reunion in Hamilton. It was the Heritage Day holiday in Alberta and Tim Nolt came into Edmonton Sport and Cycle just to open the store for me to pick up my bike. There was a large bag of old parts that had been taken off the bike. I think they managed to salvage the handlebars. I knew my bike was on the critical list when I dropped it off and after major surgery it was once again a mean, lean cycling machine.

I had brought several weeks' supply of food and some special survival supplies from home. It took me three hours to repack all my supplies to make them fit and file them based on priority access.

While I packed, Tim worked on the maintenance of his favourite bike. He told me about a Canadian who he thought was a founder or original member of Greenpeace who was wrongfully imprisoned by the government of Sweden. This individual was not even in the country at the time of the offence he was charged with. To listen to Tim talk about this person, the imprisoned gentleman from Canada sounded like an "environmental Nelson Mandela"! Tim also talked about being active in the arts community. One project he was working on was a giant mural by the Strathcona market. This mural depicted a scene from the turn of the century. What was most interesting about this project was the way they raised money to make the mural "self funding". Several people were in the busy street scene of the mural and this arts group sold "portraits" in the mural. For a price, your face could become immortalized forever in this downtown street mural. I thought it was a fantastic idea! Tim rode with me from the store, stopping by the mural. Tim took great pride in showing me where his portrait would be on a character on the balcony.

We crossed the high level bridge again, where Tim showed me piping that is used to turn the bridge into a waterfall. On Canada Day, the waterfall from the bridge is turned on. Tim rode with me almost to the city limits of Edmonton.
Lunch, (closer to supper), was donated by the Clark Restaurant, where I had the Chinese special.

Riding west on the Yellowhead, I saw a sign saying "Leduc 28 kilometres south". I knew this was a special weekend in Leduc. They were celebrating the fiftieth anniversary of the Leduc oil well becoming a gusher. This was a momentous event in Alberta history because it was an initiative that transformed Alberta into a petroleum power in the world and created wealth that gave Albertans one of the highest standards of living in Canada.

Alberta was experiencing a record breaking heat wave. Arriving in Spruce Grove, I went into the Cossack Inn. Nick, the jolly manager, immediately donated a room without hesitation. I carried my gear and my bike upstairs to my room above the tavern. With my food supplies, this was the heaviest my gear had ever been on the *To The Top Canada* expedition.

After settling in, I turned on the TV. There was a bizarre Alberta news story of a murder that took place at wedding. (This kind of event puts a positive new light on eloping.) In the Edmonton Sun, I read a well written article about the *To The Top Canada* expedition. The night was incredibly hot. My room had no air conditioning so I slept with a wet towel over me to keep me cool.

Tuesday, August 5, 1997

The weather forecast predicted a record breaking high of 33°. At Spruce Grove City Hall, I was greeted by Mayor Joe Acker and local media. I spoke with the media for half an hour. Heading west, shortly out of Spruce Grove, I was to get on Highway 43 north that would take me to Valleyview, Alberta. I said goodbye to the Yellowhead highway which I'd been on since Portage La Prairie, Manitoba. It felt like I was saying farewell to an old friend. I said a thank you prayer to the Lord, for bringing me safely these hundreds of kilometres.

I was heading straight north on 43 and I could feel the sun on my back as if a laser beam were firing on me. The sweat from the extreme heat made my eyes sting. I stopped for frequent water breaks. On one break, I noticed something I'd never seen before. In a farmer's field, there were large round bails of hay but these bails had been wrapped in white plastic. It looked as though this farmer was growing giant marshmallows. I took a picture of this unusual site.

I arrived at my designated stop, which was a small village called Gunn. The Gunn General Store, located across from Lac Ste. Anne, donated a campsite. After setting up my tent, I called an editor with the Halifax Chronicle Herald who wanted to do a story on me. I had to call his home as his Atlantic time zone was three hours ahead of me. After the call, I got a cardboard box from the store and prepared a parcel, with the help of the clerk, Heather, to send home. I am a terrible parcel wrapper. My family can always tell a Christmas gift from me before they see the tag because of the wrinkled paper and the huge amount of scotch tape. I had received a sweatshirt and honey from Spruce Grove and had won a t-shirt when flying back to Edmonton with Greyhound Airlines. On the anniversary of a Canadian writing the comic Superman, the question was, "What newspaper did Clark Kent work for?" On a full flight, I had the fastest correct answer which was, the "Daily Planet". When I was a kid, it cost me 12 cents for a Superman comic book. Today a comic book costs $2.80. I wonder if the Toronto Stock Exchange has a futures market for comic books?

Sitting in the air conditioned comfort of Doreen's Restaurant, beside the General Store, I wrote in my journal about the last two days. My tent would be like a microwave oven tonight.

Wednesday, August 6, 1997

It was day three of the heat. Back at the Gunn Post Office, while mailing out my parcel, I could hear a baby crying. I looked behind the counter to see a small baby, in a car seat wedged into a giant plastic garbage pail. The older lady running the Post Office said she heard that I had arrived in town. Obviously gossip travels faster than the mail.

After 41 kilometres, I pulled into the tourist booth at Sangudo to drop off my *To The Top Canada* news release. At a picnic table, I met Marilyn Berezowski who offered me two pears and a muffin. She told me she was facilitating a three hour seminar in Sangudo that afternoon. I volunteered to do a short opening keynote at the seminar taking place in town. After Marilyn agreed, I rode my bike into the community to the building where the seminar programme was taking place. They had a water cooler! I must have emptied their large blue bottle personally. I did my presentation, leading into their afternoon of business skills training. As I left, the seminar delegates spontaneously put their agenda on hold, following me outside to see me off.

I rode to the local Chinese restaurant in Sangudo where they were kind enough to donate an order of Sweet and Sour Chicken balls and a Pepsi.

Riding that afternoon was unbearable. The sweat was pouring off me like Niagara

Falls. My eyes were stinging and I had trouble seeing because it hurt to open them. I would go a few feet and stop and then go a few more feet and stop. After 10 kilometres of this stop-and-go effort, I paused at a roadside restaurant at Rockfort Bridge. My eyes were almost swollen shut from the pain and I wanted to splash cold water on them to reduce the swelling. The water in my own water bottles was as hot as soup, from the beaming sun. This was one of those restaurants where the restaurant is in the back and I had to walk through the china gift shop to get to it.

Under normal conditions, being a big guy, I find china gift shops to be a hazard, but today I couldn't see, which made it worse. I took baby steps, alternating eyes to peer forward, to reduce the pain, so I could make it through this mine field.

In the restaurant washroom I scooped cold water in my hands and held it against my eyes. The instant soothing of the cold was the best feeling in the world. I could now see my face in the mirror for the first time. My face was fire engine red. Not from burn because I had sun screen on but from swelling around the eyes. I had a Pepsi and a bowl of ice cream in the restaurant. On my way out of the restaurant I could see a large clock-like thermometer under the front porch. It said it was 93° Fahrenheit in the shade. As soon as you stepped off the front porch into the sunlight, the heat hit you like walking into a fire. I would guess it was 97° or hotter.

I rode another 8 kilometres and arrived at my final destination of Mayerthorpe. At the local paper, the Freelancer, I met editor Kevin Laliberte, who knew who I was before my arrival. Kevin offered his home for me to stay in as he knew the forecast for this evening was thunderstorms. He also invited me for supper, so after visiting the town office and calling Carol, I cycled towards Kevin's house. Kevin lives close to the hospital in Mayerthorpe. In front of the hospital, on the hospital grass, there is a lonely park bench with a sign painted on it. It says:

"If you depend on others to make you happy, you'll be endlessly disappointed."

Now, I don't know about you but if I was being rushed to this hospital for life saving care, this sign would not comfort me. I guess they are trying to lower your expectations before you enter. I mentioned this to Kevin as I had supper with him. He'd never noticed the sign, but laughed when I told him about it. If Kevin mentions this in his article, you may find the lonely bench has been painted over, if you ever visit. After supper, I went over to the hospital to visit patients. When I was done, I returned to the main nursing station to thank the nurses but where there were four nurses present when I came in, there were none now. I noticed this sign at the desk:

"If no one is present, please call a nurse for assistance with the microphone by pressing button on base and speaking into microphone, saying 'Nurse to the front desk please'".

Now I thought it was unusual to turn the public address system for the entire hospital over to just anybody. If I wanted a nurse fast I would say,

"Welcome to Karioke night here at the Mayerthorpe Hilton!"

We headed back to Kevin's house where we talked until 10:00 pm. I then went to bed in the basement, which was the coolest room in the house.

Thursday, August 7, 1997

Next morning I had a family breakfast with the Laliberte family. They had two very cute preschool children (and a third on the way). Brandon, who was 3 or 4 years old, was on a mission. He kept saying to me "Are you ready to go?" Yesterday, he heard his mother say I was cycling up to the Arctic where Santa Claus lives. Brandon made up his mind that he was going with me and he was going to visit Santa. When I came out to my bike in the back yard, he was on his tricycle and ready to go. His parents and I had a tough time talking Brandon out of going with me. It was a sunny day but cooler. I rode until noon hour and stopped at a restaurant by the Blue Ridge road. A kind oriental couple donated my lunch. As I left the restaurant, the oriental gentleman came to the window to see my bike. He came to attention and gave me a salute as I drove off.

The terrain soon resembled that of Northern Ontario. There was heavy forest and a series of steep hills. I arrived in Whitecourt, a small pulp and paper mill town. At the Whitecourt Star newspaper, I was being interviewed by a reporter, when the editor stopped by to listen. He wanted to know what the rest of Canada thought about Alberta. Translation, "Do they really think we're rednecks?" I answered that other Canadians thought they were on the right of the political spectrum. I told him that I had run into several people in Manitoba and Saskatchewan who said to me, "Wait until you get to Alberta!" I explained that I thought Albertans were sensible and had a balanced approach, but they did believe in the tough love approach, which meant spelling out what Quebec loses if they vote yes to separation. We finished the interview and shot a picture outside the newspaper office. The young female reporter told me as I left she thought my *To The Top Canada* expedition was "really cool". When I get up in the Arctic, it's going to be downright frigid.

The Glenview Motel donated my room in Whitecourt. The Motel owner had a young son named John who wanted to wrestle me but my thighs were starting to lock up so I had to decline. I did teach him how to do sit-ups. John's mother laughed as he struggled to do one. Supper was donated by the A&W. I then watched a great football game between the Argos and Stampeders. I worked up such an appetite by half time, that I ran across the street to Robin's Donuts and, using a head office gift certificate, indulged in some delicious fresh donuts as a half time snack. Stampeders won the game, upsetting the first place Argos. As a Tiger-Cat fan, I smiled and went to bed happy.

Friday, August 8, 1997

I had charged my new battery (replacing the one that had been stolen in Saskatoon) and plugged it into my lights. Presto, nothing happened. I double checked my connections but no luck. This was a serious problem. I decided to deal with it immediately. I called Cyclepath in Burlington, Ontario and got their mailing address. At the Post Office next door (thank goodness for franchised postal outlets), I sent the lights with the battery and charger to Cyclepath via Priority Post. With this early project done, I headed to Fox Creek in the rain.

It had become even colder. As I rode in the hills, I could see my breath. At first my body said, "I love this weather" as I was still recovering from the brutal heat of two days ago. Wearing only cycle shorts, numbness soon set in and my body changed it's tune to "Well, maybe let's not have too much of a good thing". While I was riding I saw a pickup truck with a flashing light and danger sign. This usually means a truck with an extra wide load is going to pass me. It might be an extra large bulldozer or a farmer's silo. I moved as far to the right as possible so that the truck could swing around me. This time was different. A two storey house on a float taking up 2 1/2 lanes of the road went by me at 100 kph, within inches of my shoulder. The displaced air almost threw me off my bike. Thank the Lord, I had all that weight from eating donuts the night before.

I pedaled 81 kilometres today in bad headwinds and driving rain. My personal motivation was to arrive in Fox Creek by 5:30 pm so I could see the kickoff of my Tiger-Cats who were playing at 7:30 pm eastern time against the Roughriders. I divided the trip into fractions. Three quarters to go! Two thirds to go! One half to go! One third to go! One quarter to go! At every fraction point, I would yell out the Tiger-Cat cheer!

> "Oskee Wee Wee!
> Oskee Waa Waa!
> Holy Mackinaw
> Tigers! Eat Em Raw!
> Hooray!"

I am sure that if there were any hunters in the woods, they must have thought some guy was being torn apart by a bear. I am a great believer in managing your state of mind. When I took Judo, I learned to yell "Kiai" which I think means strength of mind and spirit. There is a psychological correlation with this martial art technique. Yelling summons adrenaline which gives you sharper focus and more strength.

I arrived in Fox Creek where a beautiful new hotel called the Western Inn donated my room. I had just enough time before the game to have supper, so I popped over to the Husky which donated my meal. I called Carol and then shot back to the Western Inn. My room was 207 on the second floor so I had to hustle to unpack and haul all my gear upstairs. I carried up the last thing, which was my bike, and turned on my TV just in time to see the kick off.

In the first quarter I received a call from Charles, a local newspaper reporter, who said he wanted to interview me. I told him he would be welcome to come to see me in my hotel room. Charles said he'd be there in ten minutes. My clothes were damp from riding that day but I did not get out of them. A half an hour came and went and no reporter. I thought this would be a blessing as he would come at half time and I wouldn't miss any of the game. The second half started and no reporter. Tiger-Cats were getting killed but I enjoyed the game. I once had the job of leading the stadium cheers at Tiger-Cat games for two years as part of the Tiger Pride programme. I know most of the fans throughout the stadium. The familiar faces in the stadium crowd made me feel at home. The game finished and I took my wet clothes off. Two minutes later there was a knock at my door. I called out "just a minute" and scrambled back into my wet clothes. Charles apologized for being late. Just before he took my picture, he mentioned he was in a terrible car accident and the other person had to go to hospital. It was hard to smile for my picture. Charles' camera had slammed against the dash and wasn't working well. Charles gave me his pad and asked me to write my story. No reporter had done this before but I guess Charles was too shaken up to write. I wrote out my story. I let Charles talk so he could relax. I didn't want him to have another accident in the rain on the way home. Charles wasn't sure his camera was working so he confirmed with me that he would come in the morning to take my picture. I said good night to this nice man who had a terrible evening.

Saturday, August 9, 1997

After a good night's sleep in an extremely comfortable bed, I carried my gear downstairs and packed my bike up. Charles met me and mentioned the person he hit had been transferred to an Edmonton hospital. I made a mental note to say a special prayer for this person in the accident, whom I never met. I bought breakfast at the Husky. I had about 90 kilometres to cycle and needed major food energy.

The weather was perfect, sunny and slightly cool. I listened to two C.D's on my way to Valleyview. Bruce Springsteins Greatest Hits and the movie music track of Rocky. The fast paced music had me powering through the hills like a knife through butter. I arrived in Valleyview by mid-afternoon. Reaching Valleyview meant that I had just completed 4,000 kilometres of the *To The Top Canada* expedition.

A room was donated for two nights at the Hi Valley Motor Inn. Troy, the General Manager, approved my request without a second thought. I loved his Canadian pride! In the bar, I was re-united with my friends in the Rock-Country duo, "Secret Lives". I brought my journal up-to-date as I listened to their great music. Vina, the server, liked me and gave me free cokes all night. At the end of the evening I gave the Secret Lives band members hugs and told them I was declaring them the official *To The Top Canada* expedition rock band.

Sunday, August 10, 1997

Sunday morning my legs hurt and my back was sore but I dragged myself out of bed and went to St. Anne's Anglican Church in Valleyview. I had learned my lesson in Saskatoon. I cycled up to the small church fifteen minutes ahead of the 10:30 start time. I was greeted by the minister, the Rev. Tim Chesterton. He was a friendly English man with a beard and glasses. Everyone arrived one minute before the start of this spirit filled service. Accustomed to the more formal Anglican services in larger cities, I was caught off guard when Reverend Tim grabbed his guitar from behind the altar and played the hymn music with incredible passion. I like this minister. Keeping with the casual theme, Reverend Tim kept his coffee mug on the altar rail during the sermon. Despite his nonchalant approach, Reverend Tim delivered the most incredible sermon I had ever heard. This is a great compliment because I went to an Anglican boarding school where I heard a minister speak everyday. I've also been a regular practicing Anglican and have heard sermons from the bishop, the primate and the Archbishop of Canterbury in person. Reverend Tim's sermon was packed full of content and relevant messages. His sermon revolved around the passage from the book of John, chapter 6, verse 35, where Jesus says:

"I am the bread of life. He who comes to me will never be hungry; he who believes in me will never be thirsty."

Reverend Tim explained at length that materialism will never satisfy you and if you want satisfaction, Jesus is your answer. I knew he was right. I lived in a world where executives wanted the latest cell phone, BMW or lap portable computer just for status. My priority list had changed from my daily experience of the *To The Top Canada* expedition. This included the following:

1. Time to read the Bible and be alone with God.
2. A regular source of clean water.
3. One hot meal a day.
4. A comfortable place to sleep.
5. Time to speak to or be with the people I love.

For the rest of my existence on this earth, if I have just these five things I know that I have been blessed.

Reverend Tim also explained that just a one-time experience of coming to God will not satisfy you, but it is an ongoing relationship that is required for you to experience total satisfaction. This was an important message for me. During the *To The Top Canada* expedition, through reading my Bible and daily prayer, I had developed the closest relationship with God I had ever had in my life. The challenge for me when I return to my regular life of husband, father, business leader, sports fan, citizen and Christian, is to ensure that my relationship with God be allocated time as my top priority. After Reverend Tim's sermon, it was crystal clear what my top priority was and what I had to do in the future.

After the service the congregation met in the church basement for coffee. The local newspaper reporter attended St. Anne's and used the opportunity to interview me. At one point, a Daddy Long Legs spider was walking across the church basement floor. When one man went over to step on it the parishioners screamed "stop!" When he didn't halt, the group yelled "stop" even louder and this time everyone looked ready to jump on him. The people yelling stop were superstitious farmers. Stepping on a spider intentionally would stop the rain. Rain-starved farms meant no productivity and profit. I had to admit, I had just been upstaged by a spider.

Reg from church took me for lunch at the Burger Baron, a quiet clean restaurant. We talked for over an hour.

After thanking Reg for lunch, I headed over to the Valleyview rodeo. I was introduced to the crowd and ran a circle in the corral waving to the audience and flying my flag. Despite my best efforts, I couldn't run as fast as the horses, that were just on before me doing barrel racing.

At the Valleyview Hospital, one patient, John, had just cut himself shaving. I kidded him that it was good he was in the hospital when it happened. Afterwards, I rode to Albin and Shelley's house, whom I'd met in church. Enroute, I met Albin who was in his car running an errand. He told me to head on over to the house where Shelley was waiting for me.

While chatting with Shelley, she volunteered that she had a psychological disorder called multipersonality. Multipersonality is a very complex disorder that I had studied at university. As I recall, it can manifest as a defense mechanism against a severe childhood trauma. Aside from my undergraduate studies and seeing the movie, "Sybil", this was my first experience meeting anyone who actually suffered from multipersonality. I asked Shelley if she was receiving the best medical assistance available. She indicated she was seeing a psychiatrist in Grande Prairie. I asked if there were any support groups for people with multipersonality. She indicated yes, but not in northern Alberta. I mentioned she may want to try the Internet to see if there is a "chat area" where she could find support.

Albin came and just caught the tail end of our conversation. He mentioned he was afraid to let his kids surf the net because of the adult content. In fact, he had just come across a site that showed you one hundred thousand ways to kill a man! As a regular internet surfer, I had not stumbled upon this site.

I spoke with Albin about the I.O.P. program as well as high school chemistry, both of which he taught. Albin took his I.O.P program role very seriously, trying to salvage kids with behavior problems. Previous teachers had coined the program, "Indians On Parole". Albin was trying to give the program a fresh start and new results.

At this point, Shelley came into the room shyly and in a little girl's voice said, "Is it okay if I colour?" Albin said "yes" and Shelley sat down with one leg in the air and started colouring. Albin casually mentioned that Shelley had "multi". We continued talking about I .O.P. Albin told me about one child about whom he had nearly given up hope. Defiantly, the boy explained why he behaved badly: "Look, I can either work hard to go to university and get a degree only to find there are no jobs and I'll have to drive a taxi, or, I can have fun in high school and then go drive a taxi!"

This logic gave me insight into how frustrated and hopeless the current generation feels about their future opportunities. As a Professional Speaker who does one program called The Jobsearch Seminar, I know that the real story of opportunity is not getting through to young people. It used to be that if there weren't any jobs in your community you had two choices - move or be unemployed. There are two systems in existence now that should give any young person in Canada hope - the Internet and courier systems. Now anyone can retail any product on the Internet and orders for that product can be sent by overnight courier anywhere in North America. As a worldwide retailer, if you have a unique product that people want, you can live almost anywhere and work.

We enjoyed a roast beef supper and lingered over ice cream on the back porch watching a rainbow fill the sky. I thanked Albin and Shelley for a wonderful supper and said goodnight. In the morning, Albin would be taking a picture of my bike fully loaded, for the local newspaper.

Monday, August 11, 1997

Early next morning, I got a call from Albin on the phone to see if it was alright to come up to my room. Opening the door, I greeted Albin, Shelley and Reverend Tim. They took me to a local restaurant for breakfast where Albin treated us all. After breakfast, they helped carry all my gear downstairs. I kidded them that they were my road crew. After pictures and extending my thanks, I headed into the Hi Valley Motor Inn to thank them as well. They gave me a message that Reg had been by, while we were at breakfast. Reg really wanted to see my bike fully loaded, so I rode down to Radio Shack where he worked. Reg was delighted to see me and gave me a big hug before I left.

I rode 44 kilometres to Crooked Creek and went into the General Store. I spoke to the girl at the cash register about my expedition. Her answer to my question about how to make Canada better was "Not to get a criminal record". No wonder they call this place "crooked". As I left I said in my best fatherly voice, "I think you can do better than not have a criminal record".

After cycling to Debolt, I left my information everywhere in town (four places) and continued on. I rode through a beautiful river valley which crosses the Smoky River. On the other side, I came to Bezanson where there was a Bison game farm. At Lefty's Cafe, I enjoyed my first buffalo burger. I'd rather have a buffalo burger than a regular fast food burger, if given a choice. I camped close to the local baseball field. During the night, a storm came up that almost lifted my tent up, with me in it. I looked out to see if a twister was coming. As I peered into the darkness of the prairie night, it dawned on me that you can't see a twister in the dark.

Tuesday, August 12, 1997

I shook the water off my tent as I packed it up. Riding 27 kilometres into Grande Prairie, I stopped into the local McDonald's that donated my lunch. My media conference tomorrow would be too close to the newspaper's morning deadline, so I stopped by their office to give them a head start on my story. At a nearby fax service, I received the final draft of my essay for the soon to be published book *As Prime Minister, I Would...*, which I quickly reviewed and returned to Magna. Carol included a fax note telling me that Tiger-Cat coach, Don Sutherin, had been fired.

I then headed to the home of Wayne and Jennifer Robertson, who are no relation to me. Jennifer is the niece of Kay McPhee, who worked with my wife. In the west, I had encountered many cities that numbered their streets into a logical grid. Number streets ran north and south and numbered avenues ran east and west. Grande Prairie had adopted this great system but someone forgot to tell them it only works when your streets line up.

I quickly found 99th street downtown but as I proceeded to my hosts' home, in the 6000 series, I discovered the street ended at a park, a condominium development, and then mysteriously turned into and unnumbered street. I knew Jennifer would not be home from work until 5:15 pm so I had most of the afternoon to search for her house. I rode east-west, descending into the south until I finally discovered the correct isolated section of 99th street. When Jennifer pulled up, she asked if I had any trouble finding them. "Oh no", I replied, rolling my eyes.

Jennifer let me do my laundry before I went to bed. We talked about my expedition, so far. I told Jennifer about almost being hit by a truck in Ontario, my close call with a bear in Manitoba and almost being struck by lightning in Saskatchewan. Then it occurred to me that I was having one close encounter with death in every province. I had to be careful in the next few days, as my time in Alberta was drawing to a close. Would there be another brush with death, to keep the streak alive? The thought made me shiver.

Wednesday, August 13, 1997

I had already made friends with the family dog before I met Wayne, who had been working a late shift at Wayhauser, the local pulp and paper mill. They had the biggest dog I had ever seen. Wayne explained that was because he was part wolf. My bike was in the back yard and no one would dare climb the fence to steal it with this dog on guard.

During breakfast, I talked with Wayne about his work at Wayhauser. Wayne loved his job and the company he worked for. The company put the environment and people before profit. Not everyone felt this way. Recently someone had tried to set the mill on fire when the mill was vandalized and a railway box car was torched. Wayne didn't think it was an environmentalist, as this criminal had special knowledge of the mill. This pointed to a current or former employee. Security at the mill had been beefed up but was ineffective. Employees were only allowed in the mill when they presented their company identification card at security. Wayne was aware of one employee who had lost his card and was using his Price Club Costco card, instead, when going through security. This left Wayne concerned. A fire would put over 600 people out of work and would also severely hurt the economy of Grande Prairie.

That morning, I did my presentation at City Hall and then headed west to face hills and headwinds. Stopping in Wembley for lunch, I ordered a spaghetti dinner special and a pizza. The waitress assumed I was feeding someone else when she asked, "That pizza was to go wasn't it?" I said, "No, I'm going to eat it." It was one of those days when I felt like I was starving. Fuelled by the main courses and two desserts - fruit and a cinnamon roll - I cycled on to Hythe, where the Hythe Motor Inn donated my room.

Thursday, August 14, 1997

Just 21 kilometres out of Hythe, in the pouring rain, my trailer tire went flat. Drenched, I repaired the tire at the road side. At the last gas station in Alberta, I took the opportunity to further inflate the tires to full pressure.

I crossed into B.C. and into another time zone, now three hours behind that of Hamilton. I had planned to ride to Tomslake but there was no community on Highway 2 and with my extra hour I decided to keep riding, ending up in Pouce Coupe. At the Pioneer Inn, I was greeted by a clean cut young boy. I asked if they would donate a room. He said he couldn't say until he checked with his parents, who would be home in an hour. I told him I'd get something to eat and then come back. Across the street was a roadhouse style restaurant. There were only two people in the restaurant, Al and Wally. Al was in charge and I told him about my expedition and asked if he would donate my supper. Al was confrontational. He told me Quebec could go ahead and separate. I told him that this would hurt Canada. He told me he didn't care what would happen to Canada because B.C. was going to separate from Canada and join the U.S. Despite Al's words, I sensed he didn't mean this but was like my grandfather Harbert who loved to argue for argument's sake. Well, I was Captain of the Debating Team at Appleby College and we were the Fulford Cup Champions. Responding to Al's raised voice, I exclaimed that the U.S. doesn't have universal health care! What are you going to do if you need bypass surgery and you don't have health insurance? Al responded, "When your time comes, your time comes!" I then countered, "What are you going to do when a child is hit by a car in front of your restaurant and has no health insurance but is critically injured? Are you going to let that child die? For the first time, Al responded in a calm voice, "What do you want for supper?"

As I ate supper, Al held up a copy of MacLean's Magazine and asked if I thought this guy was proud of Canada? The cover pictured native leader Phil Fontaine, who had just won an election as the head of the Assembly of First Nations. I thought this was a funny question because I noticed that Al was helping Wally fill in an application form for Metis citizenship.

After supper, I went back across the street where the Pioneer Inn donated my room. I watched a Grey Cup rematch, the Argos beating the Eskimos. The game was neck and neck, until Eskimos first string quarterback Danny McManus was injured. Being a Tiger-Cat fan, I was cheering for the Eskimos. The Argos looked strong in this game, which didn't fare well for Tiger-Cats in their upcoming Labour Day clash with the Argos. After the game, I went to sleep happy to be in B.C., the last province in my journey to the top of Canada!

Friday, August 15, 1997

After riding the short distance to Dawson Creek, I paused at McDonald's for breakfast, which they kindly donated. I met a local radio representative who invited me to come back to her station, where I gave an interview. It was also the local TV station which was a CBC affiliate. The news director did an interview with me in the middle of the city's busiest intersections, which was "Mile 0", on the Alaska Highway. The Alaska Highway, in Canada, was built in 1944 during the war, by the U.S. Army. The highway runs from Dawson Creek to Alaska. It was built by over 11,000 U.S. soldiers and 16,000 civilians, in just nine months.

After the interviews, I went over to the Northwinds Motel, located next door to the theatre, where my room was donated. Truthfully, I had asked this motel first because I really wanted to see a movie, any movie. The only movie playing was "Spawn", which I hadn't seen. All I knew was that "Spawn" was adapted from the Canadian created comic book of the same name.

At the MLA office, I presented my Province of British Columbia certificate and asked that it be forwarded to the Premier. An effervescent Russian Canadian girl, named Sharlene, was extremely helpful to me. She let me fax a confirmation to all Fort St. John media, using her government media list for reference.

At the Dawson Creek Hospital, the patients seemed particularly sad. It might have been today's rainy weather which had apparently been falling for weeks this summer. It felt good to be able to cheer them up.

At the local tourist bureau, Mayor Blair found me. He was a very friendly man, a proud Canadian who was interested to know all about my expedition. I mentioned I was going to get lunch before my presentation at City Hall. Blair recommended I go to the Alaska Restaurant for the best food in town. Even though Blair couldn't join me, he said he would buy my lunch and asked me to tell the owner to bill Mayor Blair. I was delayed enroute to lunch, as a newspaper reporter stopped me and did a long interview. When I arrived at the Alaska restaurant, they knew I was coming. My water boy, Steve, told me about this weekend's Big Bike Ride. It was a fund raising event for the Heart and Stroke Association. There was a large bike that an entire team could pedal and at the Dawson Mall they pedaled a course, against the clock. Steve asked if I would sponsor him, which I did. Steve would be better suited to work in a sales organization, than in a restaurant.

After my City Hall presentation, Blair let me use an office so I could call home. After a long call to Carol and James, I went to a local Subway shop which donated my supper. Returning to my Northwinds Motel room, I unloaded my gear and laid down just for a moment. I fell asleep for the entire night. So much for my plans to see a movie.

Saturday, August 16, 1997

As I loaded my gear, I could see my breath in the cold, early morning air. Riding just outside of Dawson Creek, I heard a snap in the distance and saw a large German Shepherd running straight towards me dragging a long heavy gauge steel chain behind him. With a surge of adrenaline, my legs pumped as fast as they could go. I quickly outdistanced the dog. Today, I was riding 70 kilometres over solid hills. There was a long bridge over the Kiskatinaw river. The gorge was so deep it made me shiver as I cycled overhead. Despite my fear of heights, I stopped at the end of the bridge and walked back to take a picture of the spectacular gorge.

Later, after cycling into the afternoon, "spectacular" took on a whole new meaning when the Peace River Valley first came into view. Taking a picture from the top, I ventured down the steep incline towards the bottom, through breathtaking scenery. At the bottom was an even larger bridge, crossing the river to the community of Taylor. As trucks passed over the bridge at the same time, I could feel the bridge heaving from the weight. My heart pounded.

After a donated lunch at the Taylor Inn and Restaurant, I ventured out to face the climb out of the north side of the Peace River Valley. The land seemed to be calling out to me, "Welcome to the Rockies!". I had experience carrying my gear up a vertical incline from the escarpment referred to as the Hamilton mountain. I learned today that Hamilton does not have a mountain.

In Fort St. John, at the biggest Canadian Tire store I've ever seen in my life, I bought some more bike supplies for the long road ahead.

At the front of City Hall I met the media and people of Fort St. John, who knew I was coming. It was strange but no official representative of the City participated, despite my faxed letter sent by Carol as confirmation. After speaking to everyone, I placed the Fort St. John Certificate into their night mail slot. The media at City Hall had a 100% turn out, including Mark, the morning D.J. on radio CKNL, who invited me to co-host his Monday morning show with him.

The Mile 49 Bed & Breakfast had volunteered to accommodate me overnight. I was met by Gille Dupuis on his bicycle who led me to their beautiful home, with huge front windows on the first and second floor. I met his wife, Nicole, who rolled her eyes when she heard no one from the City had come to welcome me.

I phoned home to Carol. She told me about an unusual call she got after midnight. The call went like this:

Carol: Hello.
Caller: Is this Chris Robertson's house?
Carol: Yes it is.
Caller: I need to speak to him. (agitated voice)
Carol: I'm sorry but he's not here.
Caller: When will he be back? This is urgent. I have to speak to him right away.
(Carol had been sleeping, and was struggling to clear her mind so she could help the caller. Concern crept into her thoughts as she began to wonder if the urgency of the call was related to some trouble I had encountered.)
Carol: Well, he won't be back for a long time, but I can try to get a message to him.
Caller: My name is .... He's got me out of trouble before. I got in a fight with my boss. One thing led to another. I ended up punching him out. I've been arrested and I'm in the Niagara Falls jail! He's got to get me out of here!
Carol: (Speechless with the man's dilemma and how it could possibly relate to Chris on his expedition, it began to dawn on Carol that maybe this poor man had the wrong number. Just as she was about to suggest this, the man broke the silence.)
Caller: Is this the home of Chris Robertson, the lawyer?
Carol: No, I'm very sorry. You've got the wrong number. This is a different Chris Robertson.
Caller: Oh no! What am I going to do? Sorry to wake you up.
Carol: That's OK. Good luck to you. (Carol hung up relieved and amused, and feeling sorry for the poor guy in jail. She hoped for his sake that Canadian law, unlike American TV police shows, allowed him one more phone call!)

It was 4:30 in the afternoon and I was just in time to turn on TSN and watch Tiger-Cats play the Alouettes in Montreal. Quarterback Anthony Cavillo was having a terrible game and Montreal quickly racked up points from Hamilton's mistakes. I left the game to enjoy a home made pizza on the sun porch, with Gille and Nicole.

After supper we went for a drive so I could see more of Fort St. John. That night, after a hard week of cycling, I enjoyed my sleep in their extra comfortable bed.

Sunday, August 17, 1997

This morning I was greeted by a warm breakfast in the dining room. The smell of freshly baked muffins filled the house. It was heavenly.

The Anglican church building in Fort St. John is shared with the United Church. The Anglican service was at 9:00 am and the United service was at 11:00 am. After church, at the social get together in the basement, I met Dr. Jack Temple and his wife Willa. Jack had spent most of his life practicing general medicine in the north. In life and death situations, he had performed many emergency procedures because there were no specialists nearby for urgent referral. For a while, he had moved back to his hometown of Grimsby, just a stone's throw away from Hamilton, to practice medicine. He recounted a couple of stories about diagnoses he had made, that other family practitioners had missed. On the whole, he found city medicine to be too tame. His colleagues were surprised when he told them he was leaving his Grimsby practice again, with privileges at three hospitals, to move back to Fort St. John. We spoke about the bear attack at Fort Nelson this week. Two people had been killed and another couple hospitalized. Jack told me about the horrific injuries that can occur with bear attacks. One message came through loud and clear. Don't answer nature's call in the woods without your survival knife.

Willa invited me back to the house at 12:30 pm, to join them for lunch. I had to make a quick trip to the Totem Mall to send a package to Carol. At lunch we dined on fresh salmon, beets, baked potato, ice cream and chocolate cake. The hospitality of Fort St. John sure felt wonderful.

After lunch, I headed back to the B & B and greeted Nicole, saying, "Sorry I'm late, Mom." She laughed. After doing my laundry, I joined Gille, Nicole and a couple of friends for a barbecue steak supper. It was Gille and Nicole's wedding anniversary so I gave a toast to their happiness. After supper I watched TV to unwind and Gille, being a wonderful host, magically appeared with fresh popcorn.

Monday, August 18, 1997

At Radio CKNL, I was slated to do the early morning show. In Mark's studio, I sat down in front of the second mike. This was a great opportunity to talk to the people of Fort St. John about Canada. I even did the morning birthdays with station callers. One call came in from Debbie, who wanted to give me a video she made on how she thought we could make Canada better through agriculture. I gave her my home address so she could send me the video. She was disappointed that I wouldn't see it until I finished. I had to point out that my bike was not equipped with a VCR or electricity. Another call offered me a place to stay in "Wonowon", which is where I was staying tonight. I said goodbye to Mark and headed out to the Alaska highway.

Now, when I first said "Wonowon", I thought it was a place with an Indian name, but it is really "Mile 101" on the Alaska Highway.

"Mile 101" was 30 miles, or 70 kilometres away, all up and down hills the entire journey. When I arrived, the Hall family put me up in their motel which included a restaurant, gas bar and convenience store. This little complex seemed to employ almost everyone in the community. When I checked in, they told me my supper and breakfast would also be on the house. A young man, who worked in the natural gas industry, came over to my table during supper. He had heard me on the radio and wanted to wish me good luck. He once worked on a company project in Russia and since that experience he thanked God everyday for living in Canada. I told him he needs to tell Canadians his story so people really can develop an appreciation for how fortunate we are to live in Canada. After supper, I was ready for bed after challenging the hills all day.

Tuesday, August 19, 1997

During breakfast, my waitress Manny, a French Canadian, asked if she could take my picture. I suggested she wait until my bike was packed up so she could get the full effect. She brought me a banana, even though I didn't order it, to ensure I ate healthy. I enjoyed the fresh fruit. After packing up my bike, I pulled it up in front of the restaurant and recruited another customer to take the picture so Manny could be in it with me. I prefer action shots, so I picked Manny up on my shoulder for the picture.

Cycling to Pink Mountain, I passed roadside signs all day that read, "Danger - Poison Gas - No Camping - No Parking". I wondered how they feel about cyclists! As I rode into the mountains, a plane circled overhead for a few minutes. Every other vehicle that passed me seemed to be an R.V. (recreational vehicle). One RV was a little different. Instead of towing a car or a boat, this one was towing a helicopter. I guess a helicopter is invaluable when you want to find a campsite fast. It looked like rain tonight so I really wanted to be indoors rather than in my tent. At Pink Mountain, the only accommodation is the Pink Mountain Motor Inn. I spoke with the Manager, Jimmy Lee, to see if he would donate a room to help my expedition. Now it is not everyday that someone comes through Pink Mountain on a Canadian Unity mission and I could see the wheels turning in Jimmy Lee's mind as he thought about this. Unknown to me at the time, Jimmy Lee had just donated a room for three people to the Swiss runner, Serge Roetheli, who had been running for two years from Argentina enroute to Alaska. Serge, a former Olympic boxer, with his wife Nicole and friend David, were raising funds for the Francois-Xavier Bagnoud Foundation that helps needy and ailing children. I am sure Jimmy Lee thought about the chances of us both being in Pink Mountain on the same day. He had one of those looks as if to say "Am I On Candid Camera?" Jimmy, in the end, had a big heart and was proud to help Canada as he donated another room for me. Just as I got my gear inside, a downpour started, which was the heaviest since I arrived in B.C. God Bless Jimmy Lee!

Wednesday, August 20, 1997

I used some of the morning to bring my journal up to date. Serge Roetheli had a two hour headstart. It would be interesting to see when I would catch Serge. I flew down Pink Mountain at a rapid pace but didn't see him. I thought, forget about boxing, Serge needs to be on the Swiss Olympic Marathon team. After an hour of cycling, my trailer ran over something and I heard the tire pop and the hissing of escaping air. I unloaded my trailer, took my trailer wheel off and proceeded to take the tire off the rim, searching for the source of the flat. After patching the hole in the tire, I used the time to lubricate my chain which was dry. Everything back in its place, I set off again. I didn't mind this flat as it was a beautiful day. I remembered my last flat, which I had to fix in the rain.

I finally caught up to Serge at a place called Sikanni Chief. As I came up from behind, I started to sing the "Rocky" theme music for him. He raised both arms in the air to symbolize victory. I headed on, listening to my Blues Brothers movie C.D. It was comical, really. Here I was, alone on the Alaska Highway, surrounded by the rugged peaks of the Rocky Mountains, listening to Canadian Dan Akroyd and John Belushi sing the theme from Rawhide.

Rolling rolling rolling
Though the streets are swollen
Keeps them doggies rolling, rawhide

I sang along at the top of my lungs. I was probably the only cowboy cyclist in the world!

I arrived at my destination of Buckinghorse River. The only accommodation was the Buckinghorse Lodge, which was full with Natural Gas company crews. I did get permission to put my tent up on the property. While I had some supper, I learned that tomorrow's destination is non-existent. Trutch was on my B.C. map and my Canadian atlas, but, it is no longer there. Not even a gas station or a restaurant is left. I laughed because I had a certificate to present to Trutch with the community's name on it. That meant that tomorrow I had two options. One, camp by the road miles from nowhere. Two, ride farther than I ever had before, to Prophet River. I went to bed early so that Option Two could have a potential for success.

Thursday, August 21, 1997

Up early, I broke camp and packed my bicycle to be on the road at 8:30 am. As I rode along the side of the mountain, I could see more mountains looming off to my left. It was a beautiful morning, a big blue sky dotted with cumulus clouds. I was listening to inspirational music on my CD. My body was strong and I was cycling fast, totally in sync with my bike. A cool mountain breeze refreshed my face. This was one of the most breathtaking moments of my life - everything was glorious and spectacular. I thanked God as I rode. This wonderful moment was an incredible blessing.

Zooming along northbound, I was hit in the cheek by a large dragon fly, who was flying south. It hurt, as if someone had hit me in the face with a branch. I'll have to get a bumper sticker for my bike, that says: "I brake for dragon flies!"

Prophet River had been an 80 kilometre journey according to my odometer when I arrived. It was a long ride, but 107 kilometres to Dryden was still my daily record. At Prophet River, there was only a restaurant, with gas pumps and a bunk house in the back for crews. The staff person gave me permission to camp. I set up my tent and then had supper in the restaurant. After supper, I freshened up and was welcomed to watch TV in the bunk house with the crew. HBO (Home Box Office) is illegal in Canada according to the CRTC, but satellite technology doesn't stop for government policy. Many people in the north have their credit card billed for HBO via a third party, to bypass the bureaucracy. I hope the government doesn't crack down on this practice because it would detract from the quality of life of the people in the north. The sleeping quarters of the unattractive bunk house were small and cramped, but functional. I once visited a Canadian prison on government business and remember being shocked at how comfortable the facilities were for prisoners. If these ordinary working Canadians had access to the facilities of some Canadian prisons, they would have thought they had died and gone to heaven. I thought, the crew men deserve the prison facility and the prisoners deserve the bunk house.

I went to my tent, hail stones the size of ice cubes pummeling down, hurting my skin as they bounced off. It was impossible to sleep due to the constant crackle of thunder as a heavy storm had rolled in.

Friday, August 22, 1997

My ride would be long again to Fort Nelson today, but I took comfort knowing I had a bed for the weekend. John and Sue Peachey had opened their home to me. They also offered to have Barry Shainbaum, my photo journalist friend, stay with them. Barry was flying in for the weekend, to update his photographic record of the journey, hoping to sell some of the photos to Canadian magazines, such as MacLean's.

At breakfast in Prophet River, I read the Fort Nelson news. There was a story about the *To The Top Canada* expedition in the paper but the front page story was the bear attack. A Fort Nelson man, Ray Kitchen, was killed trying to come to the aid of a family experiencing a bear attack. A young boy was critically injured, and his mother was killed. A Calgary professor was being dragged into the bush by the bear, when it was shot and killed. The attack happened at a popular tourist attraction at Liard

River Provincial Park. The restaurant waitress said a friend had seen 32 bears at the Fort Nelson dump in the past few days. I would have to be especially careful of bears from this point on.

After drying off my camping equipment from last night's rain, I set out on the highway. While riding down a hill, I noticed two R.V.'s parked on the other side of the road in the middle of nowhere. The occupants were snapping pictures of something across the road. It was a bear. They had the option of running into their R.V. and locking the door if the bear charged. I didn't have this option. The bear was snarling, as if to be angrily saying, "Don't take my picture, you're making me really mad. Stop taking my picture!" The bear was 50 feet from my side of the road. I decided to shoot past the bear as fast as I could go. This strategy worked.

After travelling another 20 kilometres, a pickup truck ploughed past me and suddenly swerved left into the other lane as if it was out of control. Then it swerved back to the proper lane. I peered cautiously up the road and realized the pickup truck was trying to help me. It had tried to scare away another bear that, this time, was right up near the centre of the road. The bear didn't move. I stopped my bike a quarter kilometre away. Traffic didn't seem to frighten this bear. A Honda with Quebec licence plates, driven by an older couple, stopped and offered to help me. This would be the most important football play I would run in my life. I asked the driver to keep his car between the bear and me. He'd be the blocker and I was the ball carrier. I started pedaling as hard as I could to increase my speed, reducing the chances of the bear intercepting me. Just before we got to the bear, the Honda started to fall behind. I turned and said to the older female passenger, "Can you speed up please?". The Honda accelerated and we both rocketed past the bear. I kept going hard to put some distance between the bear and myself.

After cycling 75 kilometres, I reached the outskirts of Fort Nelson where I stopped mid-afternoon at the local Husky store which donated my lunch. At the Army Surplus store, I bought bear pepper spray and a holster to keep it close to me at all times. I also picked up a "James Bond-like" pen that shoots flares and also makes a loud bang to scare bears. Well, if I wasn't ready for bears, I would be ready to invade a small country.

I called John and Sue to get directions to their house but they were not in. I knew I would be able to see their bison farm from the Alaska Highway, approximately 5 kilometres north of town. I could see the buffalo after cycling north but there was no road. I finally found a mud path where I could cut back to a house that was across the buffalo field. I sank in the mud to above my ankles and my tires sank down from my heavy pack weight. I fought every foot of the way until I reached a country road. John and Barry found me, mud covered, on the country road and directed me to the house. John and Sue had a spectacular home with a view of the mountains and of their buffalo. I left my mud covered shoes outside and had a shower.

When I was cleaned up I joined the Peachey family. One of the first questions I asked John was to explain the difference between buffalo and bison. He told me there were no actual buffalo in North America, just bison. This news may come as a shock to the National Football League Buffalo Bills! I learned the Peacheys and Barry had just come from the funeral service for Ray Kitchen, the heroic Fort Nelson man killed in the bear attack. We then sat down to a roast beef dinner Sue had prepared. After supper, Barry went to bed early as he was still on Toronto time and he was tired. I stayed up and talked with John and Sue. I learned that John was in the lumber industry and had a company that cleared land for a mill and chopstick factory. When John learned I was a Professional Speaker who was a strategic business consultant, he took the opportunity to discuss his future business alternatives. Late that evening, we called it a night. I fell asleep quickly.

Saturday, August 23, 1997

We all enjoyed a full breakfast including elk sausages, which tasted great. After hosing down my mud covered bike, Barry and I planned to head into town. John mentioned that he had his own plane and offered to fly Barry and me around the Fort Nelson area. We agreed to meet at 3:00 pm at the airport.

At the local bike shop, I asked a young man named Brady to "fix all the things on my bike that need fixing". Even though my bike had been tuned up in Edmonton, the first leg through the Rocky Mountains had been very hard on it. I had developed problems with tires, the chain, gears and brakes. Leaving my bike, I walked to the flower shop and sent flowers to my wife as next week is our fourteenth wedding anniversary.

Barry and I visited the local radio station, CFNL. I spoke on the air with the DJ, for twenty minutes. We then went to the Fort Nelson General Hospital, visiting the patients to brighten their day. One young man told us about a psychopathic sadist who had once tried to kill him and his girl friend with an axe. As we left, he warned me to be careful through Whitehorse on September 10, because that is when "Freddy The Axe" gets released. I got shivers when I checked my daytimer and saw that, according to my schedule, I will arrive in Whitehorse the evening of September 10!

At Dan's Pub for lunch, we watched the closing ceremony of the Canada Games on TSN.

In town, there was a slow pitch baseball tournament where I addressed the players about my *To The Top Canada* expedition. At the airport, we met John and climbed into his Piper Cherokee. We weaved through the mountains west of Fort Nelson. At one point, as we were heading straight for a mountain, John had to sneeze. I thought, "Why do I feel like Buddy Holly right now?". John turned right and flew over a magnificent mountain lake. From the air, Fort Nelson is an island of civilization in an ocean of forest. On one hand it bothered me because I couldn't see any civilization that I would be riding to next week, but I took solace that I couldn't see Prophet River from the air, which is where I had just come from. After our awe-inspiring flight, I returned to the bike shop where Brady wouldn't take any money for working on my equipment.

I rode the few kilometres to the Peachey House. When I arrived, we immediately headed out to a neighbour's house who was hosting a pot luck supper for friends. At Bill and Cathy Dolan's house, we were greeted by a large banner saying "National Unity", to welcome me. After we ate, Bill who is part of a 5-piece music band named Band-X played on the porch overlooking the mountains from dusk to the wee hours of the morning. Even Barry joined the band and sang several songs, to the delight of the gathering. At one point, Sue Peachey asked me if I enjoyed being relaxed and wondered if it was hard to think of having fun when your family is so far away. I thought about the dangers of mentally relaxing. On one hand, my back, legs, and feet were in pain and only my game day mental attitude allowed me to overcome the pain. On the other hand, the total focus on my daily routine kept me from feeling the deep loneliness of separation from my family. During the *To The Top Canada* expedition, relaxation of my disciplined mental state was an evil I had to fight. Despite the constant pain which was now seeping into my body, this party was a magic moment that I will remember and reminisce about all my life, long after the pain is gone.

Sunday, August 24, 1997

Up early again, I read the story of David in the chapter of Samuel I, in the Old Testament. The story bore an important message - that even if the bear I face is as big as Goliath, I cannot be defeated with God by my side.

We headed to St. Mary Magdalene Anglican Church in Fort Nelson. At the service, the minister asked if anyone was having a birthday or anniversary this week. My hand went up. During the hymn, tears ran down my face as I realized this would be my first anniversary away from my wife. After church, I wrote in my journal.

John told us that the bison were close to the coral so it was a great time for a picture. At one point, as I was trying to take a picture, the dogs scared the herd. As I walked around outside the coral, taking John's three-year-old daughter Kayla with me, John went inside the coral to see if he could keep the bison in a central area while I snapped a good shot. The herd circled past John, around the gate and into our field. Now, a herd of bison was running straight at us. I picked up Kayla, as if she were a football during an Argo fumble, put her under my arm and ran. We hid behind a group of nearby trees as the bison thundered by. Well, that was enough bison picture taking for me.

John took us to one of his job sites to show us his operation. There was a monstrous piece of equipment called a processor, robotic technology that grabs the log, moves it to a specific length and cuts it. As I watched this computer technology, the first line of a Monty Python song came into my head, "I'm a Lumberjack and I'm O.K."

I thought, this lumberjack's not going to be O.K. because he'll be unemployed, with technology like this around.

We returned to the house and enjoyed a supper of elk steaks. I thanked the Peachey family for their kindness. They had opened their home and hearts to us this whole weekend. This is a great Canadian family . . .

Monday, August 25, 1997

Finishing an early morning shower, I pulled back the shower curtain and immediately noticed that the bathroom door had been opened. In one motion, I shut the door and stepped out of the tub, wrapping a towel around my waist. Glancing in the mirror, I was surprised to see three-and-a-half-year-old Kayla, sitting on the toilet with no clothes on! Startled, I turned around and she said, "I had to use the bathroom!" I replied "That's alright", exiting quickly. Kayla finished and left the bathroom but she gained the dubious distinction of seeing the unity guy totally naked.

Riding into town, I stopped by the radio station where they were airing a network talk show. I taped a news interview and made a music request. Later that morning, between 10:30 am and 11:00 am a song would be dedicated to John & Sue Peachey and their daughters Kayla and Jodi from Chris Robertson. I picked the current hit Canadian song, "Butterfly Kisses". It is a song about a father reflecting on his daughter growing up.

I was then off to Fort Nelson Town Square to meet Mayor Don Edwards. People had also come to greet and cycle with me. One person who showed up was the Lloydminster Mayor. This was the third time I'd seen him and I kidded him that he was like a Grateful Dead "Deadhead" groupie, following me across the country. Some pictures were taken with myself and the Mayors, in stereo. I received a gift from the town - a calculator with a picture of a bear on it. After my speech, taking pictures, talking to a reporter and signing autographs, I headed further north.

Cathy, who had hosted the Saturday evening party, came out to cycle with me until we got to her sideroad. We talked about bears as we cycled and she told me the story of when, two years ago, a bear tried to get into the Fort Nelson IGA grocery store. It had to be shot in the parking lot. Thoughts went through my mind of one of those grocery store P.A. announcers:

"Attention Shoppers, we have a bear in Aisle 1 and a special on cream corn in Aisle 2".

As we pedaled along, we were joined by another cyclist, Angie, who was German and married to a Canadian in Fort Nelson. She had just returned from a trip to Germany and had even heard the news of the deaths and injuries resulting from the Liard River bear attack on German television. Angie mentioned her family had a cabin in Toad River and extended an invitation for me to stay with them, later in the week.

After the cyclists turned off, I wasn't alone because today I was being shadowed by Barry, still covering me for his freelance pictures. Around noon, he turned his Sunfire rent-a-car around, went back to town and bought hamburgers for lunch at the Fort Nelson A & W. He caught up with me and we dined on the hot lunch. As I rode back into the Rockies, Barry especially enjoyed shooting pictures of me cycling up the majestic hills, better suited for tobogganing down, rather than biking up.

On a water break, we decided to try out my flare pen. I had armed the pen with a flare cartridge. Pointing down the road, no cars visible as far as the eye could see, I pulled back the trigger. "Click". Nothing happened. Barry was trying to take a picture of the flare in flight but we had no luck after a second, third and fourth try. Barry kidded me that the bear will have to make an appointment to have the flare pen fired at him. I tried again. This time the flare fired leaving a trail of white smoke and exploded with a bang so loud, we both jumped. I made a mental note. If flare does not fire during bear attack, pull out survival knife...

After cycling over 70 kilometres, I reached my destination of Steamboat Mountain. This mountain got its name due to it's shape. It is one of the higher mountains and had a spectacular view of the surrounding peaks.

The only business in Steamboat is the Steamboat Cafe. It is run by Ken, who seemed to be the master of evasive answers. When I asked Ken if I could camp on his property, he answered, "It's a big country and you can camp anywhere you want." I took that to mean yes. I asked Ken what time he closed his convenience store and he answered, "When I get tired." I asked him what time he opens in the morning he replied, "When I wake up."

Barry took some pictures of my tent as I set it up. He was heading back to Fort Nelson as there was no place for him to stay in Steamboat. Tomorrow morning, he was flying from Fort Nelson to Toronto. After all the bear stories I'd heard, there was part of me that wished that I could go with him back home. In my heart, I knew that I had to finish the *To The Top Canada* expedition or die trying. If the Lord decided to take my life, then I would join Jesus in heaven and die in service to my country. Maybe my death would serve Canada better, by rallying all Canadians to answer "my question" with focus. I knew for my sake and for setting an example for my son, James, I would never never quit. Quitters never win and winners never quit! I didn't plan to get killed either because I wanted to see the Tiger-cats win another Grey Cup.

I thanked Barry before he left, for coming so far to chronicle my trip. Climbing into my tent, nicknamed the "Steamboat Hilton", I went to sleep with my bear spray and survival knife by each hand.

Tuesday, August 26, 1997

Soaking wet after a night of rain, I dried my gear, packed it up, thanked Ken and headed off. The road completely turned to dirt and loose gravel, as I was in a construction zone. The ground was not well packed and my tires sank into the dirt under the enormous weight I carried. While cycling through the mountains, I saw the first moose I'd encountered in B.C. The moose was off in a distance and no danger to me. It was a struggle, up the mountain. When I reached the top, a construction flag person signalled me to stop. The female flag person told me I had two options - either put my bike in the back of the pilot truck that led cars through the maze of giant earth moving machines or wait until noon when all machine operators went on their lunch break. I asked her what would happen if I just headed off and went through with the cars. She said she would lose her job. I didn't want that to happen. I then asked to speak to her boss. After half an hour of waiting her boss pulled up. I told him I could keep up with the pilot vehicle and it wouldn't disrupt his operation. The boss gave the O.K. When the pilot vehicle came back I led the cars and raced after it. The course went over hills, through mud and puddles of water but I stuck to the pilot vehicle like glue. We passed bulldozers, steam shovels, earth movers and giant dump trucks. After passing through the construction, I rode a few more kilometres and was greeted by a second construction zone. This time the flag person waved me through and I didn't even have to wait for the pilot vehicle. I passed the pilot vehicle leading a line of cars in the south direction as I headed north. At the end of this construction zone I shot down a big hill where, at the bottom, I got a flat tire. It was my back bike tire and the messiest to fix because I had to take the chain off. My rear bike tire had to work the hardest because it had my own weight, the weight of the gear on my rear saddle bags and the weight of my trailer on it. Rather than patching this hole, I decided to put a new tube in. I pumped it up with my hand pump but could not get 65 PSI which I really needed with all this weight. I took a detour to the construction zone base camp where I found compressed air to inflate my rear tire fully.

I was off again, seemingly with all systems normal. As I rode into the afternoon, air started to seep out of my tire. My flat tire slowed my progress to a crawl. I tried to hand pump the tire but with only moderate results.

For the first time, I spotted caribou. There were two caribou at each side of the road, standing proudly with their antlers high above their heads, dark chocolate in colour. At first I thought they were statues, one on each side of the road, built to welcome travellers, but when I got close they both bolted from their frozen positions. I was more startled than they were.

I pulled into Summit Lake at about 8:00 pm, my bike was moving at a snail's pace. I decided to eat immediately as they were closing the restaurant. I then set up my tent in the twilight, the sun having disappeared behind a giant pyramid-shaped mountain. It would be midnight at home and I didn't want to phone and wake everyone. I knew I would have to fix this flat first thing in the morning.

Wednesday, August 27, 1997

Today was our anniversary. Like the day my son graduated from Holbrook School, I felt really badly that I was not at home.

As a person who worked most of my lifetime teaching members of the restaurant industry how to achieve "world class service", I found my trip into the north a study into the "worst class service". It seemed the further north you went, the worse the service got. This morning during breakfast, I witnessed a new low. A large busload of German tourists had stopped and filled up the entire restaurant. To thank these valued German customers who spent hundreds of dollars, what music was being played on the tape machine? The Summit Cafe was playing the Johnny Horton song, "Sink The Bismarck"!

I went back to my tent and packed up my gear in the pouring rain. The back tire was completely flat. At the Summit Lodge gas bar, the attendant was extremely helpful. I told him I needed compressed air to check to see if I had a loose valve stem. He turned on his air, brought me a tire tester, got water for my bicycle bottles and even got me a better valve cap than I had on my bicycle. This guy should be running the restaurant! But, in life there is always politics. In this case, if he were to become the restaurant manager, the current manager would have to be demoted or let go. Considering that the current manager was his wife, his career path was limited.

Riding in the rain, I could hear thunder but couldn't see any lightning. You haven't lived until you have heard thunder in the mountains, the echo bouncing off the granite walls around you.

More caribou darted across the road. I saw a sign stating that this was the highest point of the Alaskan Highway, right beside Summit Lake. This meant I had tackled the toughest part of the Rockies and succeeded. There were many mountains still ahead but nothing bigger than the one I had just conquered.

I rode on, arriving in Toad River by late afternoon. Toad River was a milestone because it was the three quarter mark of the *To The Top Canada* expedition. At the Toad River Lodge Restaurant, they gave me my late lunch at half price. The decor of the restaurant was ball caps and fine art. The waitress, Trish, was a talented artist and displayed her paintings of the north in the restaurant. There were also thousands of different ball caps lining the ceiling and walls.

After eating I saw the pay phone was finally free and I called Carol to wish her a Happy Anniversary and to assure her I hadn't forgotten the date. Just before the call, I noticed I had lost my wedding band! My thinner fingers, combined with taking my cycling gloves off to fix my flat tire, had been the cause. I chose not to report this news to Carol on our anniversary. This day was sad enough for Carol, without me making it worse. The flowers I'd sent on the Saturday, hadn't been delivered.

Back at my table, Trish was chatting with her friend Angie and her son Ray and daughter Terry. As we talked about Trish's art, Angie asked if I was interested in seeing more of her paintings. We all piled into Angie's Toyota pick up and went to Trish's house. There, I met Trish's husband Charlie and daughter Tara. Throughout the house were paintings of the north, including Charlie's helicopter. Charlie was a helicopter pilot, working for a company that supported environmentally-friendly logging. On remote mountains, a tree that had been cut was airlifted by helicopter to a road below, instead of building a road into the logging site. The helicopter could lift 4,000 pounds and could move up to 750,000 pounds of logs a day. This work only stopped for bad weather including bad winds, freezing rain, lightning storms or fog. I asked Charlie if there was a company bean counter pushing him to fly in bad weather. Charlie indicated the company only used very experienced pilots and fully respected their safety decisions.

Heading back to the restaurant, I got my bike and cycled 2 kilometres to Angie's cabin. I brought my gear in to try and dry it by the wood stove. Ray and I played a board game called "Explorations". It is a game where you travel the world and discover its remarkable linguistic diversity. You have language cards in your hand and you try to match them with countries on the board. I learned that I was not the world traveller I thought I was. For example, I did not know that in Afghanistan they spoke Pashto, in Senegal they spoke Wolof or, in Kenya they spoke Swahili. My eyes really opened up when I had a card for a language I had never heard of, called Loucheux. It corresponded to Inuvik, Canada. You never know where you learn more about Canada. I went to bed, after discussing strategies with Angie on how she wanted to make Canada better, by stopping illegal drug use in our country.

Thursday, August 28, 1997

Next morning, Angie decided that she and her children would go with me to Muncho Lake. They had an Uncle Jack who lived there and ran a lodge. I assumed she meant that they would ride in the truck but she planned to cycle with me. Angie and Ray had won gold medals at the Western Canadian Cross Country Ski Championships, held earlier in the year in Whitehorse. The farthest her son Ray had ever biked was 20 kilometres but today we had to go 50 kilometres.

As we pulled out, Ray noticed my Bob trailer tire was partially flat. We pulled into a nearby gas station where I pulled the tire off the trailer and filled it with air. It was either a small hole or a very slow leak because I couldn't hear or feel any air escaping. We headed out in another day of rain. After twelve miles, we stopped for lunch as the rain finally passed. Little Terry was in a small trailer being pulled by Angie. Terry was glad to be able to get out of the trailer and stretch her legs. The family's main snack seemed to be bird seed and my main snack was Oreo cookies. I don't think the children were allowed to eat many treats at home because when I asked Ray if he wanted a cookie he said, "No, I'm not supposed to." Then I offered one to Terry and asked Angie if it was alright. When she said yes, Terry took a cookie. This was a revelation to Ray, who wasn't going to miss out. Like a flash, he was in for a cookie too.

We resumed our journey as the rain started again. Angie's bike had a problem and she couldn't access her lower gear, so we walked up some very steep hills.

At one point, we pulled over so Ray could answer nature's call in the woods. Angie let Terry out of the trailer to stretch her legs. She started to walk away and Angie told her not to wander off. I kidded little Terry that I thought I'd seen a bear over there, so she'd better come back. With no fear, she continued off in the other direction. In an effort to convince her to come back, I made my best bear sound. Terry wasn't fooled but Ray came out of the bush pulling his pants up and exclaiming "I heard a bear!". Angie smiled and retrieved Terry, as we set out once again.

As we tackled another daunting hill in the pouring rain, Ray was starting to get very tired. He pushed his bike with one hand and held the back of his mother's bike trailer with the other for momentum. Every step Ray took was a personal best as he was now at double what he had done previously. Finally over the top of the last hill, we were able to cycle down to Muncho Lake and shelter.

Surprisingly, Uncle Jack charged Angie and her children for their room in his log cabin motel. With this perspective, I didn't even ask for my room to be donated. I pulled out my Visa and paid the going rate. I needed to give my gear a chance to dry before heading on to Liard River tomorrow.

I emptied my bags and plugged in my bike light battery to recharge overnight. There was a grey powder smeared over everything in one bag. I discovered it was the sparklers that a boy in Whitecourt, Alberta had given me. They had dissolved in the rain. Cleaning my bag the best I could, I left it to dry overnight. There was no television in the room, just old Alaska Airline flight magazines. I was glad to be in a bed and out of the rain.

Friday, August 29, 1997

Today I was scheduled to ride to Liard River, where the bear had killed the people. In the morning, my Bible reading was Kings I, Chapter 19, about Elijah walking a whole day in the wilderness. This was another sign that God protects those who put their trust in the Lord.

It was time to leave and I double checked my trailer tire, only to discover that it would not make the trip to Liard River. I needed a new tube and tire. This tire had served me well and had made it to Muncho Lake, B.C. from Winnipeg, Manitoba. I made the change and was on my way with three strong tires. Muncho Lake is a long lake tucked between the mountains. It was raining again. I stopped at the Northern Rockies Lodge which billed itself as B.C.'s largest log building, at 14,000 sq. ft. For lunch, I ordered orange juice, meatloaf and Black Forest cake. My bill was $21, double what I would pay at home. I wondered if I should tip 15% of the bill considering the inflated price. I decided to tip at the level that I would at home. Transportation contributed somewhat to the inflated cost but I knew the food service industry shipped goods across Canada and didn't create markups this high. These prices were determined by supply and demand economics. You could buy here or drive fifty or one hundred kilometres to a comparable dining establishment (in some cases the only dining establishment). I ventured back into the rain and rode 50 kilometres to Liard River, stopping at the home of Trapper Ray. Since Liard River doesn't have a mayor, I presented the Liard River certificate to Trapper Ray.

Trapper Ray, the resident bear expert, runs a lodge across from the Liard Hotsprings Provincial Park. He loves to chase bears. When the recent bear attack occurred, it was Trapper Ray who came in answer to the cries for help. Trapper Ray said the bodies had been badly mauled and chewed, not a pretty sight. I asked Trapper Ray why the attack happened. That fateful morning, the park campers had reported a black bear hanging around the camp. Authorities were slow to respond. All day, people had been throwing rocks and blocks of wood at the bear to keep it at a safe distance. This only aggravated the bear, to the point that it attacked. Ray believes that a bear, in most cases, will not attack unless given a reason. Trapper Ray called this black bear attack a "world record" for death and injuries from a single black bear.

I was camping out directly beside Trapper Ray's lodge. Grazing by my tent was Trapper Ray's horse, Lucy. If he thought it was safe enough for Lucy, it was safe enough for me. Every thirty seconds, I could hear rifle shots in the distance and it felt like being in a war zone. It seemed it was now open season on bears in Liard River. During supper at Trapper Ray's, my waitress, Jayme, told me about "fur spiders" in the area that were an endangered species. They are the size of a Tarantula and travel together in packs. The fur spiders had been seen pulling rabbits and beavers out of their holes. The fur spider chews off its four weakest legs for more torque and so they can run faster. You can be sure the zipper on my tent will be completely shut tonight.

After supper, I walked over to see the Liard Hotsprings. Indian legends used to talk about a tropical valley in the north. These legends were dismissed as fantasy, but the Liard Hotsprings is a rare ecosystem in Canada which is actually boreal jungle. When I arrived, the water was steaming in the swamp. With ostrich ferns everywhere, it seemed I was walking into a prehistoric, forgotten world. It looked as though I were more likely to be attacked by a raptor, than a bear. Arriving at the Hotspring pool, on this cold night, I stuck my hand in the water to find it was extremely hot. If the water were any warmer, it would be too hot for the people soaking in this natural hot tub. Geothermal heat made the hotsprings a tourist attraction that really caught on when it was first seen by the engineers who were building the Alaska highway. I walked back to my tent for the night, thinking about what other wonders lay waiting down the highway, for me.

Saturday, August 30, 1997

I awoke to a morning of fog and more rain. I packed up my soaking wet gear and rode down the highway, up and down steep, unyielding hills. My bike, with the weight, accelerated to a high rate of speed downhill. At speeds of 40 kph or more, my eyes would tear and water. I am sure cyclists are wondering why I didn't wear sunglasses. I had sunglasses but I wanted full peripheral vision to see bears or moose that may dart my way.

I stopped in the only cafe in Coal River for lunch. The girl in the restaurant said that after cooking for a large crew, she just couldn't cook anymore. She let me buy a pop and I ate lunch from my supplies.

The afternoon skies cleared and I saw the first blue sky for days. I rode 70 kilometres to my destination of Fireside, only to discover a gas bar and absolutely nothing else. I decided to keep going.

I rode until 5 o'clock and then stopped for dinner from my supplies, which consisted of granola bars, canned fruit cocktail, peanuts, butterscotch pudding and grape juice. I rode on, as I didn't want to have the scent of food in the same place that I was camping. My walkman batteries died and the headphones split from nonstop use and fell from my head. Now I was really alone, not even the sound of human music to keep me company.

I rode until 8 o'clock and set up my tent in a clearing at the side of the road. I had ridden 102 kilometres in all and my body seemed to say if you can keep the sunshine coming, I can keep pedaling. I watched the sun set behind the mountains, said my prayers to thank God for a great day, and went to sleep in my sleeping bag that was still damp from the night before.

Sunday, August 31, 1997

I awoke at 5:55 am to the sound of puppies. In a couple of seconds, my body went to full alert as I realized these were not likely domestic dogs. I couldn't see them, as my tent was closed, but these were most likely bear cubs or wolf cubs. If cubs were just outside my tent, so was their mother. One of the most dangerous situations in the north is to put yourself between cubs and the mother, as it always leads to a ferocious attack. The cubs were passing by the back of my tent, where my head was. In case of detection by the mother, I sat up so my head wouldn't be the first line of attack if the mother lunged at the tent. I timed my move from lying to sitting position with the sound of a passing car, so as to camouflage the noise of my movements. I sat quietly, until the animals had passed. Inside my tent I dressed, and packed up my sleeping bag and inflatable mattress. Then I snapped on my belt that had bear spray on my right and the survival knife on my left. I opened my tent door and stepped out. I looked 360° - no more signs of animals. I packed up my bike, as the fog from the valley drifted my way and engulfed me. I took a picture of this fog that seemed to want a closer look at me. I was glad to have my lights fully functional so I could let oncoming cars know I was coming. A while down the road, I stopped and used my supplies for breakfast, which was almost identical to my supper the night before.

Just before 11 o'clock in the morning, I entered the Yukon! A small roadside sign told this history.

The Yukon Territory takes its name from the Indian word Youcon, meaning big river. It was first explored in the 1840's by the Hudson's Bay Company, which established several trading posts. The Territory, which was then considered a district of the Northwest Territories, remained largely untouched until the Klondike gold rush, when thousands of people flooded into the country and communities sprang up overnight. The sudden expansion led to the official formation of the Yukon Territory on June 13, 1898.

I was feeling confident that I could put in another 100 kilometres or more, this day, to reach Watson Lake. I stopped into the Iron Creek Lodge for lunch. It was a friendly place with a restaurant that overlooks a postcard perfect lake. A television in the restaurant was on CNN. I was shocked to hear of the death of Princess Diana, early in the morning. Tabloid photographers had literally hounded Princess Diana to death, as the paparazzi chased her car in a tunnel in Paris, France. Her car spun out of control and crashed. I remembered my wife and I were up at 4:00 am many years ago to watch Charles' and Di's royal wedding. Sickened by the news of her death, I didn't feel like riding my bike anymore today. I asked Vern, the owner of the Iron Creek Lodge, if I could set up my tent and stay the night. Vern kindly agreed. My tent overlooked the beautiful lake, glimmering with sunlight. The death of Princess Di made me think that every moment of your life is precious and you should cherish every moment. I stopped for a moment and let my senses drink up this magical scene of the north so it would be forever etched in my memory.

Later I called home and talked with Carol. She, too, was very saddened by the Princess' death at such a young age, and felt sorry for her children. Princess Diana had been in people's lives yesterday and now, suddenly, she was gone. The swiftness of this life altering event made Carol even more worried about me. Would she have to face a police officer coming to her door, telling her I had been killed? Would I, too, be suddenly gone forever? I tried to comfort Carol the best I could. I was already practicing "maximum caution" and made a mental note to myself to stay on this course. Camping in Iron Creek in the Yukon was a good decision. I didn't know what hills lay ahead and I may fall short of Watson Lake and have to camp in the wilderness. Every time I camped in the wilderness, the danger of the *To The Top Canada* expedition escalated. I was determined to keep these nights to a minimum, by staying as close to small settlements as possible. Unfortunately, I knew there were some nights to come where this would be impossible.

Monday, September 1, 1997

I awoke to hear news about yesterday. The driver of the car that killed Princess Diana had a blood-alcohol level three times the legal limit. I worried more about a drunk driver hitting me while I was cycling than any other cause of death. The one positive about the being in the Yukon is that the low population density reduced the probability of that occurrence.

Just four days ago, I had cycled through Toad River. Yesterday, the road by Toad River had been blocked for over nine hours by a huge rock slide. The size of the slide was enormous, the fallen rock stretching 200 feet and piling to a depth of 12 feet. I am sure my guardian angels were working overtime, ensuring I was past Toad River before the rock slide rumbled to life.

A tourist reported seeing a grizzly bear off the highway between Iron Creek and Watson Lake. Speaking with Vern, he advised me it was unlikely that it was a grizzly bear. It was more likely an Alaskan Brown Bear. That made me feel better. I'd much prefer to be eaten by an Alaskan Brown Bear than a Grizzly! A colleague of mine, Professional Speaker Jack Donahue, is an international scout for the NBA Vancouver Grizzlies. I didn't want to do anything to hurt Jacks' team with negative publicity.

The shower room for campers and truckers in Iron Creek is coin operated. I put my loonie in the slot, working with the shower knobs to ensure I would have a hot, but not scalding, shower. Once the water was adjusted, I got under the spray and turned my shampoo bottle upside down. The thick shampoo slowly dripped onto my head. Just as I was ready to begin shampooing, the shower stopped. I put another dollar coin in the slot, figuring I had three minutes to finish showering with my last loonie. I finished just as the last drop of water came down.

It was a glorious, warm day in the Yukon, perfect for riding. It was a contrast with yesterday, when I'd worn my winter coat for the first time. The leaves on the trees in the Yukon were just starting to turn to their fall colours. I never really took a day off in Fireside, so I was one day ahead of schedule. I wasn't due in Watson Lake until Tuesday night but arrived early on the afternoon of Labour Day Monday. The Watson Lake Belvedere Motor Hotel donated a room. I chose them because of the large Satellite dish on their roof. There was a chance they may get CBC and the classic Tiger Cat - Argo Labour Day clash. I checked my voice mail with Carol and found CBC Whitehorse wanted to contact me. Returning their call, I did a news interview over the pay phone and we agreed I would come to their studio to join their CBC Yukon morning show when I was in Whitehorse. I then turned on the TV to see that the game was on and the kickoff was about to begin. I knew the start time was 7:00 pm eastern time and Tiger-Cat General Manager, Neil Lumsden, didn't like it because it lowered his potential attendance. A three hour game and the drive home, in traffic, would mean children attending the game would get home at 11:00 pm on the night before the first day of school. For me, this late start time worked to my advantage. Although the Argos thrashed my Tiger-Cats by the score of 46-3, the worst defeat of the season, I still enjoyed the scenes from my home being beamed into the Yukon.

There were two double beds in my room. One was a mattress bed and the other was a water bed. Even though the water bed had the best angle for watching TV, I chose the mattress bed. My body had experienced enough bobbing around today from hours of riding my bicycle over the gravel road of the Alaska Highway.

My sleep was especially peaceful because I did not have to worry about bears tonight or wonder how close was my knife and bear spray were to my body.

Tuesday, September 2, 1997

My first stop was the post office where I sent home the gifts I had received from Fort Nelson and two disposable cameras that had some breathtaking photos of the Rockies. A stone's throw away from the Post Office was the office of the Town of Watson Lake. Councillor Carol McIlmoyle accepted my presentation of the Watson Lake certificate and gave me a couple of Watson Lake pins. Watson Lake didn't have a radio station or a community newspaper but the town did have a monthly newsletter that was distributed to all residents. In the next newsletter, they would ask them to answer my question, "What will you do before the year 2000 to make Canada a better country than when you found it?"

Hungry, I popped into the Gateway Restaurant where Isabel donated my breakfast. My cash was down to $20.00 in my wallet. Checking the balance of my *To The Top Canada* account at the local CIBC bank, I found the account had a grand total of eight cents. My Interac purchases of food and bike supplies, combined with some healthy bank charges had dwindled my account bare. Twenty dollars and my Visa card would have to get me to Inuvik. I knew I would arrive in early October so I would have time to fly home and work to make some money, in order to finish the *To The Top Canada* expedition.

So, what does a person with a bank balance of eight cents do next? Go shopping! I went to Radio Shack and bought some headphones to replace mine which had split in half. I felt music was important for my sanity, as I would be riding on one of the loneliest roads in the world in the next month. The bill came to $26.74. I went to a variety store where I bought two more disposable cameras so I could record my trip on film. I bought a coke for the road and two post cards for Carol and James. This bill came to $33.26 on my Visa. Carol knew that my Visa charges would be higher now, as food in restaurants cost double to triple the prices at home. After these purchases, I'd have to give up some paid meals for the next week if Carol were to make her budget. At the local hardware store, I bought some eye bolts for my Canadian flag pole. I paid for them with my loose change. At the Nugget Restaurant, David donated my lunch. I mailed my postcards and then stopped by a Watson Lake attraction, since

1942, The "Sign Forest". If you ever wonder where the world's stolen road signs go, they all come to Watson Lake in the Yukon. Signs from all around the world that direct you to cities, give city populations and even airport signs, are all mounted by the thousands, on a forest of poles. Under the Canadian criminal code, possession of stolen property is a criminal offence. This must be another area where RCMP in the north consider it a criminal code exempt zone, like HBO TV.

At the local tourist bureau, I received directions to Johnson Elementary School in Watson Lake and cycled down to offer my services, speaking to students. On my arrival the Principal, marched over to me and harshly said, "Are you our new teacher who's late on the first day of school?" Still afraid of the wrath of principals, I quickly said, "No!" After explaining who I was, I spent the afternoon speaking to all the classes about Canada and my expedition. As I finished my presentation, the new teacher still hadn't arrived. I'm sure the Principal will have this new teacher scheduled on some subzero recess duty, this winter.

Later that day, I discovered that Watson Lake has embraced my challenge with a glorious achievement. Here in the Yukon, Watson Lake has built the Northern Lights Centre. Visitors can experience the northern lights inside a special multi-media planetarium theatre. Advanced video and laser technology deliver a world class presentation about the northern lights. Outside the planetarium, the exhibit hall is full of space-themed interactive displays by NASA. Considering how very small Watson Lake is, I have not seen a more dramatic example of a community rallying to show their pride and confidence in Canada and taking on a project to make it better! All of Canada could learn from Watson Lake's example of how to realize a glorious vision for the future!

My supper was donated by the Watson Lake Togs Store. On the Alaska Highway, I went by St. John the Baptist Anglican Church. The church was dedicated to Captain Rev. George Wolfendale M.B.E, who died a prisoner of war in Italy, from wounds he had received in June 1944. The church was building given to the people of Watson Lake by the chapel congregations of the Canadian Armed Forces Chaplaincy and was constructed in 1956. George had died not only in service to his country, but also serving God. There was a dedication with the following inscription:

A gift of the Chapel Congregations of the Canadian Armed Forces stands as a memorial to those who died of wounds while a POW in Italy June 1944. St. John The Baptist. Captain Rev. George Wolfendale, Chaplain to the Royal Canadian Engineers, First Canadian Corps, consisting of the 12th, 13th, and 14th Field Companies and the First Canadian Corps Field Park Co.

As I cycled out of Watson Lake that evening, I pondered that this little community in the Yukon had taught me more about being a Canadian than any I had encountered to date.

At the corner of the Highway 37 intersection on the Alaskan Highway, an R.V. Campground donated my space. I set my tent up next to an RV that belonged to

Nancy and Geno Sporleder. I didn't know them but they knew me. Heading up to Alaska they had breakfast at "Mile 101", British Columbia. They remembered how excited their French Canadian waitress Manny was to get my picture. Nancy invited me to their RV to join them that evening for soup and stew. Nancy and Gino were from Tucson, Arizona and loved coming up to northern Canada for the cool weather, fresh air and incredible scenery. We enjoyed each other's company and they invited me to visit them anytime in Tucson. After four full bowls of soup and stew, I called it a night. I thought I had eaten very well today for someone with eight cents in his bank account.

Wednesday, September 3, 1997

I awoke early but stayed in my tent, as I read ten chapters in the Bible in Chronicles and wrote about my previous day in my journal. When I did emerge from my tent, I saw that Nancy and Gino's RV was already gone. The people who drive RV's are like nomads and love to go place to place. Why stay in one place, when the highway beckons. Beside my bike, I found a cassette tape by LeAnn Rimes that Nancy had left me to keep me company on the road. (I'd sent my cassette walkman home to lower my weight through the Rockies. All I had was my CD player.) My wife Carol enjoys LeAnn Rimes' voice and would be glad to get this tape when I sent it home with my next mail package, from Whitehorse. Enclosed with this tape was the following short note:

> Chris:
> It was a pleasure meeting you and wish you a safe journey and look forward to seeing or hearing from you in the future.
> Nancy and Gino

It was a beautiful morning in the Yukon, the sky was blue and the sun was warm. After packing up, I headed out. There was a sign saying a new restaurant was 12 miles down the road. My speedometer, and thus my odometer, were not working so I had to estimate my distance via time. When my temperamental speedometer was working I knew I was averaging 7 kilometres every 24 minutes. I had some loose change and planned to stop for some toast and water. After two hours, there was no restaurant and I came to the conclusion that I wasn't going to see a restaurant all day. The Alaskan Highway was under heavy construction and the entire road seemed to have been moved, by Canada's Public Works department, that was responsible for highway maintenance. Because of rock slides and mountain waters washing out the road, this highway was constantly being rebuilt to keep it operational. Occasionally, I would see signs through the trees of a former Alaskan highway on my left. I had this hypothesis that some unfortunate individual had recently poured his savings into opening a restaurant on the Alaskan Highway thinking the traffic in summer would be a gold mine, only to find a year later his restaurant had been bypassed. Now he owned a restaurant on a non-existent road. Fate can be cruel. I was on the new section of highway which was under construction as I used it. There was no asphalt or gravel, just a dirt surface that was almost sandy. The road had been watered to keep dust down and the dirt turned to mud, or what I called slop. As I cycled at a snail's pace, the bottom of my tire would disappear into the slop as it approached the ground and then would reappear again. I was in my lowest gear, to battle the extreme resistance. Most people would think going this slow would drive you nuts but, to me, it was like a late afternoon car drive from Toronto to Hamilton, inching along in the bumper to bumper traffic on the Queen Elizabeth Way Highway. People stopped their cars during the afternoon to take a picture of this guy in the Yukon, fighting this demon of a highway and pulling hundreds of pounds of weight in gear, strapped to his bicycle and his trailer. Finally, by mid-afternoon, I cleared the construction zone. It was close to 4:00 pm and I had not eaten this day so I pulled over, sat in the sand and ate from my supplies.

I was riding into the mountains now and according to my map, it was a large range called the Cassia mountains. I rode for over three hours more as I wanted to reach Rancheria. I had two factors working against me, reducing day light visibility. First, the days were getting shorter and second, once the sun went behind a tall mountain in the early evening it might as well be sundown as the shadow cast me into darkness. I could now see the giant mountain shadow creeping towards me. As the shadow engulfed me, my eyes took a moment to adjust to the sudden change in light. I also felt my arms going cold instantly, as if God just clicked the mouse on his weather computer, reducing the temperature by thirty degrees. I was now just minutes from Rancheria, which is a small settlement in a beautiful mountain valley.

I met Bev Dinning, the manager of the Rancheria Hotel-Motel. Bev set a new Canadian record for her speed in saying yes to donating a room. It was as if Bev was a game show contestant and couldn't wait for me to even finish asking the question! Bev said she liked this sort of thing and gave me a choice of a room with TV or without TV. I chose TV, which will not come as a surprise to my family at home.

I unpacked and then went to the restaurant. I had the pork dinner special with mushroom soup, hot dinner rolls and freshly baked apple turnover with ice cream. It satisfied my deep hunger. I had cycled far enough to put myself one day ahead of schedule, avoiding the prospect of camping in the wilderness, at the side of the road. I counted my blessings from the Lord today, including my safe journey, a wonderful Canadian in Bev for donating my room and for Visa, the magic card that let me eat. I then relaxed and watched a little TV.

Thursday, September 4, 1997

After packing up my bicycle, I spent the morning making phone calls to Whitehorse to confirm my presentation program. Knowing a video crew was flying in from Toronto to do a one day documentary on me, I didn't want to take any chances that the officials in Whitehorse didn't know that I was coming.

Northward bound on the Alaska Highway, I stopped at a roadside spot called Rancheria Falls. In the observation area, I met retired Professor Hugh Cunningham from Florida. After talking about the Canadian quarterback Jesse Palmer of the University of Florida Gators, I asked him what he used to teach. His answer was journalism. Hugh was fascinated by my incredible journal and the extent of editorial coverage I had received. Hugh encouraged me to contact two former students of his, who considered him almost a father. The first was Dan Rather, anchor of CBS television news. The other was David Lawrence, publisher of the Miami Herald. Hugh then took my picture by the waterfall and gave me $20 to buy me lunch.

I reciprocated by giving Hugh a Friend of Canada certificate.

Riding on, I stopped at the Walker's Continental Divider Lodge for lunch. There, one of the customers asked, "Are you the guy they're talking about on the radio, who is cycling to the top of Canada?" The restaurant was full of a crew conducting mining exploration, looking for copper ore deposits. I spoke to them about the *To The Top Canada* expedition while I ate my lunch. When I went to pay for my lunch, they wouldn't take my money. I thanked them and then headed out on the highway.

I faced some serious hills as I crossed the Continental Divide. On one side water, flowed to the Arctic and on the other side water flowed to the Pacific.

The skies were completely cloudy and dark. I was sure that we would have rain that night. I wanted to get to sleep early because tomorrow would be a 100 kilometre-plus trip. At the Swift River Lodge, Jerry said he would donate a room for the night.

Friday, September 5, 1997

Still sleepy, I walked over to the restaurant by the gas bar for an early breakfast. One employee had been reading about me and my challenge for Canadians had struck a nerve. He asked me why he should try to make Canada better when the government was giving him such a raw deal. I told him Canada belongs to Canadians, not to the government. He proceeded to list the areas and decisions of government he wasn't happy with. After he went on extensively, I summed the situation up for him this way. Canada is like our backyard. The problems with government are like weeds growing in our back yard. You have a choice. . . You can complain about the weeds or you can dig them out. This analogy seemed to focus his frustration into positive energy. He wished me good luck. As I left Swift River, I found it very cold. My fingers were numb in my cycling gloves. I made a mental note to wear my cycle mittens tomorrow. It was another sunny day in the Yukon.

After cycling a long distance, I stopped for a break. When I was cycling I was moving fast so I didn't worry about bears. When I stopped, I became a stationary target. I developed a strategy where I would only take a break on the top of a large hill. If a bear appeared while I was stopped for a drink, I would release my brakes and with all my weight my bike would (hopefully) surpass the bear's speed down hill. I finished my break and moved on. After cycling a fair distance, I noticed a man, across the highway, emerging out of the heavy forest, miles from anywhere. I stopped in case he needed help. As he walked towards me, I could see a staff in his left hand and a rifle behind his right shoulder. Now, I was thinking, I may be the person who needs help. He told me his name was Sam Johnston and he had a cabin in the woods. Sam was a former chief of the Tlingit band. At the Indigenous People's Games in Victoria, which is a competition for all Indian communities in North America, Sam had won a gold medal in archery. Sam had also served eight years as an elected member of the Yukon legislature. He also was the Speaker and had the unique distinction of being the first Native Canadian who was a House Speaker anywhere in Canada. Sam wished me good luck and said he could tell that God was with me and I would successfully complete my journey. I said goodbye to Sam. He disappeared into the woods as quickly as he had appeared.

Arriving in Teslin after riding 70 miles, I had pedaled the longest distance I had ever travelled in one day. It was 4:15 pm and I cycled down to the Village Office. I presented my Teslin Certificate to the staff person and said I would appreciate her passing it on to the Council. She said she'd be happy to do so, when she could. I sensed anxiety and asked if there was a problem. She told me that the Mayor had resigned and left town. The other councillors had also quit and left town. There is an election in October and it is hoped candidates will come forward to vie for election or acclamation. It looked as though you could move to Teslin tomorrow and be the Mayor the next day.

I called Carol from the Village office to let her know I had arrived in Teslin. She told me Mother Teresa had passed away today, a great humanitarian lost to the world.

I found the Fox Point Lakeshore Resort, which is on the west end of Teslin, on the Alaskan Highway. Kelly Morris, one of the managers, is also a corrections employee. Her convenience store features native artwork she had purchased from inmates at the correctional facility. I talked to her about setting up a Virtual Trading Post on the world wide web.

While talking about the minimum security facility of the Teslin Correctional Centre, Kelly mentioned that the inmates were allowed to go hunting. I had to inquire about this practice. Do you give hunting rifles to the inmates? She said no, only to the correctional officer or the elder with them. This seemed like a good answer but the whole idea still struck me as funny. Do I want to go hunting deep into grizzly bear country with no rifle? I could see someone who had been jailed for fraud, out on a hunting trip, seeing a grizzly bear:

> "There's the biggest grizzly bear I have every seen coming towards us. Shoot him Correctional Officer Jim! Are you there, Jim?"

This seemed like cruel and unusual punishment to me. I didn't feel well that evening, I had a headache and stomach cramps. I went to sleep early, to ward off the discomfort.

Saturday, September 6, 1997

Heavy fog blanketed the terrain outside my window at the Fox Point Lakeshore Resort. It looked cold and it was. I wore my winter clothing to be ready for this brisk morning, my breath visible in the air as I prepared my gear.

As I cycled west, the Alaska Highway was the quietest I had ever seen it. The only sign of civilization were the names at the side of the road. Similar to Northern Ontario, where people spray painted messages on the Canadian shield rock, in the Yukon, messages were spelled out by arranging football size rocks on the high ditch at the side of the road. Names, messages of love, names of homes, and tributes to rock bands were all spelled out with rocks placed strategically so that all highway travellers could read their message. The really enthusiastic rock spellers also sprayed their rocks a fluorescent colour.

After 51 kilometres, I stopped at Johnsons Crossing Campground Services, over-looking the Teslin River. Caroline Smith, the owner, immediately said I could camp for two nights. My legs were sore with a pain that felt like shin splints and my right knee felt as if it were swelling. I needed the rest as next week would be busy in Whitehorse and preparing to ride on the Klondike Highway.

Banners in the campground celebrated the 100th anniversary of the Klondike Gold Rush of 1897. There was an outdoor pay phone which I used to call Carol. She told me about Princess Diana's funeral, including the huge crowds, the Anglican service, Elton John's tribute, Prime Minister Tony Blair's reading and the family eulogy. The sadness made Carol miss me more. On a brighter note, Carol reported it looked like Tiger-Cats were beating the Alouettes at half-time today! I would have to wait until tomorrow to find out if we had our second win of the season!

Usually at the end of a day I find myself very busy. I may be going motel to motel to find a room, getting permission to put my tent on some land then going through the exercise of setting up my overnight camp, checking my route for the next day, phoning home, making an evening speaking appearance, doing laundry, reading ten chapters in my Bible, writing in my daily journal or just collapsing from an exhausting day. This evening was different. Knowing I was ahead of schedule, no TV and leisure time on my hands, I enjoyed a campfire supper I cooked for myself, including chili style beans, fruit cocktail and an instant cheese cake I whipped up. It was a relaxing end to a busy period where I had been on the go for thirteen days. Except for my Bible reading and laundry, I had absolutely no plans for tomorrow and that suited me just fine.

Sunday, September 7, 1997

Today, I encountered another coin operated shower. I knew from my last experience that I couldn't waste a second of time. I stripped off my clothes, put my soap in the soap dish, put the shampoo on my head and then put the money in the machine. The shower came on but there was no hot water. I tried every feasible adjustment to the dial but the water was ice cold. I decided I would only put my head in the water to finish washing my hair. If I wasn't awake before, I was awake now, as the cold water jolted me to shiver. The coin operated shower had beaten me again.

I phoned home to learn that my family had enjoyed a hotdog barbecue at church for Celebration Sunday at St. Christopher's and had spare ribs cooking for supper. I was looking forward to regular home cooked meals, once I completed my *To The Top Canada* expedition.

This was my last rest day for the next 23 days. I had to ride over 1,000 kilometres over Canada's toughest roads to make the end of the Dempster Highway, which was Inuvik. Once in Inuvik, I would plan my final strike at Tuktoyaktuk. Ready for the challenge, I went to sleep with the pregame concentration of a linebacker before a championship football game!

Monday, September 8, 1997

I headed out into the coldest day yet. Even with my gloves on, I could feel the cold numbing my fingers. I stopped into the RV office to thank them, as I pulled out. They had a gift for me, of a Canada T-Shirt. They gave me specific instructions to wear it on Thursday in Whitehorse on TV so everyone in Johnson Crossing could see it! I thanked them and told them I would. After packing my shirt, I headed out on the Alaskan Highway. You could tell it was getting colder, by the sign of a convoy of American R.V.'s exiting Alaska as though escaping the plague.

The mountains around this area were majestic. The trees on the lower slopes were a palette of reds, golds, and greens. The higher slopes were treeless and the sunlight reflected off the granite like a mirror.

In the early afternoon, I neared my destination of Jake's Corners, when I heard the rhythm of something hitting my rear spokes. I immediately stopped and looked for a dangling strap from my packs. Nothing. I slowly moved my bike forward, watching and listening carefully. It was my rear tire rubbing against the frame of the bike. I took all my gear off my bike and turned it upside down. I checked to see if my quick release wheel had come loose. The lock was firm and the wheel was in the right spot. I spun the wheel and studied its spin. The rim was warped. When this last happened, I hadn't recognized what was coming next. In Saskatchewan, I'd seen the same symptoms before the rim split. This was the early warning sign that total system failure was imminent. I rode the last few kilometres to Jake's Corner.

I went into the restaurant to think about my options. Rose, the waitress and Terry, the cook, listened to my dilemma and offered my lunch of pop, soup and a toasted sandwich. In this restaurant, there were exotic birds flying loose around the restaurant. Normally this would be the type of unusual occurrence I would investigate further but I thought only about my bike. I got the local yellow pages and was directed to an outside pay phone that didn't require money to place a call. As a matter of fact, Terry said the phone jams when people put money in it, so not to do it!

There was one ad for Wheel and Brake Cycle in Whitehorse that said they serviced mountain bikes. I called the number but it rang a long time and then only the fax would answer.

I tried another bike shop and described my problem to a girl. She said they only sold bikes and the person I needed to talk to was Ray at Wheel and Brake. I tried Wheel and Brake again. I got the fax again. I tried another bike shop in Whitehorse. This time a man said the only person who could help me was Ray at Wheel and Brake, but, they were closed today.

I returned the phone book to the restaurant. Terry, the cook, said he'd be driving into Whitehorse tomorrow with his truck and would give my bike and me a lift. I thought about this option and the time I was going to lose. After some thought I suggested another plan. It was 2:00 pm and I had several hours of daylight left. I would ride towards Whitehorse with my wheel rubbing. If my rim split, I would camp by the road and Terry would pick me up when he saw me on his way into Whitehorse tomorrow morning. Any progress or distance travelled today would be road that I would not have to come back to, if I had to return to some point on the Alaskan Highway where I left off.

We agreed this was the plan. I rode hard because it seemed that at higher speed there was less rubbing. By late afternoon, I had made incredible progress. In Saskatchewan, I had my summer tires, but now I had my more rigid winter tires. The tire was holding up to the constant rubbing. After riding twelve hours that day, I had covered 109 kilometres. I stopped at the Highway #2 intersection, for a late supper. I walked into the restaurant and found every customer, and my waitress, smoking. My need for a good meal was exceeding my current need for clean air. I ate and then cycled another few kilometres to Wolf River campground. I pitched my tent just after sundown. When I entered my tent, it was completely dark. I turned on my flashlight, read my Bible in the book of Nehemiah. It was the story of how the city walls of Jerusalem were rebuilt by Nehemiah, a wine steward of the Persian emperor. God answered Nehemiah's prayer to return home to Jerusalem from exile, to restore the holy city, that was broken like my bicycle. In the same way, my prayer had been answered. Something good had come from my adversity today, in that I had travelled two days' distance in one and now had the perfect opportunity to arrive in Whitehorse early and solve my problem on my own terms. I counted my good fortune and blessings.

Tuesday, September 9, 1997

Awaking early, I read the book of Esther in the Bible. It is an incredible story of suspense and comedy that I enjoyed. I then packed up and headed the 30 kilometres into Whitehorse. I arrived at Wheel and Brake early, before the opening time of ten o'clock. I waited for Yukon Ray to save the day. When Ray saw my bike he took one look and said, "That wheel is done". I brought all my gear into the shop with my bike. Ray had only one rim that fit my bike. I gave him the go ahead to build me a new wheel.

While Ray built the wheel, I went across the street and offered my services as a speaker for a school assembly. The principal knew me before I said a word. We agreed I would speak to the students at 9:00 am on Thursday. I visited my local bank for an Interac machine to get some cash. Carol had seen my low bank balance and had put $100 in my account. I withdrew $80 and used this money to go shopping for food at the local grocery store, as my supplies were down to zero. I stocked up for the trip in Inuvik.

After picking up my bike, I looked for a room for the night. At my third inn, the Family Hotel said they had a single bed they could give me. The owner led me into a small conference room which had been partitioned off with office dividers. Behind each divider was a small bed. The bed he showed me had old linen and hadn't been made. I wasn't fussy because it was a bed and it was warm inside. I moved my gear into the cramped space. Experiencing claustrophobia and restlessness, I went out and saw a movie G.I. Jane, enjoying the two hours of simple recreation and leisure.

Wednesday, September 10, 1997

It was nice to be able to shave, in order to be ready for my day of meetings. I had meetings with the newspapers of Whitehorse. The big story in the newspapers was that, in response to the four grizzly bears killed in the city of Whitehorse in the last week, the Emergency Measures Organization had started broadcasting all bear sightings on 91.1 FM. The station was exclusively for bear sightings by conservation officers, RCMP and helicopters. It sounded a lot like a Toronto traffic report. "We've got a bear in the Logan subdivision area." The Whitehorse residents had dubbed the station "bear talk radio".

I enjoyed lunch as the guest of Marilyn Margeson, the Anniversaries Coordinator for the City of Whitehorse. Marilyn was my liaison with the City and was coordinating my *To The Top Canada* program at City Hall, on Thursday.

I went to the Gold Rush Inn to meet the TV crew flying in to cover my day in Whitehorse. I discovered the camera man and audio man made it to Whitehorse but the program director and producer were delayed when their flight was cancelled, due to aircraft technical difficulties. As it was their first time in Whitehorse, I showed the two TV people our program locations. I took them by CBC, City Hall, Yukon Government Building and Whitehorse Elementary French Immersion School.

At my donated room at the Bonanza Hotel, I was contacted by Radio CKRW, who set up a remote interview with me at 7:05 am tomorrow in front of the hotel.

A Whitehorse GPS reading showed that I was over 4,000 air miles from my house. I was feeling homesick. I called home and our sitter, Cathy, answered. James was in bed and Carol was at an evening business function. Later in the evening, Carol phoned me about a problem at James' new school. A boy with a history of violence had threatened James with scissors. I suggested that Carol set up a meeting with the principal, first thing in the morning. If she had any doubts that the school could facilitate a satisfactory solution, we would put James in a safer school. I got off the phone feeling helpless because I was not in Hamilton. I had faith in Carol to make the best decisions in regards to James' welfare.

I went to sleep, not worried about grizzly bears but about the welfare of my son in an environment of urban violence.

Thursday, September 11, 1997

I awoke at 5:30 am and started my day reading my Bible in the book of Psalms, finishing with the 23rd psalm.

> The Lord is my Shepherd
> I have everything I need
> He lets me rest in fields of green grass
> and leads me to quiet pools of fresh water
> He gives me new strength
> He guides me in the right paths
> as he has promised
> Even if I go through the deepest darkness
> I will not be afraid, Lord,
> for you are with me
> Your shepherd's rod and staff protect me
>
> You prepare a banquet for me
> where all my enemies can see me
> You welcome me as an honoured guest
> and fill my cup to the brim
> I know that your goodness and
> love will be with me all my life
> and your house will be my
> home as long as I live.

150

After reading I washed up, packed up and got my bike ready for my 7:05 am CKRW interview in front of the Bonanza Hotel. Rock, the morning announcer, came down the street. He did the sports and then interviewed me for ten minutes. After the interview, Rock gave me his card and the station's 1-800 number and asked me to call in updates, from time to time.

I then went to CBC radio, where the TV crew had already arrived to tape my morning interview on the Yukon Morning Show. This 7:45 am interview reached all across the Territory and was the radio station most people in the Yukon listened to as they had their breakfast.

At the Whitehorse Elementary School, the students had come together, in the gym, to welcome me. O' Canada was sung by all the students. To my delight, their version was sung in three languages. They started in French, switched to English and then finished in the local native language of Southern Tutchone. I was inspired by these children! Their O'Canada was as follows:

O'Canada

O Canada, Terre de nos aïeux,
Ton front est ceint de fleurons glorieux,

With glowing hearts we see thee rise
the true North strong and free,
From far and wide, O Canada,
We stand on guard for thee.

Ut'akwädjch'e dak'anata ch'e.
O Canada, nk'atsanuta shi.
O Canada, nk'atsanuta shi.

The gym was full of students, from kindergarten to grade 7. They were animated and enthusiastic.

After the school program, I met Nicole from the Yukon Cycling team and we were joined by cyclists from the Vanier Catholic School in Riverdale which is just on the other side of the Yukon River, from downtown. We rode by the Yukon River along beautiful paved bicycle paths that were built for community enjoyment.

At City Hall, a piper was playing when I pulled up and there was a large crowd, all holding Canadian flags. There were two Mounties in full red dress uniform. One was on his horse that had a maple leaf shaved on its rear thigh. The other Mountie was accompanied by his husky dog and sleigh. I was welcomed by Mayor Kathy Watson, who spoke about the special role that Capital Cities have in promoting National Unity.

After my presentation, I was swarmed by people who wanted to shake my hand, get autographs and take pictures.

A large box arrived for me, in care of the Mayor. It was from Carol and it was large because it contained my size 12 triple E winter boots. With bungie cords, I secured the box to my trailer.

At the Whitehorse General Hospital, I met the new CEO, Ron, who had just driven to Whitehorse from Oshawa, Ontario. He had a real appreciation for the distance that I have come.

After visiting patients and nurses, I met the television crew at the picnic table by the river. I answered questions about the *To The Top Canada* expedition and about my essay for the book, *As Prime Minister, I Would....* The four person Toronto-Vancouver TV crew were frustrated at times because during different questions in the interview, a passing car would see me and honk their horn in support of Canada and myself. Then, we would have to start all over again.

After the interview, I rode through the streets so they could get footage of me in action. It was beautiful with the leaves turning colours, the mountains and the Yukon River. We then went to the Talisman Restaurant where the crew bought my lunch. Afterward, the crew would be flying home. I thanked them and excused myself because I had to be at the Yukon Government Building at 2:30 pm.

I was met by Piers MacDonald, who is the Government Leader, the equivalent of a Provincial Premier. As a matter of fact, he was leaving shortly for the Provincial Premiers' Unity Conference. I told Piers I would be praying that their effort meet with success. I presented Piers with the Yukon Territory certificate to commemorate the *To The Top Canada* expedition passing through the Yukon Territory. He presented me with a Yukon flag and a Yukon pin.

At the Vanier Catholic School, I presented them with a Friend of Canada certificate to thank the students for riding with me today. Downtown, I paused on Main Street to take a picture of a Klondike Miner and the statue's inscription which read, "Dedicated to all who follow their dreams".

The Gold Rush Inn gave me a room that overlooked Main Street and had a huge jacuzzi! After unpacking, I was hungry and went to a new restaurant on their open-ing day. The restaurant that donated my supper was Helen and Vangie's Restaurant on Main Street. They serve Filipino and Western food. I had their "meuudo plate" for supper.

Back in my room, I soaked in the jacuzzi for a half hour. After some television, I felt hungry again and went down to the saloon and ordered a clubhouse sandwich. A Canadian Armed Forces Search & Rescue Pilot spotted me and said, "Aren't you the guy cycling to the top of Canada?" We talked for a while. He said he was going to check, when he got back to his base in Yellowknife, if it was possible for them to fly me out of Tuktoyaktuk when I arrived. He wanted me to know that as far as he was concerned, he was "in". I thought that would be nice because I really had no firm plan to get out of Tuktoyaktuk. I thought I might hitch a ride on a truck down to Inuvik and then fly back to Toronto using my Air Canada frequent flyer miles.

I spoke with Carol on the phone. She had spoken to James' principal who assured her that the problem would be immediately resolved, ensuring a safe school environment. With this news, I'll sleep better tonight.

Friday, September 12, 1997

As I was getting ready for the day ahead, a reporter from the Toronto Sun newspaper called my room. He had the advantage of being three hours ahead of me in the Eastern time zone. We talked for an hour. When the call was over, I checked out of the Gold Rush Inn. Thanking Bev and Paul from the hotel, I headed off to Whitehorse Elementary School. The children had created artwork and letters for me and they wanted me to pick them up in person.

One by one, the children came up and presented their mementos to me. Afterwards, we went outside and took a picture at the front of the school with all the children, my bike and me. Packing all the artwork into a large courier envelope, it was time to send another care package home. This time it had a notebook that I had filled with my daily journal from Edmonton to Whitehorse. I wanted this package to go by courier so it could be traced if it was late or got lost.

At the Loomis courier office, I asked for ground transportation rather than air because it was cheaper. The girl on duty was aware of my expedition for Canada and she gave me a free upgrade to air delivery. I thanked her very much and pulled out my Visa card to pay. She said, "We take cash or cheque". As if I was saying the magic word, Abracadabra, I said again, "I have Visa". I didn't have cheques and I only had a five dollar bill. I also knew I had exhausted the money in my Interac account when I bought food for my supplies to take me north. Then the girl said, "I really like what you are doing for Canada so this one's on the house". My package was now going by air and for free. I went to my bike and got her a Friend of Canada certificate to thank her. I guess the words, "I have Visa" really are magic.

The exterior of the Whitehorse McDonald's is built out of logs. They donated my late breakfast, which was my first meal of the day. This was the last McDonald's, as I headed north. Before the expedition, I had contacted McDonald's Head Office in Toronto to ask if McDonald's would donate food to me in exchange for becoming an official sponsor of the expedition. Their answer was a "no", because of the many other community commitments they already had. During the expedition, I had approached the individual managers and franchisees of McDonald's to donate meals. Every local McDonald's said "yes" to me. I was proud of the Canadian franchisees who said "yes" to the *To The Top Canada* expedition.

Leaving Whitehorse, I cycled up to Two Mile Hill. I would miss this friendly city, and best of all, I hadn't met "Freddy the Axe"!

Once on the Alaskan Highway I rode my last few miles. I travelled over 1,400 kilometres on this famous road, from Mile Zero in Dawson Creek.

I now turned on to the Klondike Highway that would take me over 500 kilometres, to Dawson City. From the north, I faced the strongest head winds since Alberta. I went to a lower gear and toughed out the distance.

Around 4 p.m., I stopped and had supper from my supplies. When I was finished, I stowed my garbage in a plastic bag and tied it to my trailer. I then continued cycling to camp in a different spot than I had eaten, to minimize the chance of attracting bears. A few miles down the road a car pulled over. The man introduced himself as Peter Jenkins. Peter had seen me the previous day at the Government Building, speaking with government Leader Piers MacDonald. Peter explained that he owned the Eldorado Hotel in Dawson City and would like me to stay as his guest. I thanked him and pulled out a Friend of Canada certificate for him in advance of my stay. I also asked him for one small favour. I gave him my bag of food garbage to deposit in a bin up the highway. I may not see a bin before I camped and this was another precaution against bears.

Fox Lake is a small dot on my map but in reality it is a long lake that runs parallel to the highway, seemingly never-ending. If the Yukon has a rowing team, this is a perfect lake for them to train in.

I rode until the sun went down because I wasn't sure whether roadside camping is illegal in the Yukon. I set up my tent on a gravel area at the side of the road, not minding the uneven surface because my self inflating mattress keeps me comfortable. It was very quiet, except for the odd passing car. Once in my tent, the air thickened with the deafening sounds of animals. It was as if the animals were practicing their sounds through loud speakers. Regardless of the noise, I was tired and I was going to sleep after a long day.

Saturday, September 13, 1997

Although my body was warm in my sleeping bag, I could feel the very cold air biting my face as I awoke at 7:30 a.m. Packing up my gear took longer than usual because my bags were stiff with the cold. I had to take my hands out of my mittens to tie bows, handle my key to unlock my bike and to close zippers.

Heading north on the Klondike highway, I rode into the Braeburn Lodge around 9:30 a.m. They were famous for their large cinnamon buns. If they were just a bit bigger, I could have taken a couple and used them as bicycle tires. I opted for something smaller. Toast and pancakes. When they came, they were the biggest pancakes and slices of toast I'd ever seen. Even though I was very hungry, I just managed to finish what I had. My waiter said that when he came to work he had looked at the thermometer, at 7:00 am. The temperature was ten below zero.

I headed out from the restaurant full and completely warmed up. The sun shone brightly and the leaves were magnificent to see. My bright yellow jacket was the exact colour of all the trees around me. I looked like I was dressed for Halloween as an aspen tree.

I could see one animal saying to the others, "Hey guys, you're never going to believe this. There's a tree riding a bicycle."

I stopped my bike when a wolf crossed the road with her cubs. One cub stopped in the middle of the road and looked at me. The mother came back, grabbed the cub by the scruff of the neck and pulled him off the road. I waited five minutes and then continued. I was scheduled to ride by the Nordenshield River but I was making excellent time so I rode to Carmacks, which put me one day ahead of schedule.

I pulled into the Sunset Motel in Carmacks. Emmie, a Native Canadian, was running the bar and was in charge of the motel. She donated a room for me. I carried my gear into my room and listened to CBC radio, or as the marketing people wanted us to call it, Radio One. On the news, I learned that Mother Teresa was buried today and the Prime Minister's wife was Canada's representative. I listened to the fiftieth anniversary of a CBC jazz show called Hot Air. I closed my eyes and imagined I was at Queens Quay in Toronto listening to jazz, sipping a Pina Colada and watching boats sailing in the harbour.

After I rested, I regained enough energy to get my clothes ready for tomorrow and ate supper from my supplies. I fell asleep again as soon as my head hit the pillow and this time, for the rest of the night.

Sunday, September 14, 1997

At 8:00 am, I ate my breakfast which I had laid out the night before - two nutribars, one can of fruit cocktail and a McCain Orange Juice. I shaved and showered and was on my way at 8:55 am. I cycled around Carmacks, looking for the Anglican Church. I found someone who directed me to St. George's Church and told me the service started at 11:00 o'clock. I had a couple of hours to kill so I said my prayers and oiled my bike chain. Around a quarter to eleven, a pick-up roared up the gravel driveway, carrying two ladies. They told me the minister wasn't coming but a lay person would be taking the service at 11:00 a.m. At ll:15 a.m., no one had shown up so I unlocked my bike and decided to move on to my next task.

I ran into Lana who told me everyone was in the Terry Fox Run today. She pointed out a city official cycling my way so I stopped him and presented him with the Carmacks *To The Top Canada* Certificate.

Lana then invited me back to the community centre for the Terry Fox Run hotdogs and refreshments. My stomach was saying, "Yes! Yes!" but I declined because I knew the Run would not finish for several hours and I had to cycle to Minto. If they had given me a two hour head start, there would have been no hot dogs for the Terry Fox Run participants. I thanked Lana and headed for the Klondike Highway.

Just after crossing the bridge, I had to climb two serious character building hills that put me at a higher elevation, looking down on the Yukon River.

Suddenly, I heard a terrible scraping sound and felt the weight of my trailer increase. I hit the brakes fast. My trailer fender had come loose and pulled itself under my trailer wheel. I had crazy glued the bolt so this wouldn't happen. Upon closer inspection, I found that the crazy glue held the bolt exactly in place. A hole in the trailer the size of a loonie had worn through big enough for the large washer to escape. The fender was finished, so I pulled out my Allen wrench and undid the mounts that held it partially in place. I put the fender on my trailer until I came to the next garbage can.

I stopped at Five Fingers lookout, a spot on the Yukon River where the river splits into separate channels. I put my fender into the garbage can. Three men from Iceland, on a month's vacation, talked to me about my journey and my bike. One was a construction worker, one a doctor and the third never talked but just smiled. I ate lunch from my supplies, which they also found fascinating. When I was packing up my food bag, the doctor offered to take my garbage and throw it out for me. I strapped up my bag and the doctor came back with my garbage and said he couldn't open the garbage container. I walked over and said this is a special Canadian garbage container. It keeps bears and doctors out. While I was looking directly at the doctor my hand flipped the hidden bar and the lid opened with the greatest of ease. The doctor looked at me and said, "How did you do that?" He then sheepishly put my garbage in the can. We said goodbye and they got in their rental car and headed off to Vancouver. I headed north. The day offered breathtaking scenery that I tried to capture with my disposable camera. I was also challenged by many mountainous hills that tired me out.

When I had gone approximately 50 kilometres there was no sign for Minto, my destination for the day. I saw a highway sign that stated the mileage for Pelly Crossing and Dawson City, but no Minto. I was starting to think Minto may be another Trutch. The sun was high in the sky at 6:00 pm so I decided to try for Pelly Crossing which was 55 kilometres away. Another few kilometres was Minto R.V. Resort with a sign saying "closed", across the driveway. All the trees around it had been burned in a forest fire. A little further on was a sign pointing down a dirt road saying, "Minto 1 kilometre" but I didn't explore it in case Minto had suffered the same fate as the forest.

I was now racing against the sun. With 30 kilometres down and 25 to go according to the highway distance sign, the sun was starting to set. The sun had set below the mountains to my left but the mountains to my right were still reflecting sunlight on me. By 8:30 pm, I had 15 kilometres to go but no direct sunlight. I made sure my rear red caution bike lights were flashing. The mountains on my right glowed a rich, red hue and the biggest full moon I had ever seen in my life rose just above the horizon. I stopped for a quick picture. Cycling the final kilometres into Pelly Crossing, I watched this incredible living postcard. I pulled into Peaches Ice Cream. It was run by Sandy, who was especially friendly. I asked her if there was a motel in town. She said no but I was welcome to stay and camp by her food stand. I accepted her offer and ordered a hot dog and a drink. While the hot dog cooked on the grill, we talked. I told her about my mission and she told me about her food stand which was named after her dog, Peaches. Peaches once chased a squirrel off a canyon cliff, fell 40 feet and lived. In her eyes, it was a miracle that her dog was alive and certainly some of that good luck may help her business.

When I went to pay, she decided not to charge me. Earlier in the summer a Portland, Oregon couple named Ralph & Cheryl Davis had stopped for milkshakes at Peaches and thoroughly enjoyed themselves. When they got home they had about $15 Canadian dollars they could not use. They wrote Sandy a note saying how much they liked her and sent the $15 Canadian so some deserving person could have a meal on the house. Sandy decided I was that deserving person. I was ready to sing God Bless America to thank this very kind family from Portland, whom I had never met, but who had bought me some supper.

After eating my hot dog, I quickly set up my tent as it was almost dark now at 9:30 pm. Although it had been a tough day, I thanked God for not giving me any challenges I couldn't handle.

Monday, September 15, 1997

At 7:30 am, I read my Bible in the cold morning air, from the insulated comfort of my sleeping bag. Stepping outside, the icy frost had covered my tent again. I decided to do my morning tasks and leave my tent up so the sun would have a chance to melt the frost and dry the tent.

At the local RCMP detachment, I rang the buzzer. When an officer came to the door, I explained I was on a national unity mission and asked to use the phone. He pointed to a side office and said he had to go because he was on a call himself. I called Dawson City, to let City Hall know when I would arrive. I then called the Eldorado Hotel, where Peter Jenkins had already told them about me. They accepted my reservation for Wednesday night. I called home, as it was lunch hour, but there was no answer. Carol is just six doors from work and likes to have lunch at home. With no answer I knew she must be having an especially busy day. I called my voice mail business line and left the address of the Eldorado Hotel for Carol so she could send me more Friends of Canada certificates. I knew I had just enough certificates to get me to Dawson City.

I then waited behind the counter to thank the officer. He was in another office, being talked through the operation of a new computer he was setting up. It was clear to me that he'd be tied up a very long time so I let myself out.

At the local band office, I presented the Pelly Crossing certificate. In the same building was the Post Office where I was able to send home another camera and some copies of the Yukon News.

After packing up my tent, I rode across the Pelly River, which had been used by the Northern Tutchone Indians all their lives. It was only discovered by the western world in 1840 as a travel route. I was amazed that it was only 157 years ago and here I was, conquering this land with my *To The Top Canada* expedition. I felt in awe of what I was doing.

There were more character building hills as I left the river valley of Pelly Crossing. During the morning, I spotted a large black fox-like animal at the side of the road up ahead. I pulled out my Fox 40 whistle and blew it three times. The fox had the same reaction as the caribou. He came out to the middle of the road to have a better look. I yelled and he disappeared into the ditch. I waited a few minutes and then carried on. On my original schedule, I had planned to ride from Minto to Stewart Crossing so I assumed it would be 25 or 30 kilometres away from Pelly Crossing. It turned out to be 65 kilometres away and I had a full day of riding. If I had stopped in Minto I would have been riding over 100 kilometres today. The Lord works in mysterious ways. . . There was only a Chevron station and an RV Park in Stewart Crossing. I declared the Service Station owner the Mayor of Stewart Crossing and presented him with the Stewart Crossing Certificate.

At the service station, Minnie the local school bus driver pulled over when she saw me. Minnie was like an angel who suddenly appeared in my life with the message to stay on course. Minnie told me I was doing a good thing for Canada and stuffed $10 in my hand. I gave her a certificate to thank her. I called home and spoke briefly with Carol.

With my back muscles in pain, I set up my tent and prepared for tomorrow. I knew the next two days to Dawson City would be a gruelling ride. There was never the question in my mind of whether I would do it or not, I simply prepared to do it. No questions asked. Before bed, I read Psalm 91 which gave me peace of mind as I would head further into the wilderness of the north.

Whosoever goes to the Lord for safety
whoever remains under the protection of the Almighty, can say to him,
"You are my defender and protector. You are my God; in you I trust."
He will keep you safe from all hidden dangers and from all deadly diseases.
He will cover you with his wings you will be safe in his care;
his faithfulness will protect and defend you.
You need not fear any dangers at night

or sudden attacks during the day
or the plagues that strike in the dark
or the evils that kill in daylight.

A thousand may fall dead beside you
ten thousand all around you,
but you will not be harmed.
You will look and see how the wicked are punished.

You have made the Lord your defender
the Most High your protector and so no disaster will strike you
no violence will come near your home.
God will put his angels in charge of you to protect you wherever you go.
They will hold you up with their hands to keep you from hurting your feet on stones.
You will trample down lions and snakes.

God says, "I will save those who love me and will protect those who
acknowledge me as Lord
When they call to me, I will answer them; when they are in trouble,
I will be with them.
I will reward them with long life; I will save them."

Tuesday, September 16, 1997

The night had been surprisingly warmer, for the Yukon. I didn't feel warmer but at least there was no layer of frost on my tent. With a busy day ahead, I packed up quickly. My map showed no place to stop today so I popped back into the Stewart Crossing Chevron station looking for a breakfast snack. Using the money I had received from Minnie, I purchased a microwave bacon cheese burger and a grape juice. Despite the fact that it sounds like a terrible breakfast, it did cover each of the required food groups.

At the Stewart Crossing bridge, I turned left towards Dawson City. The road soon climbed steeply back into the mountains. At one point, the gravel road turned to dirt, a large road grader turning it over. I followed the road grader for a couple of kilometres, riding in the tire track which was the only part of the road that was compressed. Back on gravel, I cycled on further on the Klondike Highway. It was a cool morning and I could see my breath as I cycled. After a while, I saw a Visitor Facility sign which was the standard Yukon sign that a roadside restaurant was just ahead. I pulled into the Moose Creek Lodge. At the front door, I was greeted by a "closed" sign. I took a sip of water from my bottle and had decided to ride on, when owner, Don Lefter, came around the corner. Don said his generator had gone down so he had to close until it was fixed. We went through the kitchen door and Don's wife, Joanne, put on the kettle to make me a hot chocolate. Don had heard I was coming and was glad I stopped in. Both Don and Joanne were originally from the Simcoe, Ontario area. They came to the Yukon and fell in love with the life. They did move back to southern Ontario once, but only stayed for three months before heading back to the Yukon, where their hearts are. Like many Yukoners I met, they felt they lived in heaven on earth. After a slice of Joanne's carrot cake, I headed on the road again.

I was glad I had a brief rest. It left me fresh for a very steep hill, north, that I climbed slowly as I left Moose Creek.

My legs were getting sore. I had tinges of pain in my quads, hams, calves and shins. My right knee was feeling the strain from all the hills. These hills weren't as high as the Rockies so I wondered if the source of the pain was the cold weather or just the cumulative effect of cycling for hundreds of days.

That afternoon, there was another bonus of a place to stop for a break at McQueston River. I went into the small restaurant and asked if they took Visa. They would not. I counted the money I had, which was $4.00. I ordered the $3.50 hot dog and water. The lady also gave me a free drink. Then she realized she had accidentally put a hamburger on the grill, instead of a hot dog. She told me I would get a hamburger instead, at the hot dog price. Hamburgers were $5.00 each. She took my last four dollars and kept the change. I enjoyed my homemade burger on fresh homemade bread for the bun.

Out on the Klondike again, I ran into a sun shower which was the first rain I had experienced since entering the Yukon. The rain was spilling from a small cloud that I quickly outpaced, to be back in the sunshine again. Riding along, I was startled by a police horn and pulled over. It was a Yukon Conservation Officer who read about me in the Yukon News and wanted to shake my hand. With my left arm stretched out, I took a picture of both of us. I then headed on and thought I would try for Flat Creek, the next lodge on the highway. To do this, I would have to cycle a personal best of 139 kilometres with all my gear, in one day. As I cycled, the forest terrain slowly turned into swamp country. The swamp was covered with heavy brush. As my legs got tired, I passed the time by singing songs out loud as I cycled. I sang hymns, Beatle songs and television themes. After eleven and a half hours of cycling, I pulled into the Klondike River Lodge in Flat Creek where the Dempster Highway begins. A year ago, if you had told me I would cycle 139 kilometres in one day, I would find that hard to believe. I celebrated, by ordering a hot beef sandwich. Debbie, at the Klondike River Inn, donated my room for the evening. I felt joy at my accomplishment and stayed up and watched the satellite TV movie, *Shawshank Redemption*. I'd seen the movie when it first came out but enjoyed the great acting again. The important message of this movie was, "never lose hope". I had never lost hope that I could make it to the top and today's accomplishment convinced me again that I could do anything!

Wednesday, September 17, 1997

Today was a side trip. I could have bypassed Dawson City because it was not on my direct route to Tuktoyaktuk. It meant I had to make an 82 kilometre round trip out of my way. In my final decision, I considered the people of Dawson City important Canadians. They deserved the chance to be a part of the *To The Top Canada* expedition. I rode to Dawson City in the coldest weather I had encountered yet.

Dawson City was a special experience. I saw this town that was born from the Klondike Gold Rush on the Bonanza River. Gold was discovered in 1896 and the Gold Rush reached its peak in 1898. In 1998, Dawson City would celebrate the Centennial of the Klondike Gold Rush. The City still had the spirit of the Klondike, capturing the flavour of this exciting frontier. There were no paved streets, just dirt roads. All the buildings looked like they were fresh from 1898. There were no sidewalks. Wooden boardwalks lined the streets. I pulled up to the Eldorado Hotel where I was a guest, which turned out to be the finest hotel in Dawson City. I talked to the local butcher who had heard about me. He was asking me a question when a tall cowboy with a mustache came out of The Sluice Box Lounge and answered his question about me and then elaborated more details about my trip. Impressed with his knowledge, I introduced this cowboy by saying, "Meet my agent." The cowboy smiled, got in his pick-up, and sped off. The butcher had moved to Dawson Creek from England. The butcher knew Canada was the very best country in the world. He wished me good luck in delivering my pro-Canada message to all Canadians.

After checking into my room, I went out to buy thermal socks and thermal underwear. As I bought the socks, I noticed some headbands. I tried a green one on and liked it. I said to the store clerk, Diane, that I would take one but I'd take a black one that would match my helmet. Diane said, "It is so important to make a fashion statement when you are riding through the Arctic." I laughed but I knew she was right. Here I was about to ride into the toughest climate on the planet and I was looking at colours. Diane asked me to say hello to a friend of hers in Tuktoyaktuk, named Uma Tuma.

After buying some more food to top up my supplies for the Dempster Highway, I went back to the hotel for an early supper. My supper of salisbury steak, garlic toast, and pecan pie with ice cream was delectable. When I went to pay the bill, my waitress insisted that my meal was on the house.

In my room, I lay down for a rest and then called home. Carol was glad to hear my voice. James was already in bed but snuck out to talk to me. I was glad because once I headed out on the Dempster, I would be out of touch for days. Carol told me of how they had accidentally locked themselves out of the house but, my cool son, James analyzed the problem and found a window that was unlocked and got himself in the house to unlock the door. I was very proud of him. We talked for over an hour and it felt great to trade stories with my family.

After the call, Carol sent me a fax from Magna International Chairman of the Board, Frank Stonach. It was my invitation to the Magna for Canada Scholarship Awards Gala on Friday October 24th at Roy Thomson Hall. For the first time, I found out who were the other Invitational Participants in the 1997-1998 book, *As Prime Minister, I Would...* They were: Ted Byfield, The Honourable Nellie Cournoyea, Pauline Couture, Arthur Erickson, The Honourable Willard Z. Estey, Edward Greenspan, John T. Mayberry, Steve Smith a.k.a. Red Green, Dr. Ken Walker a.k.a. Dr. Gifford-Jones, and Adam Zimmerman. Here I was, part of this list of distinguished Canadians and no money to do my laundry. I walked over to the CIBC bank Interac machine, where I found that Carol had put $60.00 in my account. I withdrew $40.00. On my way back from the bank, I decided to check out Diamond Tooth Gertie's Gambling Hall. Now, I know this sounds dangerous, considering my funds were very short but I just wanted to look around without gambling. In 1971, Diamond Tooth Gertie's opened as Canada's first and only legalized casino at the time. (Now, the Ontario government is opening casinos like Walmarts). It was originally a community hall that was converted to a casino. You could play Red Dog, Blackjack, Money Wheel, Texas Hold "Em Poker or the slot machines. A balcony, overhead, had additional tables and chairs for people who wanted to watch the show. From the balcony hung all the flags of Canada, representing all provinces and territories. The stage that faced the casino had a show where Diamond Tooth Gertie came out singing with Can Can Style dancing girls. The opening number was belted out by Diamond Tooth Gertie, who sang about Dawson City where "men were men and women were women".

I spoke with Bill Holmes, Slot Security Supervisor. He told me he was the "Toe Master" of a Dawson City club where you had to have a drink with a human toe in your glass. If your lips touched the toe, you received a certificate. The club had over 1000 members. I declined joining.

Walking back to the Eldorado Hotel, I took a GPS reading and found Dawson City had the following coordinates for the farthest western point I would reach:

64° 03.25 North of the Equator
139° 25.18 West of Zulu

Another reading told me that I have to travel in a jet 4329 kilometres on a course of 63° to get to my house in Hamilton. I was a long way from home.

I got a roll of quarters and a small bag of soap from the front desk. It was close to midnight so I decided to do my laundry when my 6:00 am wake up call came.

Thursday, September 18, 1997

At 6:10 am, I was awakened by the sound of quiet knocking at my door. My phone was off the hook, so my wake up call didn't get through. Someone in the Eldorado

Hotel was watching over me. I sprang up and took my clothes down to the washer and started a wash. Back in my room, I shaved, showered and packed the food I bought yesterday. I then called the Hamilton Spectator in my home city. Dana, the editor, asked me to call back in an hour. I switched my clothes to the dryer. I called back to the Spectator as requested and did a 50 minute interview over the phone. I had just a half hour to finish packing, carry my gear downstairs, pack my gear on my bicycle and get to City Hall. First my large orange bag. Then my small orange bag and my Canadian Flag, then my large back pack, then my saddle bags and trailer flag, then my trailer, then my bicycle were carried out from room 333. I just made it on time. I met with Mayor Glen Everitt and Lambert Curzan, Chairman of the Klondike Visitor Association. Glen told me a story that after a CBC radio commentary for Canada Day where he satirized Canadians' dependence on foreign made goods, one angry listener cut down every American flag in town and put it on his front porch. Many people visited Dawson City from Alaska and American flags made the Americans feel at home. That day, the American Consulate General was in town to meet with the Mayor. I wondered why the American Consulate General would want to meet a municipal politician. I asked why he was in town. It was just a goodwill meeting to discuss US-Canada issues like the B.C. fish war and the recent announcement that Canadians may now require visas to enter the United States. It sounded like a power lunch, in which relationships are being put in place to meet the objective of a future agenda. The U.S. had the most to gain from the break up of Canada. I'm sure they would love Alberta, B.C. and the Yukon to join the U.S. in the west. Alaska would no longer be the isolated state.

Strategic reasons caused the Americans to build the Alaska Highway, through Canada, in the first place. This was a friendly get-together but I'm sure American diplomatic intelligence had studied influential Canadian politicians and determined who would be disposed to supporting them at a future time. I am glad to report that my intuition tells me Mayor Glen Everitt was strongly and firmly Canadian.

A Fedex courier, that Carol sent me on Monday, would not reach Dawson City until Friday. Unfortunately I would be leaving today. Kerry, at the Front Desk of the Eldorado Hotel, agreed to take it over to Brenda, the manager at the Northwest Territories Visitor Centre. She would try to give it to someone going up the Dempster Highway who would deliver it to me. I felt this was a lot of effort to get a slow moving $80 Fedex package to me. The package contained more Friend of Canada certificates, that I could give out to appropriate people in the Northwest Territories.

At 12 noon I stopped for my first meal of the day, in the Bonanza Restaurant in the Eldorado Hotel. When I went to pay, they wouldn't take my money. I thanked them and rode out of town with my large Canada flag flying. I kept it flying for the 10 kilometres to the Dawson City Airport, outside town. If I passed by the American Consulate General, I wanted him to know he was in Canada today!

I arrived back at the Klondike River Lodge at about 4:00 pm. I enjoyed my last hot meal for a few days. I called home and spoke with Carol and James before I headed up the Dempster Highway and out of touch. I told them both I loved them very much. It was a call I couldn't hang up from, even after saying goodbye. After a pause of silence, I said, "Are you still there?" James was still on the line, as he couldn't hang up either. I told him I love him, and said goodbye one more time.

There were several signs on the Dempster Highway. One read, "Next services 389 kilometres". Another read, "Drive carefully as there are no emergency or medical services available on the Yukon portion of the Dempster Highway". I crossed the single lane wooden bridge and was on my way, over 700 kilometres to Inuvik. The road was mostly dirt, which I rode slowly on for approximately 10 kilometres. The sun seemed to be going down much earlier than I expected, as the September equinox was soon approaching. I set up my tent on a gravel clearing at the side of the road. The small flies were bad tonight. I didn't understand how there could be flies, even when temperatures were below freezing at night. I put all my gear in my tent, climbed in and closed the zipper. Just after I got in, it started to rain. In my tent, I opened my self inflating mattress and my sleeping bag. As I went to sleep, I thought about the next leg of my journey where I would cross the Arctic Circle.

Friday, September 19, 1997

I got on my way mid-morning. Experience had taught me this was a good thing. A little time in the morning is what my tent needed to dry off. When I did not let the tent dry, I inevitably spent a wet, uncomfortable night.

I read my Bible and wrote in my daily journal and nibbled on a breakfast of fruit cocktail, potato chips, a nutribar and grape juice.

The Dempster Highway took the crown away from the Northern Ontario Trans Canada highway as Canada's worst road. The sloppy surface was causing me problems including shifting gears and knocking my bicycle chain off twice. After the second incident, I realized all my gears were stripped. My 21-speed bike was now reduced to just two gears. My trailer, full of food and water, made it almost impossible to climb hills as I rode through the Ogilvie Mountains. Tears ran down my face from the pain of pedaling uphill. It soon became clear to me that I was not going to make it to Inuvik unless I made some changes. I thought about getting a new bike but the closest place to get a bike would be Whitehorse, over 500 kilometres away. The hardware store in Dawson City might have a bike, but not necessarily a bike that would accommodate my special needs. I didn't like either of these options because the chance of success was low and they both would mean lost time.

If I could just get to Inuvik with my bike, I would have plenty of time to source the best bike for the ice trail to Tuktoyaktuk. I would have two to three months of downtime in Inuvik and I was planning on flying home during this period, with the help of the Magna Corporation. In southern Ontario, I have lots of choice so I could make the very best decision.

I struggled to make it to the 66 kilometre mark up the highway where a Yukon Highway Maintenance Yard was my camping spot. I set up my tent and then went through all my bags and removed all non-essential gear to lighten my load. I even removed some food and some water to lower my travel weight further. The only three things I kept were my Bible, the Canadian flag and four certificates that were the last to present. The highway guys headed into Dawson on their Friday night. I would have to wait for their return, to ask a special favour. I loaded my non-essential gear into a bag and would ask them to forward it to Eagle Plains. I figured I would stay in the Eagle Plains Motel and then ask them, whenever they could, to send it on to Inuvik.

All I would carry now was minimum food, camping gear, bare minimum bicycle repair supplies and my clothing. I oiled my chain with mother-like attention. Just a little over 600 kilometres away, I thought I could make it, slow and sure. Ultimately I knew my fate was in God's hands. I read my Bible after a supper that was the same as breakfast.

Saturday, September 20, 1997

It was a very cold morning and the frost was very heavy. I went inside the maintenance residence from my tent, to warm up. I met Richard, the chef. I had a breakfast of two bowls of cereal and four slices of hot toast. It was a real treat. Richard had the contract for the food concession and lived in the maintenance residence. His wife had a retail store and lived in Whitehorse. Richard was trying to get a new system where the Internet could be accessed via satellite. He could then "chat" with his wife on a regular basis. I asked Richard if he would take my bag of extra weight and hold it until someone was going to Eagle Plains and send it with them. Richard agreed. I thanked him and then went to pack my things up. As everything was covered with frost, I read my Bible and the chapter of Ecclesiastes. In this chapter, a philosopher king of Jerusalem concludes that life and all our efforts are useless. I did not subscribe to the philosophy because I believe one person can make a difference. I believed I was making a difference in Canada and knew that Jesus Christ would make a huge difference for all of mankind.

I packed my gear slowly, hoping the sun would pop up and melt the frost. In the end, I packed my gear, frost and all. The first sign of the sun came at 10:25 a.m., when it popped over the mountain. Riding by Tombstone Mountain, I saw a couple of men with pack horses preparing to go hunting. An Indian man had warned me the bears were bad at Tombstone, but I didn't see any.

With no low gear, I had to walk my bike up the mountain. I left the forest behind on one side of the mountain and was in tundra on the other side. With the absence of trees, grass and snow, the tundra looked a lot like desert. Only small bushes grew in swampy areas.

After going up hill, I earned a long down hill coast on the other side. I had to be careful to go slowly because the road was full of potholes and rocks. I couldn't afford to wipe out and hurt myself, as help was a long way off. I stopped for something to eat at 3:00 pm. This would be my lunch and supper. It was extremely cold, with strong winds and no shelter. As I pulled out my food and sat on the ground, I tried to look on the bright side. There were no ants to spoil my Yukon picnic. I was glad to drink my juice, as my water bottles were still frozen into ice blocks from the night before.

I cycled along the Jackstone River, where I could see wild horses drinking. Further up the road a couple of hunters were bringing a dead moose back to their truck. When I drove closer, I could see they already had another moose in their pick-up.

I had cycled 76 kilometres in total, as I pulled off the road at 6:00 pm. I set my tent up and I knew it would be a mean night. The wind was whipping between the mountains where I was camping. In my tent, before it got too cold, I changed into some dry clothes. My new red thermal socks had turned my feet red.

I was 212 kilometres from Eagle Plains and I wondered if I would complete this distance in two days or three. My written schedule didn't have me arriving until Wednesday night but I knew if I didn't have too many mountainous hills, I could do better.

Sunday, September 21, 1997

The sun was kind to me this morning and rose over the mountain at 9:15 a.m. I ate some breakfast and got on the road as soon as possible. I cycled by giant, round rock mountains, void of vegetation from the base up. It was like an ant's view of a boulder on the ground. The road wound by the mountain on my left and the Red River on my right. Crossing the Ogilvie River, I stopped into the Ogilvie Highway Maintenance Yard. Even on a Sunday, all the men were out working. I met Daniel, the cook. Daniel was taking freshly baked rolls out of the oven and putting in shortbread to bake. Daniel had been trained as a culinary chef at the Royal York Hotel in Toronto. Without a doubt, these men eat well. Daniel offered me some lunch and I accepted. After lunch, I was on the road again.

The marshes were dotted with dysfunctional looking evergreen trees. They made the Charlie Brown Christmas tree look lush. I didn't know if it was a strange marsh variety of evergreen, an evergreen disease or, if I was approaching the tree line where trees could no longer grow in the north.

I nicknamed the place "spooky forest" because the trees gave me an eerie feeling. I was pulled over by an RCMP camper vehicle. Driving was Constable Don Dupasquier. Don was the Mountie on a horse at my Canada Rally in Whitehorse. He was amazed that I'd come hundreds of kilometres so fast. There was no regular police patrol on the Dempster Highway. To have such a patrol, the RCMP would have to have set up stations and residences similar to the ones the Yukon Government had created for highway maintenance. This was cost prohibitive for the RCMP. In response to this challenge, the RCMP had come up with an innovative approach. If an officer wanted to visit Inuvik on their own time, they could take the RCMP camper vehicle for free, as long as they patrolled the Dempster Highway as they drove and dealt with any situations that warranted police action. Don, like me, was enroute to Inuvik for the first time in his life. I took a picture of us and he pulled out his video camera. Don had asked to be transferred to Whitehorse after visiting the Yukon area as a member of the RCMP musical ride. We said goodbye but knew we would see each other when Don headed home from Inuvik, as I would still be pedaling to get there. I pedaled until dark and then set up my tent high on a mountain I had just climbed by walking one quarter of the way up. I had a good day, having covered 92 kilometres. I was now 120 kilometres from Eagle Plains. Depending on the hills, I had a chance to make it tomorrow.

Monday, September 22, 1997

In my tent, I was reading when I heard a snort. It was just outside my tent and sounded like a horse's snort, but deeper. It was a moose! My high self confidence had me believing that when I came face-to-face with a bear, I would come away the victor. Now, with a moose I had no such notion. In a confrontation with a moose, I lose, end of story. With this frame of reference, I decided to go on quietly reading my Bible. When it came time to finally emerge from my tent, I opened the door zipper and instead of poking my head out first I used my knife to gently lift the flap. The coast was clear. I packed up and hit the road.

Immediately, a steep hill forced me to walk. It took most of the morning to reach the summit. I think, after referring to my map, I'd just climbed the Continental Divide. At the top, I could see the river below but it just looked like a thread from my high vantage point. On top, I had to ride 16 kilometres of plateau before descending. It was colder at this altitude and it didn't help that there were high speed winds in my face the whole time. I could feel my fingers and toes getting numb. I cycled harder, to try to get to a lower altitude faster where the air was warmer. I came close to crashing three times this day, as my bike would slide in the deep soft dirt on the road. I had to reduce my speed. After the Continental Divide, there were rolling hills which I usually enjoyed. This time, because of the poor road conditions, I couldn't zoom down one side and coast up the other side. Due to my slower speed and stripped gears, I had to walk and push my bike, trailer and gear, up hill after hill. I managed to cover 65 kilometres by the end of the day when the sun set. There was good news and bad news to look forward to. The good news was I had, by my standard, a short distance to Eagle Plains tomorrow. I would look forward to a hot meal and a place to clean up. The bad news was the Continental Divide would swing back my way, intersecting my path again just as I crossed the border into the Northwest Territories.

Tuesday, September 23, 1997

I had spent a restless night. The wind was blowing hard and every sound made me think a bear was nearby. In the north, I slept with a knife, unsheathed, and my bear spray holster open always in the same spot, just to the right of my head. I never let myself fall into a deep sleep in my tent. My life may depend on my vigilance. It was a cold, cloudy morning and hail was pelting down. At least hail would bounce off my tent, and not leave it wet the way rain would. I hated packing up a wet tent.

On the way to Eagle Plains, I had to walk up three large hills. The largest hill took over an hour, to the top. I passed a south bound road sign that said Whitehorse was over 800 kilometres away. I found it hard to believe I was really this far north.

Fatigue began to overtake me. I found it hard to keep going and I found I was getting short of breath in the afternoon. Yesterday, I had two small meals from my supplies and then my food was all gone. I hadn't eaten at all today but I was still asking my body for maximum effort. My fatigue was my body's way of saying - no more!

I found that Eagle Plains was not a flat place, to lessen my cycling burden. Eagle Lodge was on a hill that was a final challenge before I could rest. Eagle Lodge was built in 1978 as a self-contained settlement with a motel, restaurant, bar, service station, offices for government departments, store, highway maintenance shop, trailer park and helicopter pad.

The next services after Eagle Lodge were over 180 kilometres up the Dempster. The Yukon Government wanted Eagle Lodge built as a stop half way between Dawson City and Inuvik.

I didn't ask for a donated room because I needed to get a full night's rest to recharge my batteries for the push to Inuvik. I pulled out my Visa and checked in. Then I tried to call my wife at a conference, at the Constellation Hotel in Toronto. She wasn't listed as a registered guest. This is because she was most likely sharing the room with another management person, but I couldn't remember who. I knew Carol was worried about me because this was the longest stretch of the expedition where I would be out of touch. I had the hotel operator connect me with the room of the conference organizer and left a voice mail message asking her to let Carol know I'd arrived at Eagle Plains in the Yukon. Specifically, I asked the organizer to tell Carol, "The Eagle has landed". If someone left that message on my voice mail at a conference, I would think I was being set up for a practical joke.

At the front desk, my Friend of Canada certificates were waiting for me. My Yukon friends' courier system was more reliable than Fedex. In the restaurant, I relished a hot turkey sandwich and pie. It was double the price of back home but I would have paid almost any price to get a hot meal.

After carrying my gear to my room, I took my clothes off and noticed that a toe on my right foot had been worn raw. I didn't feel any pain because of the cold. I took a long hot bath to let it soak and then pulled out my first aid kit and bandaged it up. After a short rest, I gathered up my laundry and headed to the laundromat. Especially with pushing my bike up every hill, my shirts were all soaking wet from sweat. I will be the first to admit that I am not the most domestic guy in the world. I washed roughly half of the clothes I carried with me. It seemed my red thermal socks had turned all my other clothes pink. I think I'll wear the pink clothes when I'm not scheduled to be around people. The pink makes me look like I'm the Yuppie Canadian Unity guy. So much for trying to make a fashion statement in the Arctic.

Wednesday, September 24, 1997

I awoke with a feeling of excitement. Today I would be leaving for Inuvik, that would take me to the end of the farthest road north. I prepared by buying some food supplies from Leslie at the Eagle Lodge kitchen. I called home at 9:15 am, hoping I'd catch Carol home at 12:15 pm eastern time. No luck. I left a detailed message in my voice mail box. I had committed to be in Fort McPherson by Friday and in Inuvik on Wednesday, October 1st. I was now on another time table so I had to perform regardless of road conditions, bike problems or mountains. There were no excuses now.

I checked out with Stacy at the front desk and she promised to redirect my bag from the Klondike Maintenance Yard to the RCMP station in Inuvik. Who needs Fedex anyway.

I cycled out of the Eagle Lodge and back on the Dempster Highway. Riding down the north bound hill for 20 minutes, I crossed the Eagle River. Then I had to walk my bike up a hill which took me 90 minutes. New gravel on the road was like trying to ride your bike in a room that was three inches deep in marbles. I am sure it was fine for cars and trucks, but it was treacherous for a bike. I did not complain because I felt great and up to the challenge, whereas the day before I felt extremely weak, to the point where I was concerned for my life.

My water was fresh from the Eagle Lodge, which was a treat because it was warm. Drinking water that had frozen the previous night was painful because the 1° water would feel like a cold sword as you swallowed it.

Thirty-five kilometre down the road, I reached a landmark. It was the marker where the Arctic Circle crosses the Dempster Highway at 66° and 33 minutes. I rode up to the marker and checked the position on my GPS. It came back as the following position:-

66° 33.90 N
136° 18.45 W
570 metres above sea level

Well, the sign was in the right place. I had my lunch of an apple and a Pepsi when a sport utility van, towing a house trailer, pulled up. It was a family from Halifax, Nova Scotia. Now this is what I call a Canadian family, that visits the entire country! They had seen me in Whitehorse and had already been to Inuvik. They asked me to pose with the children for a picture. On the count of three, I had the children say "Whiskey" to make them smile for the camera.

For the next 25 kilometres I had a relatively straight, flat road with a uniform surface. With the wind at my back and sunshine warming me, I used the good road to cover some serious distance. Coming up one hill in the early evening, I ran into a couple of guys in a pick-up truck. There were just slowly driving the road looking for reindeer antlers that they'd put in their truck. They were doing well at collecting discarded antlers because their pick-up was almost full.

As I rode, the low Arctic sun was setting and throwing off a large shadow of me, cycling. I think I created a new art form because I tried taking pictures of my shadow while I was cycling, holding a pose that made it look like I was cycling and not taking a picture of my silhouette. If it's not a new art form, it could be a new demonstration sport at the next Olympics. "Shadow cycling"! You heard it here first!

When the sun disappeared behind the mountain, I pulled into a gravel yard off the side of the road and set up my tent. I had ridden approximately 79 kilometres and it was a good day.

Thursday, September 25, 1997

I awoke to a sky filled with dark, grey clouds. It looked like it would rain any minute and I wanted to get my tent packed away while it was still dry. I hit the road, knowing I was close to the Northwest Territories border. It was just spitting briefly. It was as if the Yukon was trying to maintain its perfect record of no heavy downpours on me.

The Richardson Mountains posed a half hour of arduous walking, pushing my bike all the way. On top, I was greeted by a marker welcoming me to the Northwest Territories!

As I cycled into the Northwest Territories, it started to rain heavily. I tried to think of different things to take my mind off the rain. It seemed I would have to cycle into Fort McPherson before I could come to a public pay phone where I could call Carol. There were many hills, as I passed through the Continental Divide again.

At one point, I met RCMP Constable Don Dupasquie heading south. His RCMP vehicle looked like my bike, completely dirt and mud covered. Don asked me if I had any trouble with bears. When he camped overnight at Rock River Campground in the Yukon one night, a grizzly bear began angrily rocking his camper. Don didn't arrest the bear for assaulting an officer but I bet if that bear had tried to pick the lock on the camper, it would have been arrested for break and enter. Don had worried and wondered about me, alone with no vehicle for protection.

I had stopped at Rock River Campground the night before to eat supper from my supplies but then rode on until sundown on the Dempster. Don told me the RCMP had their own program on Fort McPherson radio. Don was a guest on the show and had told everyone I was coming. He told everyone to honk when they saw me but not to go by too fast, so I wouldn't choke on the Dempster dust.

As I headed out of the mountains, I encountered Arctic ice fog. It deposited ice on my bike, my gear and me. I pulled warmer clothing out of my bag and bundled up. The ice fog crept into my lungs as I rode and it felt like a vice on my chest.

I rode to the Pelly River Ferry at about 8:00 pm. Jack was driving the Ferry and Abe was working the ramp. It was a three minute crossing. I guess operating a Ferry was cheaper than budgeting a multi million dollar capital expenditure to build a bridge. There was really no road from the Ferry, it was just a mud field. So much mud had accumulated on my bike, that the wheels would not turn at one point. I forced my bike one kilometre down the road to a campground where I set up my tent in the pouring rain. A lot of my things had got wet after several hours of rain and ice fog. In total, I had covered 85 kilometres but tomorrow I had to decide if my bike, which was on its last legs, could make the trip to Inuvik.

Friday, September 26, 1997

I had changed into "pink" sweats the night before because they were dry. It had been a long rainy night at my Peel River campground but fortunately the rain had stopped by morning. It was still cloudy and cold. I found a long flat rock and used it like a chisel to scrape mud off my bike. Anyone who can bottle and sell Arctic mud is going to take a major share of the crazy glue market. It was extremely hard to get off. After an hour of chiselling, my bike was ready to be packed up.

I headed on to the Dempster where I started to slowly accumulate mud again. My bike protested under the strain. Click, click, click as my chain would slip from the chain wheel. I knew my chain was stretched past recommended limits and the spokes on my chain wheel were also worn down. Would the mud be the last straw that would stop my bike? I gingerly rode 10 kilometres toward Fort McPherson, at a quarter of my regular cruising speed, on the Dempster. (If you can cruise on the Dempster, at all). Late in the morning, I pulled into Fort McPherson, riding slowly but proudly with my Canadian flag flying.

I went to the Coop Cafe, grocery store and hotel. Managers Ken & Kathy Davidson agreed to donate a room for the night. I went to room nine on the second floor. Shaved and washed, I put on clean clothes before heading out. I went for lunch in the cafe as my first meal of the day. I arrived at 12:15 pm. At this restaurant, you ordered at the cash, paid your bill, and then went to your seat where your food would be brought to you.

There were 12 to 15 tables in the restaurant and all, except one, were full of native Gwich'in Students from the local school. The native waitress was working very hard bringing food out of the kitchen. She would walk rapidly and, as soon as she had delivered an order, she would dart into the kitchen to get another.

I had worked as a short order cook for a summer job and I knew how you could get backed up when all the orders came at once. At ten to one my order hadn't come, nor had the orders of many students who had ordered before me. At five to one, a group of students went to the kitchen door to quietly ask about their food. They had to be back at school at one. About three minutes later their food came out and they quickly ate it and headed off to school. I knew they would be late. Someone may think these student were irresponsible by not being punctual. I knew better. I knew the students wanted to be on time for school.

After my lunch came, I headed over to the new multi-million dollar Chief Julian School. It provided grades from kindergarten to Grade 12 and was also a campus for Arctic College. It was a new school, with state-of-the-art facilities that any Canadian would be proud attend.

After introducing myself to the principal, she took me to the different class rooms to speak to students about my *To The Top Canada* expedition for Canadian Unity.

The children were dressed like most Canadian school kids, wearing their favourite sports team emblems. I saw Nike, Maple Leafs, Blue Jays and Chicago Bulls clothing. I did find the students tired, which I attributed to it being a Friday afternoon.

One native teacher, Ruby, especially thanked me because her class had been working on a study segment on how to make the community better. My presentation gave the students the motivation to go out and practice what they had learned. Another teacher, Brian, was from Burlington, Ontario and he invited me to his house for supper. I also spoke to Kate's class. She was the teacher I had met on Steamboat Mountain in B.C. The principal, Janey, said she really had enjoyed my presentations and felt that it was an extremely important message the students needed to hear. I left the school feeling good about the impact I had made.

Fort McPherson was the first Hamlet I had visited. I didn't know what made a hamlet different from a village, town or city. I was told, at the Hamlet office, that they did not have the right to charge property taxes and their total revenue came from a Territory Government grant and some community user fees.

CBC News had called looking for me, but first I went next door to the local Gwich'in radio station, CBQM, and went on air with Bertha Francis. Bertha told me she saw me cycle into town and she went to the window because she wanted to yell out "Welcome to Fort McPherson" but I was already by when she got to the window.

I talked at length on the radio about how wonderful Canada is but how we still had a responsibility to make it better. Bertha then came on and also praised Canada. It struck me as interesting when she specifically said their community was blessed with an abundance of caribou and berries. I wondered what the reaction of a Canadian Bay Street stock broker in Toronto would be if I told them I was going to bless them with an abundance of caribou and berries. They would probably ask if there was a futures market for those commodities. I had just learned a special lesson about the word "contentment". I then went to the RCMP office and thanked them for mentioning earlier this week that I was coming into the community.

At the band office, I met Chief William Koe of the TeeTl'it Gwich'in Council. Chief Koe indicated he would pass my important message on to everyone at Council.

At the RCMP station, Officer James washed the mud off my bike with the power washer and locked my bike in the police garage for the night for safety.

I walked back to my hotel and caught a little television news. A Canadian stamp had been released today commemorating "the goal" scored by Paul Henderson that allowed Canada to win the first Team Canada-Russia hockey series. Paul remarked about how many Canadians still come up to him and each of them remembers exactly where they were when that goal was scored. I was in Oakville Trafalgar Hospital watching on my hospital bed TV, recovering from a concussion I had received in an Appleby College football game. My Mom was with me in the hospital, watching the game. When the goal was scored, the patient in the next hospital bed beside me opened the hospital window and started yelling out the window in joy! I had met Paul Henderson on the speakers' circuit and like myself, his life was committed to Jesus Christ. Miracles are possible through Him.

Brian picked me up and we had a visit at his house, enjoying hot dogs cooked in a campfire in his driveway.

I remarked to Brian how nice their school was. Brian was troubled by the new school because it was the third in two and a half years. The school had been set on fire by students. To Brian, the new school sent a message that if you want a better school, burn your old one down. This was a reward to a destructive act. We then had a discussion about school life in a native situation. Brian also drew on his experience at God's Lake, a native community 600 kilometres north of Winnipeg.
Although we were now giving Native Canadians the very best in educational facilities, students were still deeply handicapped by problems in their society. Many students, although still young, had to be the parents in their family because of substance abuse and addiction problems with their parents. Brian had students who missed school because they had to look after their younger brothers and sisters. Unfortunately, some of these children would also look forward to the time when they didn't have to be responsible and they could slip into the comfort of substance abuse.

There was also wide spread abuse of public funds and the feeling that items like "braces" were automatically free and there was endless money. I asked what would happen if the Auditor General put C.A.'s in every band to help the bands achieve full financial integrity. The C.A.'s would be driven off or killed was Brian's answer. I found this perspective unsettling. Later in the evening, Kate, the teacher I met at Steamboat, dropped over. Her perspective is that the children come from dysfunctional family situations and you had to accept it would affect them in the classroom. She tried her best to take every student as far as the circumstance of the environment would allow her to. It was twenty minutes to midnight when Kate took me back to the hotel and dropped me off. I was tired and needed my sleep.

Saturday, September 27, 1997

Down at the cafe for an early breakfast, I discovered it didn't open until noon on the weekend. There was complementary use of the washer and dryer, so I put my clothes in. I very much appreciated this service. I knew my bike couldn't be picked up until after 10:00 am at the police station, so I used the time to write in my journal. Taking my wash out of the dryer, I noticed my good normal colour sweat pants had a large rip in the crotch. Two choices loomed, neither of them pretty. I could wear my slightly pink sweat pants that had been washed with my red socks or my air conditioned sweat pants. I opted for the pink pants.

At the RCMP station, Constable James Buhler was on duty. I asked him about the school fires. The first one was a break-in by young adults in their twenties, who were looking for money to support their drinking habit. One of the offenders cut himself during the break in and was bleeding in the school. In order to leave no evidence of his DNA from his blood, he decided to set the school on fire. The second incident involved a 17-year-old who didn't want to go to school. He paid two boys, who were 14 and 15, a grand total of $15 to burn the school down - and they did. After losing two schools, you would think there would be respect for their new school.

Within a month of opening, outside lights had been broken and graffiti sprayed on the outside wall saying Metallica Rules. James smiled, adding that the person couldn't even spell Metallica correctly. I collected my bike, bought some supplies at the Coop store and thanked Ken and Kathy before I left.

When my mud covered, chain slipping, gear-absent bike rolled into Fort McPherson, I thought it was time for it to visit the glue factory. Now that it was clean, especially the chain, I was starting to think there may yet be hope for my bike.

I rode north on the Dempster Highway, through a construction zone. One of the construction flagmen was listening to radio CBQM and playing Bingo over the radio.

I rode on and I was told there would only be three hills I would have to walk up on my way to Arctic Red River. I discovered there were very many more hills.

The MacKenzie River is as big as the St. Lawrence, in Quebec. There is a "T" where the Arctic Red River joins the MacKenzie River. A ferry does nonstop triangles between the Dempster Highway to the south, Arctic Red River to the east and the Dempster Highway to the north. Each crossing takes approximately 20 minutes. Just like the famous Hollywood sign, Arctic Red River has a huge sign on a hill that says "Tsiigehtchic", which means Red River, in Gwich'in. Once the ferry let me off on the Arctic Red River side, I cycled up the hill into the community. Everything was closed as it was about 8:00 pm. I rode up to the band office, where there was the only outdoor pay phone. I called Carol to let her know I had made it to Arctic Red River. I then rode my bike over to the church that sat at a point high on a cliff, overlooking both the MacKenzie River and Arctic Red River. I could see the local fishermen coming in after checking their nets for Arctic whitefish. I could also hear the howls of many husky dogs that were kept outside in the community. The howls were long and loud and had a harmony all their own. I set up my tent and crawled in, as it was now dark. The drawl of the ferry engines, continuously crossing, and the howl of the huskies lulled me to sleep.

Sunday, September 28, 1997

Today was a special treat because I had "breakfast in bed". With no real chance of bears climbing the cliff, I had kept food in my tent. My breakfast consisted of a can of mixed citrus juices, three oatmeal raisin cookies and a can of fruit cocktail. With everything in Arctic Red River closed, I had enough to have two small meals a day until Monday night. By Tuesday afternoon, I expected to ride into Inuvik. Hopefully, I could hold out until then. It was raining in the morning so I stayed in my tent the whole time, hoping the rain would pass. I wanted to pack my gear when it was dry. The wind was blowing very hard. When I climbed out of the tent, I'd have to be careful that my tent and all my gear didn't blow over the cliff. I went to the front of the church, to go in and say my Sunday prayers. It was locked. I talked with a gentleman named Serge, from England, whose life pattern consisted of working for a year and then travelling for a year. This year, he wanted to drive the Dempster and see Inuvik. From high on our hill, we could see the ferry was coming to Arctic Red River. Serge headed out, in his car that he had bought for $500.

Packing up my gear, I took the last item out of my tent when I heard a swoosh. Out of the corner of my eye, I could see my blue tent fly by, four feet off the ground. With lightning fast reflexes, I caught the exterior tent pole. If I had weighed less, I would have been the first person to parasail over the Arctic Red River. I walked the tent to the side of the church where there was protection from the wind.

When all my gear was packed on my bike, I rode to the Chief's house to present the Arctic Red River *To The Top Canada* certificate. I was told that the Chief's house was the one with the Teepee on the second floor balcony. I discovered this was true. When I went to the door and knocked, I heard someone yell "yeah". The door was unlocked, so I went in.

When I came through the door, the Chief's family was watching one of those giant TV's that cover the wall. Peering at me in my helmet and bright yellow jacket, the family looked as if they had seen an alien.

I introduced myself and explained about the *To The Top Canada* expedition. The Chief didn't move from his chair. I walked over and gave him the certificate. The Chief didn't talk much, so I thanked him and excused myself. There must be an Indian proverb that says, "When a strange white man suddenly comes to your house carrying a 10 inch survival knife, do not make him feel welcome and hopefully he will leave". I rode to the outdoor pay phone to call home before I left. I'd promised Carol I'd call before I left Arctic Red River, as I would be out of touch for a few days. I made it a quick call because I knew the ferry was coming. Riding down the hill, I could see the ferry approaching and I would easily beat it to the landing spot. Then, the ferry changed directions and did not come ashore. It seemed they wanted a longer coffee break on the other side or, maybe, they wouldn't dock just for a bicycle. I waited at the shore for an hour, pelted by freezing rain. With no physical activity, I soon became cold and wet. A pick-up truck joined me. I was glad because they'd have to stop now. They came ashore. I leaned my bike against a wall and went to the washroom. It was small but heated. I put my mittens on the radiator to melt the ice. I stayed in the washroom the whole crossing, to warm up as much as possible.

When I started north on the Dempster, I saw the road had turned to sloppy mud. My tires sank in it under all the weight. The mud collected at my brakes as my wheels turned and formed mud balls as big as baseballs. At times, the mud between my tires and fender would be so thick, my wheels could not turn. I had to get off my bike and use my knife to clear the mud.

The freezing rain was blowing hard and to the south, right into my face. I was ready for cold weather and I was ready for wet weather. Unfortunately, when they both came at the same time, there was a problem. My winter gear wasn't waterproof. Once I was wet, I was losing body heat fast.

After cycling approximately 10 kilometres, I knew I had to get under shelter or risk hypothermia. The sides of the Dempster were like mushy swamp, making them unsuitable for camping. My body had gone numb a long time ago and time was running out. I prayed to the Lord for one of those elevated turn around places or any place suitable for me to set my tent up so I would be out of the way of Dempster traffic. I didn't want to have my tent on the one lane Dempster, where I could be hit by a transport truck or someone drinking and driving. In three minutes, I saw a cut off road. I pulled my bike in and set up camp. My tent was at the side of this road. I put my orange food bag on one side of my tent on the road to warn cars. On the other side was my bike and trailer, with reflectors and large safety flag.

I pulled dry clothes out of my bag. As I took off my damp clothes, I used them to dry off my sleeping mattress that was water soaked. I then pulled my dry sleeping bag out of my white water proof bag and got in. It took a long time but my body finally returned to its normal warmth. I fell asleep, with my head on a damp camp pillow.

176

Monday, September 29, 1997

I opened my tent door and snow fell in with a thud. It had snowed during the night and everything was covered with a thick, packing snow. Before heading out, I had to use the saw side of my knife to cut the hard frozen mud off my bike.

Once on the road, I encountered even worse mud conditions than the day before. On one of my stops to clear mud, a small truck pulled up behind me. It was James, from the Fort McPherson RCMP, off duty and heading into Inuvik to have some work done on his truck. He asked me if I was alright. I told him I was fine. James, I'm sure, knew that the last two nights had been terrible weather and I wondered if he was being a good Samaritan, heading into Inuvik now to look out for me. I had made a decision that with all my dry winter clothes gone, except for what I was wearing, instead of camping tonight by Caribou Lake I would go all the way - 112 kilometres to Inuvik. I asked James to call CBC in Inuvik and tell them I would be ahead of schedule and would be arriving this evening. By 11:00 am, I was both hungry and thirsty as I hadn't eaten yet. I stopped and finished all my supplies. My meal was a can of fruit cocktail, three oatmeal raisin cookies, a can of grape pop and a can of apple juice.

Everyone had told me it would be down hill to Inuvik but from about 50 kilometres out, I started to have to climb several hills and upward inclines. At about 8 o'clock that night, as I was climbing one hill 20 kilometres from Inuvik, I encountered a family I'd met earlier on my travels. Joseph, Clare and their two children were coming out of Inuvik. They stopped and were excited to see me. "You've made it", Joseph called out. You're just less than 20 kilometres. "You've made it to the top!" Clare said, "Let's clap for Chris!" The whole family clapped and cheered in their truck. I asked if they had a beverage I could buy, as I was very dehydrated. Joseph gave me a one litre bottle of coke and said, "It's yours". As we talked, I opened it and drank it all down. They took the empty bottle. I thanked them because they were like angels bringing me refreshment when I was ready to drop. I then continued up my last hill, walking my bike and counting every time my left foot touched the ground to take my mind off the pain in my side and the blisters on my feet. At the top of the hill, I could see the Inuvik airport which I knew was 10 kilometres away from Inuvik.

I then got on something I hadn't seen since Whitehorse - an asphalt road. My bike glided into the airport. I had to call CBC to let them know I was arriving. When I got to the terminal building, I discovered it was locked and closed for the night. I then went over to the control tower, which was open. I met Gerrard, the air traffic controller on duty. I asked if I could call CBC on his phone. He agreed. Gerrard was busy, as it seemed a few smaller planes were going and coming. I called the CBC reporter's line. There was no answer and no voice mail. I called the CBC newsline and got no answer. I called the CBC general reception line and got no answer. I thanked Gerrard and asked if I could use his washroom. When I got back, Gerrard gave me a computer print out to commemorate my arrival in Inuvik. It showed the current temperature was 1° C and the current temperature in Windsor, the closest airport to Point Pelee where I began was 18°C. I appreciated his interesting gift and went to my bike and got Gerrard a Friend of Canada certificate.

I then headed towards Inuvik, as it was 10:00 pm and the sun had set. On the good road, I quickly mastered the distance. Everyone in Inuvik seemed to have a dog and every dog barked at me from their cage or dog house as I rode into town. I'm sure most people thought a bear was strolling around. I don't know what it was about my bike and trailer, but it drove dogs nuts.

I checked in at the Eskimo Inn. After carrying my gear in, I popped across the street to the Rooster, the only place open late at night. I had a bacon burger and three cold drinks. I declined ordering the Caribou and Muskox, also on the menu. When I finally settled in my room, it was 12:30 am. I don't know whether it was the excitement of arriving in Inuvik or all the Pepsi I drank, but I couldn't sleep.

Tuesday, September 30, 1997

In the morning I met with Susan, the Manager of the Eskimo Inn. Wanting to stay until Friday, I asked her if I could pay for two nights and have them donate two nights. She agreed. I needed something dry and clean to wear during my presentations this week which meant laundry was next on my agenda. Contacting the travel agent for the Magna Corporation, I was delighted to learn that they had booked a flight for me. I would leave Inuvik on Friday on NWT Air, at 3:55 pm and fly to Edmonton via Yellowknife. Transferring to an Air Canada flight, I would stop in Calgary and fly to Toronto arriving at 6:07 am on Saturday morning. I smiled at my good fortune - I had a free flight home. I called Carol at work to tell her I had arrived in Inuvik and to give her my flight details. She started to cry, knowing that I was safe and she would soon see me. I was choked up myself as I spoke with her. I offered to get an airport shuttle van home, as 6:07 am was early to arrive, requiring them to be up before 5:00 am to drive from Hamilton to get me. Carol said they'd be at the airport to meet me.

After retrieving my laundry, I went to the Rooster for lunch. The owner, Mohammed Elkadry, donated my lunch. I spoke with his wife Alia. They were from Lebanon. Now, climate-wise, I think of Lebanon as the Miami beach of the Mediterranean. So, how does some one end up moving from one of the warmest places on Earth, to one of the coldest? The answer was, to drive a cab. Taxis in Inuvik are an essential service. People go from building to building in taxis rather than risk facing sub-zero temperatures. Even people who have cars prefer taxis for short trips rather than go through the fuel and time to warm up and de-ice their vehicles. When Mohammed first started his cab business, Alia told me he could clear $1,000 on Friday night. He charged people almost $5.00 to cross the street. If you had groceries, he charged a premium of $1.00 per bag. Today, Inuvik's taxi industry is more regulated and on a

Friday night, a cab driver clears $500.00. Driving a cab was good to Mohammed, earning enough to purchase a local restaurant, a retail convenience store, six houses and some tracts of land. Alia's heart is still in Edmonton with their first house, of which she is so proud. Her oldest daughter Kathy, who is 19, is looking after her children in Edmonton. Although Mohammed had become a taxi tycoon with a net worth of one million dollars, the money did not buy happiness for Alia.

In the afternoon, Candice, at CBC radio, asked me to read a day from my journal for a CBC North program. I chose a portion of my day in Fort McPherson, in order to share its special message about materialism and contentment that I had learned from the Gwich'in community. While I was at the Western Arctic CBC station, they made arrangements to meet me early in the morning for a television interview.

The dinner at the hotel that evening cost me $30. Although the price was not entirely a surprise, I still found paying that much for one meal to be shocking. I spent the evening catching up on the television news. Senator Pat Carney was making headlines for saying that British Columbia should not rule out separation as a future option. I found her comments obscene. As an individual living off Canadian taxpayer's money in an unelected senate, making a destructive anti-Canadian comment, she was a disgrace to our country. I am sure Progressive Conservative Sir John A. Macdonald, the first Prime Minister of Canada, was rolling over in his grave in disgust.

It was one more event that told me that we can't depend on politicians and government to save Canada. Canada's future depends on the good deeds of Canadians making non-governmental initiatives happen to save our country. The *To The Top Canada* expedition is vitally needed by our nation at this time.

Wednesday, October 1, 1997

I left Point Pelee seven months ago and today is my official arrival in Inuvik. I met with CBC television. They seemed to relish taping the evidence of my struggle against the dreaded Dempster Highway. They filmed the mud and my broken bike with its stripped gears and stretched chain. They captured me walking up the hill pushing my bike, trailer and over 200 pounds of gear, as I did for every hill on the Dempster through the Ogilvie, Tombstone and Richardson Mountains, the entire way.

When I arrived at the Inuvik Town Office, Mayor George Roach presented me with mementos of Inuvik, including a personalized certificate that commemorated Chris Robertson crossing the Arctic Circle.

Meeting with a supervisor in the Department of Transportation for the Northwest Territories, we discussed the Ice Trail from Inuvik to Tuktoyaktuk at length. The most important fact that I learned was the exact distance - 187 kilometres. In southern Ontario weather, it would be a two day drive but just crossing the street in Inuvik, with either your face or hands exposed, could lead to frostbite in less than a minute. Although the ice surface would be less than ideal for a bicycle, this was not a battle against the land. This would be a battle against the weather. The coldest weather on the planet could quickly kill. Ice trail gale force winds had pushed over fully loaded transport trucks and trailers. There would be no room for error. An error could mean death.

At the Government of Canada Parks office in Inuvik, I used their E-mail system to send a message to the Parks Canada staff at Point Pelee, letting them know I had arrived in Inuvik.

Greetings Everyone!

Today on October 1, 1997, just a short seven months after leaving Point Pelee National Park, I have arrived in Inuvik in the Northwest Territories. This is the farthest north that roads will take you in Canada. I am now waiting for the ice trail to freeze on the MacKenzie River and then I will go the final 187 kilometres to Tuktoyaktuk. Last year, the ice trail opened on December 21, 1996 but it has been a warmer fall and may not open until early January 1998. When it does open, I'll be ready to go the distance to become the first person in history to travel from the very bottom of mainland Canada to the top, under their own power. I still remember the very first day of March 1, 1997 at the Point Pelee Visitor centre like it was yesterday. I've travelled over 6,300 kilometres and have spoken to over five million Canadians asking them to answer my question: "What will you do before the year 2000 to make Canada a better country than when you found it?" I look forward to returning to my home in Hamilton, Ontario. You may be interested to know that the Magna Corporation has chosen me as one of 10 distinguished Canadians and asked me to be a co-author of the 1997-1998 book, "As Prime Minister, I Would...". It wasn't enough that I had to ride my bike all day, now I had homework in the evenings! I just wanted to send you this note to update you on my status. If you could do me one favour, I would ask that you let the media in Southwestern Ontario know I made it to Inuvik. Thanks for all your help!!!

Kindest regards

Chris Robertson
To The Top Canada Expedition.

I wanted them to know that all their efforts in helping me begin the *To The Top Canada* expedition had paid off with success! That evening I ate in the hotel bar. Their menu was more economical and I ate lightly. James, a customer and sales person for the local Northern department store, agreed to tape the CBC news for me on his VCR. James was born in the Arctic but given up for adoption. He was adopted by an Edmonton family and grew up with a mother who was a teacher and father who was a lawyer. He came to Inuvik to discover his cultural roots when he reached adulthood. In the bar, a woman named Ruby sent a drink over to James and myself. I drank the

Zambooka, the first alcoholic drink I'd had during the *To The Top Canada* expedition. Ruby is Inuvialuit. She was in Inuvik for a seminar training session on how to be a community facilitator, helping develop a consensus to create Self Government for the Inuvialuit and Gwich'in nations. I wished her good luck with her initiative.

After some discussion, Ruby expressed concern that her people face an uphill battle, that they have been exploited and that there is a plan by those in the south to keep her people subservient. I'm one to never let an untrue allegation go by unchallenged. As a person from the south, I voiced my belief that there is no agenda to keep the people in the north under our thumb. Ruby rhymed off a laundry list of past exploitations. It's important not to confuse the past with the present. I'm sure that, earlier in this century, there was exploitation but that is not the public will today. To dwell on the past would be analogous to my saying I find it hard to deal with Germans in 1997 because of what Hitler did in the forties. There comes a time where you have to move forward. James was quietly listening and I asked him for his perspective. James, who grew up in a major urban centre, agreed with me. He cited the example of his white parents ensuring he went to the library to read books on Arctic culture so he could discover his biological heritage. He knew that his "southern" parents felt more than respect for him and his northern family. They felt love.

The subject changed to the Internet when James pulled out his laptop Canon computer with the latest Windows program. A while later, Ruby said she was talking with her Seminar Leader who had overheard our conversation. He invited me to come to the seminar at 4:00 pm, the next day. I accepted the invitation. The time had gone by quickly and I excused myself, to get ready for a busy day tomorrow.

Thursday, October 2, 1997

I would only be allowed to check two bags on Air Canada and a piece of hand baggage. I had to reorganize all of my gear into two groups. First, those items that I would fly home with. This was a challenge, since I had over 200 pounds of gear and Air Canada allowed a maximum of 70 pounds. Second, those items that would be left in Inuvik. My challenge was to find someone willing to store this extra gear. The hotel had a small holding area under the stairs for guests but my gear had filled this area up completely. I don't think the hotel would look kindly on not being able to offer this service to any other guests until January.

Turning to God for all my problems, I walked down to the Anglican Church of the Ascension in Inuvik. The minister's name is Larry Robertson (no relation). Rev. Robertson quickly agreed to help me. Larry showed me a new church that was under construction beside the current church. The current church had been built as a temporary building that was still in use, 12 years later. The congregation had outgrown the small church. Larry was a man of action. He found a building that was owned by the Northwest Territories and being used as a warehouse for the hospital. He asked if the church could buy the building. The Northwest Territory Government said they couldn't sell it to a private organization without going through a tender process. Unwilling to take no for an answer, he asked if the Northwest Territory Government could give the building to the town if they requested it. This time, the answer was "yes". Larry arranged for this to happen. Once the transaction was completed, the church bought the building for $1.00 and then paid $30,000 to move the building to their property. (Larry negotiated a new roof as part of this deal.) Now, the church community just had to carry out leasehold improvements. In a small community, despite Larry's shrewd negotiation skills, this is a hefty financial commitment for the Inuvik parish. I applauded their efforts to create a new church building, a wonderful legacy to leave Canada in your lifetime.

Larry was constantly on the go, functioning not only as the church minister but as almost the social safety net for the community. He counselled Inuvialuit, who did not understand when they were arrested and he acted as a character reference for them before the judge. Larry tried to help unwed teenage Inuvialuit girls who had gotten pregnant. Larry said to me: "You know Chris, the last thing we need around here is more blond Eskimos." There was anger in his voice because Larry had seen the hardship caused when men from the south took advantage of these young girls. I have worked with church ministers and am somewhat knowledgeable about their daily routine. It became apparent to me that Larry is working harder than any church minister I've ever met. Larry fought hardship and adversity with God's love. Larry worked longer days than anyone I'd ever known, never once complaining. The only time I saw fear in his eyes and heard his voice quiver was when he said: "Chris, I don't know where we are going to find the money to build the church." In that moment, I knew I had to help Larry. I will not let Larry carry this burden alone. I told Larry that when the expedition is done, I will try to help him raise some money to make his dream, of the first permanent Anglican Church in Inuvik, come true.

Larry told me he had a Scout meeting this evening and I offered my services to speak to the troop. I told him I'd bring my bike trailer and gear over just before the meeting, which took place at the Sir Alexander MacKenzie School gym.

After lunch at the Dempster Cafe (good food, reasonable prices, good service and great music), I caught up on my Bible reading. I was reading the Chapter of Ezekiel, which left me feeling great about my relationship with God. In the Old Testament, the stories seemed to portray a God who punished people when they sinned, showing mercy only when a prophet negotiated a kinder punishment. Jesus was the epitome of mercy to his people. When God spoke through Ezekiel in Chapter 33, Verses 10 to 20, the message was that when a person stops sinning and follows a good and righteous life, he is saved in God's eyes. I'm not a saint. Like most people, I've done some things I'm not proud of in my life. This passage felt like the Lord had taken a weight off me. Like I'd said to Ruby, "Let's forget the past. Let's focus on the present and future."

At Ruby's seminar, I spoke to her colleagues of my admiration for their efforts to make Canada better, by trying to create an Inuvialuit-Gwich'in Self Government to better serve the community. I told them I was confident that they would be successful because the majority of Canadians want to see the aboriginal people treated with respect and fairness. As a thank you for their efforts for Canada, I presented the twenty delegates with Friend of Canada certificates. They were all very appreciative and invited me to join them for a buffet dinner that included caribou meat, which I enjoyed. I was glad to share this positive message.

Loading my gear into my trailer, I towed it, wheel barrow style, to the Anglican Church. Together, Larry and I walked over to the school where I was on the program at the beginning of the Scout meeting. The boys responded to my presentation with enthusiasm and asked me many questions. After all the questions were answered, I excused myself and went back to my hotel. I was anxious to go to sleep because when I woke up I would begin my journey home to see my family again. I missed them so badly, just thinking about the trip made my eyes water.

Friday, October 3, 1997

After closing my two large back packs, I turned my attention to my bike. My objective was to turn the handlebars parallel with the front wheel and remove the pedals so I could take my bike home with me. It would be important to ride in Hamilton to maintain myself in the condition I was now in. My own tool kit allowed me to quickly adjust the handlebars but I didn't have the right wrench for the pedals. Walking my bike down to the Home Hardware store, I borrowed the right tools but my pedals wouldn't budge. The clerks invited my to bring my bike into the store, all of us trying, with no success at getting the pedals off. I commented that I'd simply have to tell the people at NWT Air that the pedals don't come off. Both store clerks knew the baggage handler for NWT Air. One clerk looked at the other and, in a minute, the call to the baggage handler was made. The clerks assured me, "Everything's cool". I thanked both of them for resolving my last concern of the day.

On my way out of town, I picked up the videotape of the CBC news footage from James, at the Northern store. A Lebanese cab driver, with a station wagon, took me to the airport. I had been quoted $22 for a ride to the airport but he only charged me $10.

When I checked in at home, by phone, Carol told me several people had heard on the radio that I had arrived in Inuvik! They were anxious for me to get home. Reminding Carol to hook the bike rack to the car when she came to pick me up, I hurried to board my flight.

It was a 737 jet but it only had a small seating area in the back of the plane. The entire front half of the plane, except for the cockpit, was a cargo hold. In two weeks, the ferries on the Dempster highway would stop. Then, for two months, Inuvik would be cut off from the rest of the world in terms of supplies, except by air. I'd flown other Air Canada connectors such as Air Ontario and Air Nova but NWT Air seemed like the best for service and meal quality. It was a pleasant discovery. Enroute to Edmonton, we stopped at Yellowknife. Inuvik had no airport security but there was security in Yellowknife and all Inuvik passengers had to deplane and go through security there.

In Yellowknife, we picked up some fellows going to Edmonton, who had too much to drink in the bar. They were loud, obnoxious and their language turned the air blue. I met a lot of people who discussed the substance abuse problems of native Canadians during the *To The Top Canada* expedition. No one seemed to put the "substance abuse label" on Caucasians. I'd met many native Canadians from many nations across Canada but I can honestly say none of the first nation people acted like the rude Caucasian men that were on this flight to Edmonton. I ignored them so as not to give them an audience, and read the paper.

In Edmonton I grabbed a snack before my next flight. The departure time was 23:15 for my next flight, to Toronto via Calgary.

The Air Canada agent saw my *To The Top Canada* t-shirt and realized I was the national unity guy. She upgraded me to business class. The flight attendant brought me champagne just after take off. It was a great way to finish the day.

Saturday, October 4, 1997

It was 2:15 am on the ground in Calgary when we had a brief stop to pick up more passengers. I couldn't sleep with the excitement of coming home.

Arriving in Toronto, I was the first person off the plane, running down the strangely quiet Terminal 2, at six o'clock in the morning. James, Carol and Smooch, my dog, ran through the security doors to the baggage area, when I opened them. We all had tears in our eyes, as we hugged each other.

My family was surprised at how much weight I had lost. I left Point Pelee weighing 272 pounds and now, after fighting the Rockies, Ogilvey, Tombstone and Richardson Mountains and the Continental Divide, I was down to 217 pounds. I had lost 55 pounds. It seemed my wife had got back the man she married.

Getting behind the wheel of our car felt very strange. Yesterday, I had been walking on the snow and today it was incredibly warm weather, in the mid-seventies. The grass was a lush green and the leaves were still on the trees. We pulled into the driveway of our west mountain home and, to me, it looked like the most wonderful place on earth.

Carol showed me the Saturday Hamilton Spectator. She had inserted my picture and an announcement welcoming me home.

Exhausted from the long flight, I lay down for a rest. My dog Smooch lay on my chest as if to say, "I'm not going to let anybody take you away". There was a part of my spirit that was still in Inuvik, above the Arctic Circle. It would stay there, calling me to return, to finish my expedition. I now waited for the mighty MacKenzie River to freeze so I could continue on the ice trail, to travel through the Arctic and arrive at my final destination of Tuktoyaktuk. For now, I was happy to be under Smooch's house arrest.

In the afternoon, Carol had to go to work, so James and I went to a movie. It felt so good to be with my son again, talking and laughing and voting together, thumbs up - thumbs down, Siskel and Ebert style, at the movie previews. The movie we watched was "Jurassic Park The Lost World". During the movie, I thought about Canada and how the majority of Canadians have never experienced life above the Arctic Circle. In a way, the Arctic is Canada's Lost World. I will not forget the spectacular geography or the warm people of the Arctic. This Lost World has found a home in my heart.

Saturday, October 11, 1997

Carol had organized an open house to celebrate my arrival home, and the success of the expedition to date. As she prepared for the evening, cooking and cleaning, I was busy putting over 400 expedition photographs in chronological order, in two photo albums. A giant map of Canada was on display for our guests, with a red line tracing my path through the 47 cities where I'd given speeches during my *To The Top Canada* expedition.

The guests started arriving early. Soon our house was humming with activity. Along with the giant Canada map, helium balloons, welcome home gifts and news coverage of the expedition from across the country were on display in the living room. The dining room and kitchen were set up for refreshments. In the family room was a display of photographs, my beat-up bicycle, and mementos I had received from cities across Canada. A reporter from the Spectator came to interview me. At first, we had trouble connecting as I was so busy answering questions from our guests. Carol broke through the crowd and told me I'd better speak to the reporter because she was now interviewing James about the expedition. I came into James' den to find my son busy with his own press conference. He answered the reporter's questions clearly and knowledgeably. James had lived the expedition for the last seven months. He knew where his dad was at all times and he developed a geographical knowledge of Canada far superior to the one I received when I went to school. I was proud of my son as he fielded the tough questions with ease.

Joining the interview, I found that the reporter only needed a few quotes from me as James had provided all the logistical information on the *To The Top Canada* expedition. Carol grabbed me again - it was time to cut the cake. A giant chocolate cake (my favourite) had been prepared with a large Canadian flag and an illustration of me on my bicycle.

Carol said a few words welcoming everyone and thanking them for coming. I said a few words, taking this opportunity to especially thank Carol. I explained how, at the beginning, I envisioned an organization to support me that had fifty people giving me full logistical support. When it finally came time to leave, my organizational chart looked like this:

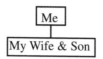

I told everyone that Carol and James had sacrificed much with me being away. In my eyes they are great Canadians. I cut the cake and then was swarmed by people who thanked me for what I had done for Canada. I actually didn't get a piece of cake until the open house was over and everyone had left. The evening had been a wonderful celebration, ending a full hour and a half after the scheduled finish time. It was the first of a few special events that would take place while I was home.

I thought constantly of the tasks to be accomplished, in order to be prepared for Tuktoyaktuk. My "To Do" list included:-

1) Repair my bike or source a new bike for the ice trail trip.
2) Order metal stud tires from Finland.
3) Write a clothing company to see if they would donate special subzero clothing.
4) Write a shoe company to see if they would donate special sub-zero boots.
5) Write the Eskimo Inn to see if they would donate a room for a few nights in January.
6) Write Tuktoyaktuk to see if they would donate a room for two nights when I got to Tuktoyaktuk.
7) Write truck rental company to see if they would donate a truck to follow me on the ice trail.
8) Write to Air Canada to see if they would donate a flight home.
9) Keep media informed of the current status of the *To The Top Canada* expedition.
10) Ride my bike to keep myself in good physical condition.

There would be challenges in the days and months ahead. Tonight's celebration was a release from my busy agenda. It was nice unwind with friends and family.

Friday, October 24, 1997

Carol and I enjoyed breakfast in bed at the Holiday Inn on King in Toronto. It was the hotel that Magna International had designated for the VIP's participating in their "Voices Of A Nation" celebration, at Roy Thomson Hall.

The previous night, we had dinner with Frank Stronach, Chairman of the Board of

Magna. The group had taken over the Veronas Restaurant, for a private dinner. For the first time, the Invitational Participants had a chance to meet one another. This year's Invitational Participants were:-

Ted Byfield - President, United Western Communications Ltd.
The Honourable Nellie J. Cournoyea - Chair & C.E.O., Inuvialuit Regional Corporation
Pauline Couture - President, Pauline Couture & Associates
Arthur C. Erickson - Architect
The Honourable Willard Z. Estey - Supreme Court Justice
Edward L. Greenspan, Q.C. - Solicitor
John T. Mayberry - President & C.E.O., Dofasco Inc
Chris Robertson - Professional Speaker
Steve Smith - (aka Red Green) - T.V. Personality
Dr. Ken Walker - Physician and newspaper columnist
Adam H. Zimmerman - Retired Chairman & CEO, Noranda Forest Inc.

Frank Stronach was just across from me at the dinner table. One of directors of the Magna Board, who worked for the Royal Bank, asked how much it really costs to make a car. Frank estimated the materials make up 20% of the retail cost of a car.

In dinner discussion, Frank talked about how we need to stimulate the economy. He mentioned that he doesn't see new factories being built in Canada, only U.S. companies building warehouses for their Canadian distribution. Frank was right.

Frank was making an impact on Canada's future because he was creating a forum for new ideas to make Canada stronger. You can be sure the book *As Prime Minister, I Would . .* is being read by the Prime Minister and every aspiring Prime Minister in the country. It was fascinating to spend the previous evening with Frank Stronach one of the greatest entrepreneurs in Canada's history.

Carol and I met for lunch with a Professional Speaker, Leslie Lorette, who is a friend of mine. There are no media outlets, let alone media network services, in Tuktoyaktuk. I didn't want to arrive in Tuk, completing a great Canadian accomplishment, with no way of letting the country know about it. Leslie was taking a detailed media list from me and would be notifying the media that the *To The Top Canada* expedition had been completed, after receiving my confirmation call from Tuk. Most of the country's media networks are based in Toronto. My Bell Canada long distance bills had been so high, they were off the chart. Carol had paid these bills, that were hundreds of dollars every month, as the phone was my only link with home. Faxing a media release in Toronto for Leslie would be a local call, whereas for us it was another long distance call we couldn't afford. My cousin Beverley Godin, in Pembroke, was doing the same thing for me in the Ottawa area. I deeply appreciated their help.

At the downtown Toronto photography studio of Barry Shainbaum, we were delighted to have a visit with Barry and see more pictures taken in Point Pelee, Bracebridge and Fort Nelson.

Back in our hotel room, we dressed in our formal wear. I had rented a tux - the one I had at home fit me when I was 272 pounds! All the VIP's met in the "Green Room" at Roy Thomson Hall. Carol and I sipped wine as we mingled with everyone. This was a far cry from the Dempster mud.

Frank Stronach made a special presentation to the Invitational Authors. He praised us as authors, noting that the world is full of critics, but there are very few people who have solutions and the courage to submit their ideas to scrutiny.

At the reception upstairs, the black tie audience was enjoying a pre-show cocktail party, while being entertained by a musical duo (flute and harp). The audience was a "who's who" of Canadian celebrities.

In the magnificent hall, we were seated in the second row, right behind Frank Stronach and the wonderful university students who had won the essay contest, to become the ten student essayists in *As Prime Minister, I Would...* During the program, footage of all of the co-authors was shown, including the video of me in Whitehorse. The presentation was greeted with long applause.

After the formal presentations, we were treated to a wonderful concert by the group Great Big Sea. One of the members of the Newfoundland group, looked into the audience of black tie tuxedos and formal gowns and announced that we were the best dressed audience they had ever played for!

After the official program, the audience was treated to a fabulous buffet. My wife Carol couldn't believe it when the man in the buffet line in front of her, former Ontario Premier Bill Davis, personally served her, by dishing up her plate. All evening, people approached and asked me to autograph their copy of *As Prime Minister, I Would...* It was a wonderful celebration of Canada, and I appreciated the kind words and acknowledgement. Still, my mind drifted back to Inuvik, where I had unfinished business...

Sunday, January 4, 1998

It was time for me to fly back to the Arctic to continue my expedition. The alarm clock went off at 5:00 am. James, who had stayed up until midnight the night before, considered the early waking cruel and unusual punishment. The car was packed with my gear last night. All we had to do was put the bike on the car's bike rack and we were ready to drive from our home in Hamilton to Toronto's Pearson International Airport

On the ride to the airport, I thought of the last three months and all the work that had gone into getting ready for the final, but most challenging, week of the expedition.

. I was wearing my Sorel Arctic boots which would keep my feet warm in temperatures of 100 degrees below zero Fahrenheit. The boots were too big to pack, so I had to wear them. Marks Work Warehouse was like a Canadian angel, helping me get the boots from the manufacturer. They used their retail clout to have one pair made, just for me. My shoe size is 12 triple E. When I went to my local Marks Work Warehouse store to pick them up, they told me there was "no charge." I tried to get a himalayan suit but the supplier could not find a suit in Canada or the United States that would fit my 200 pound-plus build. I was going to wear my snowmobile suit, with several levels of clothes underneath and my bright yellow jacket over top. I had practiced cycling over 100 kilometres wearing this clothing and my new boots. I felt ready.

My bike had been rebuilt "again." New gears, new breaks, new rear rim, new extra bright tail light and new Arctic tires from Finland, with over 200 metal studs per tire. The repairs cost me over $1,000. A large Hamilton corporation donated $500 towards the repairs. They wanted to remain anonymous because they have a donation policy whereby they don't contribute to individuals and their personal projects. The CEO and President over ruled the policy because he thought that the *To The Top Canada* expedition was a very important initiative for Canada. I was flying back to Inuvik, courtesy of Frank Stronach and the Magna for Scholarship program. The return airfare from Inuvik to Toronto was over $1,700. Air Canada gave me a reduced fare of $300 and NWT Air gave me a free fare for the flight home. When I arrived at the airport, I discovered the special freight charge to ship my bicycle had gone from a 1997 price of $25 to a 1998 price of $65.

After checking in for my flight and checking all my gear, we popped out of the airport and went over to the Airport Marriott for breakfast. Carol and James laughed as I walked into the luxurious surroundings wearing my enormous, white Arctic boots. When James first tried my boots on, he looked like an Apollo astronaut and he said, " Neil Armstrong is on the moon!" The staff gave me, and my giant boots, double-takes because there was no snow on the ground in Toronto. We had a nice breakfast in the luxury of the Marriott. I was a little shocked that breakfast for 3 cost $40, but it was another way of thanking my family for all their help to get ready for the last leg of the expedition.

After breakfast, we walked to our car at the Marriott parking lot to return to the airport. Carol was squeezing my hand hard as the time of my departure approached.

At the airport, before I went through the domestic security checkpoint in Terminal 2, we went into the airport chapel. Carol and James prayed for my safety and I prayed for the Lord to comfort them and free them from worry.

We gave each other long hugs, with tears in our eyes, and kissed good-bye. The expedition made me realize how wonderful it was to be home. I had cherished the last three months.

Through security, I walked down to gate 83 and immediately boarded my flight. Our flight was a half hour late taking off. The in-flight movie was "The Game", starring

Michael Douglas. It is the story of a man who is subjected to more stress than any person can stand. This was not the best choice of a movie for a flight running late, with a tight connection in Edmonton.

As we flew over the Prairies, I looked below to see the ground carpeted in white snow. The real winter had arrived.

In Edmonton, I walked down to the NWT Air gate and immediately boarded again. Over the intercom, the pilot announced that we would be on the ground for 45 minutes, while connecting passengers and their baggage were brought on board. I was very patient, knowing that the baggage included my survival gear and bike. The flight stopped in Yellowknife where we changed planes, bound for Inuvik. The pilot let us know the current temperature in Yellowknife was 38 degrees below zero Celsius.

I had noticed in Toronto, from my window seat, that four trucks were de-icing planes, where there was no snow. In Edmonton, where I could see 2 to 3 cm's of snow lying on the wings, there was only one de-icing truck. The single truck de-iced us, coating the wing with an orange material, all over. If I was in the Operations Department of Air Canada, I'd send a couple of Toronto's de-icing trucks to Edmonton immediately.

The service on NWT Air was fantastic. The flight to Yellowknife was almost full, yet I found the flight attendants to be energetic, pleasant and specifically concerned that all my needs were looked after. I flew economy to Yellowknife, as there is no business class. The service in NWT economy was better than the business class service I received on my flight from Toronto to Edmonton. I had used one of my Aeroplan Prestige Upgrade Certificates to fly to Edmonton, in business class.

There was no movie on this flight, and I found my mind wandering. It occurred to me that I had seen an ad, in my local television guide, for a Discovery Channel special that would be on television tonight back at home. There was a giant picture of a walrus with long tusks. The headline read: "Sinks boats. Kills polar bears. Stalks humans. Film at 8pm." The detailed description read as follows:

"Few people would relate this behavior with the walrus. Due to its remote habitat, the floating ice pans of the Arctic Ocean, this fascinating creature is shrouded in mystery. Now, for the first time ever, you can see rare footage of one of the high north's most formidable mammals. Discovery's Sunday Showcase presents "Toothwalkers: Giants Of The Arctic Ice". Tonight at 8pm."

I had never heard of a killer walrus before reading this advertisement. As if polar bears, the coldest temperatures on the planet and riding a bicycle over ice on the Arctic Ocean wasn't enough danger. What were they going to throw at me next? Space aliens... I just smiled at the thought.

In Yellowknife, we deplaned to switch aircraft. Although it was 2:30 pm in the afternoon, the sun was low in the sky at the sunset level. The moon was high. As I walked to the terminal building, the snow crunched under my boots. The cold air immediately gave my bare face a slight stinging sensation. This was really cold and I wasn't in the Arctic yet.

On my final flight to Inuvik, I watched the sun set into a sea of blackness that covered the north. It was an eerie feeling, knowing that, for the first time in my life, I would not see the sun for a week. No bright yellow round orb to light my way. There would be no warmth on my face. It was now one more reason why I had to get to Tuktoyaktuk to finish the *To The Top Canada* expedition. My ultimate reward was to win back God's privilege and have the sun shine in my life again.

When I arrived in Inuvik, it was completely dark. I looked for Rev. Larry Robertson, who had offered to pick me up. At first, I did not see him. My bike arrived with no plastic on it. It looked different but I couldn't put my finger on it at the time. I called Larry, to learn that he had only just arrived home himself, after the weather had stranded him at Sacks Harbour for a week. His church vestry meeting that day was cancelled because the church wasn't sure he'd make it. Larry was at the Inuvik airport in ten minutes.

On the drive back to town, Larry told me that the Sunrise Festival fireworks had been rescheduled to this evening. It seems my report of the sun's demise was premature. After having no sun for an extended period of time in the Arctic, tomorrow would be the first sunrise. The sun was scheduled to rise at 1:38 pm and set at 2:23 pm. This meant a full day of work would be 45 minutes. (They must pay a lot of over time in Inuvik).

The fireworks tonight would be the only fireworks this year in Inuvik and was sure to be attended by all the community. This meant that my tentatively planned Canada Rally, for tonight, might have no attendance. We agreed to change the Canada Rally to Monday evening, at 8:00 pm. Our plan was to let the radio station know so they could inform everyone in the community. We stopped by the church and made a large sign on the church door saying the Canada Rally would be postponed to Monday at 8:00 pm, due to fireworks tonight.

Larry dropped me off at the Eskimo Inn, which had donated my room for the entire leg of the Inuvik-Tuk journey. It almost felt like coming home, now that I was back. I locked my bike in the cage area under the stairs. I had twenty minutes to get settled before Larry would be picking me up to go to the Sunrise Festival fireworks.

We drove to a large clearing, outside of town. It was an area the size of a large grocery store parking lot, that had been plowed by the town. The Inuvik Volunteer fire-fighters were dressed in their gear, their fire trucks parked by three fifteen-foot high piles of wooden pallets.

The parking lot soon filled up with cars and trucks, all facing the wooden pallets with their motors running. The firefighters set the pallets on fire and the flames from each of the three piles rose fifty feet in the air. Everyone got out of their vehicles, leaving their motors running and leaving their vehicles unlocked and walked to the giant blazing fires. The heat kept us warm as it was 8:00 pm in January, in the Arctic and I estimated the temperature was forty degrees below zero. If you faced the fire, the heat was too much for your face. If you turned your face away, the cold quickly froze your exposed skin. I quickly developed a technique of rotating my face from cold to hot and back to cold. Then, the fireworks began. They were spectacular. I have seen a lot of fireworks in my lifetime but, with the exception of Disney World, I have never seen a better display. Something Disney will never be able to do is show the effect of fireworks in -40 degree temperatures. For some reason I don't understand, it made the fireworks display more intense.

When the festival was over, I went over to Larry's house and enjoyed butter rum hot chocolate. It was the best I'd ever had.

Monday, January 5, 1998

Awake at 5 am (which was actually 7 am eastern time), I organized my gear for the day. As I got my bicycle battery out, I realized what had looked different on my bike at the airport. My special Arctic lights had been removed. I called NWT Air, to report that they were missing. I would now have to rely on my night vision and the lights of the truck that would be driving with me. This would be the first time I had a support vehicle but now it was an essential tool to ensure my safety. Even with the support truck, there was still a stronger potential for danger without adequate bike lighting.

The threat of a polar bear attack was very real. Their colour camouflages them against the snow. They can be almost on top of you, before you know it. The only analogy I can give to describe this challenge would be if you cycled your bike through the African Lion Safari compound, with the family car behind you. How safe would you feel?

My breakfast at the Eskimo Inn was cut short, when the CHUM national news radio network called to do an interview.

I was then picked up to go to Delta Auto Rental, to rent a truck as a safety vehicle for the trip to Tuktoyaktuk. Warren Flight was to be my volunteer driver for the next four days. At Delta Auto Rentals, I met Judi Falsnes, the owner, who worked out of her home. I signed all the forms, taking responsibility for the vehicle. This meant that if the truck broke through the ice, never to be seen again, I had just bought the truck. Judi had already been a big help to me, by finding Warren, to be my volunteer driver.

Warren and I headed to the Western Arctic CBC building, where they were expecting me at 9:30 am. I did one interview in the studio. Another CBC reporter returned to the Eskimo Inn with me, to record some bike sounds. The reporter, named Candice, followed me up to my hotel room where I was going to get my gear to pack in the truck. She was fascinated with my flare pen, which is used for bear defence. She turned on her portable tape recorder and taped an extensive, lengthy interview. I noticed, as I spoke, that the hotel cleaning lady was in my bathroom. Now she was trapped because she didn't want to disturb the interview. Even after the interview, she was too embarrassed to come out of the bathroom. I just grabbed my gear and headed out.

The temperature was 38 degrees below zero. Candice ran behind my bike and taped the sound. It was so cold that the snow crunched as my tires came in contact with it. I can only describe it as if your bike was riding over Captain Crunch cereal. As I rode out of Inuvik, away from the town lights, I soon learned how black it was in the Arctic. It was 10:30 am and pitch black. I went down a small hill and turned onto the ice trail on the MacKenzie River. Nearby were boats, frozen into the ice. I could hear the deep sounds of ice cracking as I rode. My heart raced at the thought of drowning in freezing water. It didn't help that at home I had recently seen the movie "Titanic", produced by Canadian James Cameron. The sight of Titanic passengers freezing in the North Atlantic was gruesome. After a while, I calmed down.

Warren is from Trinity Bay, Newfoundland and this was his first time on the ice path to Tuktoyaktuk. Warren came to Inuvik 10 months ago, to find work. In Newfoundland, there was no employment in the fishing industry. It's not that he didn't have a job, but as a fisherman he would go out and drop his net and there were just no more fish. Fishing policy in Canada had been decided by political agendas, not by ecology. As a result, fish stocks have been devastated. Despite the personal hardship of leaving his home in Newfoundland to find work, Warren still had a huge heart. Warren was giving me four days of his time to help Canada. He loves his country.

The ice trail was tougher than I thought. The ice made a rough surface and the snow drifted deep at certain points. I shifted to an easier gear and pedaled on. At times, my front tire cut through the snow like an ice breaker. I thought the ice trail would be plowed regularly, but that was not the case. Frequently, my front tire would be brought to a halt but I kept pedaling which caused my rear wheel to spin left and right. I passed two pick-up trucks and a skidoo in the morning. I saw Polar bear tracks criss-crossing the ice trail. They were larger than the Grizzlie tracks I had seen. I was shivering. I had to take my ski goggles off. In this extreme cold, the fog on my glasses from exhaling turned to ice immediately, on the glass surface.

As I cycled, I kept my mind busy doing math calculations. How far to Tuktoyaktuk? What is the total distance I've travelled in my expedition? What would be my estimated arrival time in Tuktoyaktuk? I hummed every song I know. I wondered if the musical, "Annie", has ever played in Inuvik. The title song, "The Sun Will Come Out Tomorrow", may be greeted with skepticism, in the land of six month darkness. The sun was supposed to make a short appearance today. At 1:00 pm, it got a little lighter, still dark grey, with heavy cloud cover. It looked like the sky, at home, just before a bad thunderstorm. I saw no sun on Monday.

I had hoped to ride 70 km today but could only do 51.9 km by 6:00 pm. It was time to return to Inuvik, as I was leading the Canada Rally this evening. I found a large snow boulder on the trail to use as a landmark. I loaded my bike onto the truck. It took us 45 minutes to drive the 51.9 km on the ice trail, back to Inuvik.

We first went to the Arctic Tire to fuel up the truck. This is the only gas station in Inuvik. As the pump rung up a small fortune, I looked closer to investigate. I was shocked to see regular gas was 93.9 cents per litre. I had witnessed, first hand, the power of a monopoly and the cost of living in the Arctic.

Warren took me to the Anglican Church, where I wanted to retrieve my bike trailer. Also waiting for me was my bag, which I had to abandon in the Yukon, on the Dempster Highway, to reduce my weight after my gears stripped. The RCMP had coordinated its safe delivery to the Anglican Church, much cheaper than Fedex!

I told Larry I would change at the Eskimo Inn and be right back. It was now after seven and I didn't have time to shower. I got out of my wet clothes and into my dry ones. My clothing kept the cold out, but it also had the effect of turning my survival clothing into a sauna, as my body heat from cycling had nowhere to go. Sweat completely drenched my body and my inner layer of clothes. If I ever stopped cycling and generating heat, my wet clothing would quickly freeze and I could die. I grabbed my presentation materials. Warren drove me back to the Anglican Church, and then took the truck home. He had a place to plug in the truck's block heater and I didn't.

At the Church, I put on a cassette of motivational music, to help inspire people as they walked into the church. Rev. Larry liked the music, but I could tell by his smile that this was something new for Inuvik. We had a very small turnout, but the program was enjoyed by all who came. Rev. Larry said we were competing with Inuvik T.V. Bingo. If I had known that, we could have played bingo at the Canada Rally.

I walked back to my room at the Eskimo Inn from the church. This was a mistake. I forgot my gloves, and with my presentation materials to carry, I couldn't put my hands in my pockets. My fingers soon started to hurt in the subzero temperatures. I used my conditioning to run to the hotel, to lessen the pain period.

With my first free time of the day, I called Carol to report on my progress. She was worried sick, knowing this was my first day on the dreaded ice trail. After reassuring her I was fine, it was time for supper at 11:00 pm. I had to eat because I knew I needed the food energy tomorrow. I ran across the street to the Roost as the hotel restaurant was closed, and ordered take-out. This time I wore my mittens.

Back in my room, I ate supper. I didn't enjoy it. My mind was preoccupied planning contingencies if I had to stay in the Arctic longer because of slow progress on the ice trail. Today I fell 18.1 kilometres short of my goal. I had planned to ride 70 kilometres on Monday, 70 kilometres on Tuesday and then just under 50 kilometres on Wednesday. I decided that Monday just became my 50 kilometre day, and Tuesday and Wednesday would have to become my 70 kilometre days. I did not sleep well, tossing and turning all night.

Tuesday, January 6, 1998

My wake up call came at 6:00 am but I was already awake and tired from a night that gave me no rest. I'd asked Warren to meet me at 7:00 a.m., to head out to our last point on the ice trail. It was hot in the truck so I kept my gear off until we arrived. Then I suited up and, at the snow boulder, I headed out for another day at 8:00 a.m. It was colder today, 40 below zero, but the sky was clear. I could see the stars and, for the first time, I saw the northern lights clearly. Everywhere in the black Arctic sky, there was bright, fluorescent lime green northern lights - Aurora Borealis. They just hung in the air, like a department store of ultra bright green curtains. The sky got bright at 1:30 p.m., a hint of sun on the horizon. It was as if God had snipped a sliver of the sun and placed it on the Arctic snow.

During a warm up break in the truck, I heard the radio interview that was taped in my room yesterday, on the CBC national radio news. The announcer began with the headline "Right now, Chris Robertson is cycling on the ice trail from Inuvik to Tuktoyaktuk, in 40 below zero temperatures for Canadian unity." I replied, "No I'm not. I'm in the truck taking a break!" Warren commented, "You just can't trust what you hear on the news these days."

Yesterday, I told Warren about the hotel cleaning lady trapped in my bathroom during the interview and he laughed. After hearing the actual interview today, Warren informed me that at home last night, he discovered the trapped hotel cleaning lady was his wife, Roxanne. I told Warren to tell Roxanne that her story would definitely be in my book.

I passed a very large snow plough truck. As it went by, the sound of ice cracking below me was the most intense I had heard yet. My heart jumped up to my throat, again.

I had to ride 70 kilometres today and I wasn't leaving the ice trail until I'd done it. My body got extremely sore and stiff. My cycling pace slowed to a crawl but I kept going. Twelve hours later, at 8:00 p.m., I cracked the 70 kilometre barrier. There was no distinguishing mark to use to identify this spot. I discovered my GPS would not work in temperatures this cold. Warren had the idea to use an empty chocolate chip cookie bag with some snow in it, on top of a snow bank. Hopefully, no animals in the night would have a craving for chocolate chip cookies and respond to the scent. We also measured the kilometres back to Inuvik, as a "B" plan.

Warren put the pedal to the metal, getting us back to Inuvik just after 9:30 p.m. Our first trip was a return visit to the gas station. I could hear the gas pump singing, "We're In The Money!", as I was being soaked again. Warren dropped me off at the Eskimo Inn. I was too sore from battling the ice trail to run across the street for supper. I noticed they delivered, so I ordered a pizza. The delivery charge was $4.00, for walking it across the street, but I paid it gladly. I was so tired I could only eat 2 slices. In my bathroom mirror, I noticed my cheeks and around my eyes were frost-bitten. It felt like a bad sunburn.

I laid down, exhausted. This time, I fell straight to sleep.

Wednesday, January 7, 1998

At 5:30 a.m., I packed up everything to vacate my room at the Eskimo Inn because I planned to be at the Tuk Inn this evening.

On the drive up the ice trail, we listened to a fun, inspirational tape I made for my personal use. It had songs from Indiana Jones, Superman, Mission Impossible, Flashdance, Top Gun, Rocky, Apollo 13, Beverly Hills Cop and Star Wars. I was so pumped, I forgot about my sore muscles and stiffness, I felt ready to go to Tuktoyaktuk without a bike, if I had to. Based on having to drive further up the ice trail to a starting point today and based on my experience yesterday of taking 12 hours to go 70 kilometres, I had left a message for Western Arctic CBC and on my voicemail that I expected to arrive in Tuktoyaktuk at 8:45 p.m.

It soon became clear that the excitement of my final cycling day had afforded the benefits of adrenaline pumping. I was flying. By mid morning, I had mentally revised my anticipated arrival time to as early as 3:00 p.m. I was in awe of my own progress. I found a radio equipped ice trail truck that relayed my revised arrival time to CBC. It was colder today, at 50 below zero. On the radio, during a short break, they said the windchill was about 80 degrees below zero. I could see sweat leave my forehead and actually crystallize to ice, immediately in the air, before it hit the ground.

At one point, I took my hand out of my glove for just five seconds to snap a picture of Warren with the Canadian flag by the truck. In that short time, my fingers started to sting from the cold.

Soon, the ice trail diverted from the centre of the MacKenzie River, right out into the Arctic Ocean. The ice trail doesn't hug the shoreline on the way to Tuktoyaktuk. Instead, it goes 5 to 10 kilometres out from the coast. Now I was really worried about the ice. My fears were well founded. An ice trail maintenance truck, heading south, stopped to warn me of cracks in the ice and sea water gushing up. The maintenance worker said, "We always have this problem around high tide." I worked to avoid the deep cracks and studied the trail closely so that the many cracks would not swallow my bike tires.

On the ice trail, three Inuvialuit men in snowmobiles, pulling large homemade wooden toboggan trailers, stopped to say hello. They were out hunting. After an hour of cycling on the Arctic Ocean, I could see the lights of Tuktoyaktuk in the distance. I took out my Canadian flag and rode towards Tuk, flying the Maple Leaf proudly. A huge, beautiful three quarter moon hung low in the sky directly over Tuktoyaktuk, almost as a beacon leading me in. I rode slowly, to savour the moment in the final kilometres. All the places and all the people I'd met during the expedition flashed through my mind. My eyes filled with tears as I got closer. I was realizing my impossible dream.

I pulled into the Tuk Inn at 3:25 p.m. and walked over to the truck to thank Warren. I shook his hand. Warren's quiet, constant help was a source of strength and peace of mind for me.

I walked into the Tuk Inn and met John, the owner. He assigned me my room for the night. Before he did this, he had to think for a moment. Court was in town and he couldn't put the Crown Attorney and Defence Lawyer beside each other. I asked if there had been a problem before. John told me that a Defence lawyer once was mad about losing his case, believing that the Crown Attorney had listened through the hotel wall when he was conferring with his client. I wonder how Canadian Raymond Burr, who played lawyer Perry Mason, would have handled this case.

The only phone available to customers in the hotel was in the office. John let me use it to call home. Carol answered and I said, "Will you accept a collect call from Tuktoyaktuk?" Both Carol, and James on another extension, screamed in delight. Carol couldn't believe my fast progress. I told her I could smell victory. Carol knows that I face every challenge with laser focused determination. She said she had a long list of media from across Canada that wanted to speak with me. I told her I needed to get out of my wet clothing first, then I would call her back. I was soaking wet, from head to toe. My constant body heat, generated by the incredible exertion, was the only thing that prevented me from succumbing to the Arctic cold.

After changing into dry clothes, I called Carol back and got a long list of reporters across Canada who wanted to do phone interviews. I returned their calls for the next two hours.

In the Tuk Inn restaurant, Warren and I enjoyed the special of chicken noodle soup, roast ham and potatoes, with pie for dessert.

In my room, after supper, I filled out a number of postcards that I had promised to send from the Arctic. As the quiet set in and my adrenaline slowed, my body hurt with aches and pains everywhere. It didn't bother me because these were honoured aches and pains, to be worn as badges of valour.

Thursday, January 8, 1998

With my first scheduled appointment of CBC North radio talk show interview at 8:30 a.m., it seemed to be an easier morning here at the Tuk Inn. The room we were in had a sign on the door that said, "Susan Aglukark Slept Here". The celebrity status of this entertainer had been immortalized with this Tuk Inn door acknowledgement. Other people had stayed at the Tuk Inn, including Metallica and Courtney Love had their names on the doors. John indicated the Metallica guys were nice, and although John didn't say anything, I could tell Courtney Love had been "high maintenance" for him. I wondered if after I'd left, John would be adding another sign saying, "Chris Robertson Slept Here". I was concerned because this may give people the impression I was sleeping with Susan Aglukark!

I read the final books of the Old Testament. There were stories from Prophets who talked about how evildoers would be punished, so you must return to the path of righteousness. I knew that this message could apply to me. In the three months home, waiting for the ice trail to freeze, I had been seduced by the pleasures of civilization. I had done some good during the break, like coordinating Project Santa Claus. This was my personal effort to help 34 people in seven single parent families experiencing economic hardship, to have a nicer Christmas. In my heart, I knew I was still a long way from being the person God wanted me to be. In the second last book in the Old Testament Zechariah Chapter 14 verse 6-7, I read:

"When that time comes, there will no longer be cold or frost, nor any darkness. There will always be daylight, even at nighttime. When this will happen is known only to the Lord."

This was the "Arctic"! The reference to the end of cold, my enemy for the last three days. The reference to daylight, even at nighttime, only happens in the land of the Midnight Sun where I was, in Tuktoyaktuk. The significance of this message hit me like a baseball bat and took my breath away. My Bible is 1395 pages long. What was the mathematical probability of finishing on exactly the last official day of my *To The Top Canada* expedition. I had become "bored" reading the book of Numbers, had switched to the New Testament, reading it completely and only then had I come back to read the rest of the Old Testament. What were the odds of finishing by reading this exact passage, at this exact moment in time. The message was clear to me. God was giving me a second chance...

At breakfast, I heard the phone ring. The cook swore at the interruption because he was busy with a full restaurant and no waitress. The call was for me. He handed me the phone in the kitchen and ran back to his food, before it burned. It was CHUM radio, again. The satellite phone line from Tuktoyaktuk to Toronto was not that good. I also had to contend with the noise from the giant HVAC fans over the kitchen grill. I could barely hear the program host. I tried my best to answer his questions or the question I thought he was asking. This would be the first of many radio and newspaper calls I received. After other interviews, Warren and I headed out in the darkness.

I rode to the Nursing Station, which is like a small hospital and presented the staff with my best wishes and Friend of Canada certificates. On my way to the RCMP station, I was pulled over by Mayor Eddie Dillon in his pickup truck. Mayor Dillon welcomed me and said he would meet me at the Mangilaluk School at 10 am, twenty minutes from now.

At the RCMP detachment, I learned that there were five officers and one clerical person. I left my best wishes and Friend of Canada certificates for all of these people serving Canada. Time was tight and I wasn't exactly sure where the school was, in Tuktoyaktuk. I asked Warren to drive ahead in the truck, find the school then come back and lead me there to save time. Warren drove off. I took my giant Canadian flag which I was holding up proudly and started riding towards the general direction of the school. In five minutes, I was at the Mangilaluk School, no Warren in sight. A person from the Hamlet Office came over to me and said, "We're not quite ready yet. Could you just wait until 10:30 am and bring your bike, when you come in?" I was glad for the reprieve, with Warren lost and the Tuktoyaktuk certificate in his truck. Ten minutes later Warren, pulled up, not via the road but by driving the truck over the school yard. I kidded him, "I guess we know which is the faster vehicle."

Warren took my slides and cassette music into the school. I followed, in two minutes. The school gym was packed with Tuktoyaktuk people, young and old. As I wheeled my bike into the gym, there was a tunnel line for me with the Inuvialuit drummers playing their drums, on both sides. Everyone else clapped and cheered when I appeared. There was a huge, multi-coloured CONGRATULATIONS banner on the wall, running the whole length of the gym. Tears came to my eyes, at this outpouring of warmth from the entire community. There were chairs set up behind a microphone. In the chairs, sat the Hamlet Council and the Elders.

Mayor Eddie Dillon welcomed me and saluted my determination and dedication to Canada. He then asked me to say a few words to the school about my journey. Before I let the Mayor sit down, I asked him to come forward and receive the *To The Top Canada* certificate for Tuktoyaktuk.

I summarized the certificate for the audience and then gave a short synopsis of my journey and the purpose of the *To The Top Canada* expedition. I invited everyone to join me and experience my journey in a three-minute multimedia presentation. I had slides of my trip to Inuvik arranged to inspirational Canadian music. When the first slide came up, the entire audience let out a loud "aaahhhh". The projector was shooting across the gym and the giant image looked like the Cinesphere a large Imax theatre at Ontario Place. Then the next slide came up a couple of seconds later and everyone said "oooooooo". It occurred to me, suddenly, that this may be the first time some of the Tuktoyaktuk residents were seeing images of southern Canada! My presentation was a hit. Mayor Dillon presented me with a fur hat and a Tuktoyaktuk plate. The local RCMP came forward and presented me with a Tuktoyaktuk T-shirt. It was

Canada-red, with a logo of the RCMP musical ride, but the mountie was riding a polar bear instead of a horse! Then Mayor Dillon introduced the drummers and invited the dancers to come forward. They performed to seven dances, in my honour. At the beginning of the seventh dance, one performer asked audience members to join in. After the song started, I went up. Listening to and feeling the rhythm of the drums, I closely watched the young girl beside me and copied her movements. The audience cheered their approval.

At the end of the performance, I thanked the dancers, the drummers, the elders, the Hamlet Council, the RCMP, the Mayor, my driver Warren, the teachers, the students, and all the people of Tuktoyaktuk. A crowd of people surrounded me, shaking my hand and patting my back and shoulders. This was a moment that money could never buy. You can't buy respect, admiration and love which were the most important gifts I had received today. I just let the feelings sink in, knowing I would enjoy memories of this moment for the rest of my life.

The school principal asked if it was possible for me to visit students in the classroom. We planned for me to join the students in the afternoon, following some more scheduled media interviews.

Warren and I headed to the Post Office, where I mailed post cards to people from the top of mainland Canada. Warren and I ran back to the Tuk Inn, where we quickly gobbled down a couple of hot roast beef sandwiches. John said it was the first roast beef he'd sold in three months. I didn't want to ask him why.

At the Hamlet Office, Mayor Dillon let me use his office for a number of telephone talk show interviews. When the interviews were done, we were into the very short period of the day where there was light in Tuk. Warren and I blitzed the community in five minutes, taking all the pictures we could. Soon, it was dark again and we were off to the school. They had a written schedule prepared for me, outlining where I was to speak, to every grade from 1 to 12. I spoke to every class. Some classes had artwork to present to me, "drawings of Chris Robertson". I treasured every one. Then, it was back to the Tuk Inn, where John had time to prepare my bill. Speaking from his heart, John told me he had lost money last month but supported what I was doing. He said I was the most enthusiastic person he'd ever met. He said it wasn't much, but he donated our suppers from last evening and reduced the price of our room rental. I appreciated John's kindness.

Warren and I returned to the Hamlet Office, curious to take up an earlier invitation to see the "Ice House". Now, I thought maybe Tuktoyaktuk had a winter carnival and the Ice House was some kind of an ice sculpture. When they pulled out the legal waiver forms to sign, before we entered the Ice House, I knew I was into something more serious. We were taken over to a small shack. After entering the door, we saw a hatch over the ground. When the hatch was opened, it revealed a deep well, where a ladder dropped down vertically and, after 50 feet, disappeared into darkness.

It was a narrow, wooden ladder covered in ice and snow. My large Arctic boots barely fit on the wooden steps. I followed our guide into the sea of blackness, deep under the ground. At the bottom, I turned on my flashlight to reveal catacombs of cave tunnels that were very small. I had to crouch, so as not to hit the ceiling. At some points I had to turn my wide shoulders to fit through the cave tunnel. Ice crystals hung from the ceiling and walls, long and thin. They resembled thousands of ice butterflies, suspended from the ceiling. At the bottom of the walls, I could see the swirling stripes of the brown permafrost. It looked like a combination of flavours of chocolate ice cream, from Baskin Robbins.

The floor of one cave room was strewn with frozen whale meat. I could clearly see the whale's tail. In another cave room, we came across more frozen meat on the ground, including a complete whale's head and frozen geese, feathers and all. I hadn't seen these items in the President's Choice product line in my local grocery store. It felt strange to be in the Arctic, in a remote community, underground, like a bat. A perfect setting for a scene from "The X-Files".

After taking some pictures with our guides, we all climbed up the ladder to the surface. After walking back to the Hamlet Office, from the Ice House, I thanked everyone for a wonderful day and for the unique experience of being in the Ice House. It was now dark, late and time for Warren and I to leave Tuktoyaktuk and make the return trip to Inuvik. I was scheduled to fly home from Inuvik, on Friday.

The trip, in the truck, took us two and a half hours. At one point, the truck skidded out of control and spun around on the ice. We slid till the vehicle came to a stop. No harm was done. This was the first time this had happened in four days. Warren drove a little slower, as he didn't want to be responsible for any accident.

Once back in Inuvik, we fuelled the truck up, dropped my gear off at the Eskimo Inn and then returned the truck to Delta Auto Rental. Not including all the gas I'd purchased, the rental was over $700. It sounds expensive but I considered it money well spent. This truck made the difference between me living or dying in the Arctic.

Warren drove me back to the Eskimo Inn in his personal pickup. I called Carol to let her know how my day had gone. She told me she already knew because she not only heard me on CBC, but everyone was calling to say they heard me and to offer congratulations.

I was happy to know that my Canadian unity message was spreading across Canada, like wildfire.

After the call, I celebrated the completion of the expedition quietly by ordering a delicious steak at the Eskimo Inn. It had been a day for the history books. God bless Canada!

Epilogue

In the 21st century, Canadians need to convey to every leader, every parent and every teacher that they have a responsibility to teach all children one important lesson. Every Canadian has a "responsibility", during their lifetime, to make Canada a better country than when they found it. Every Canadian must look into their hearts and decide what special project they will undertake, to show their pride in Canada. My advice, to you, is to dream of your most glorious Canada and then make that your destination.

For example, it would be nice if you chose to volunteer at a food bank, but it would be glorious if you decided to end all hunger in Canada! Don't be afraid to set glorious goals, like being the first person in history to travel from the very bottom of mainland Canada 6,520 kilometres to the top under their own power. What glorious goals would you set for Canada, if you knew you could not fail? I want you to know you never fail, until you stop trying. So just keep pedaling and wonderful things will happen in Canada. Imagine a country of 30 million Canadians working together, to create a synergy, making Canada better 30 million ways for all of us...

It was my honour, during the *To The Top Canada* expedition, to start this national discussion by speaking to over five million Canadians, in speeches and media appearances across Canada. Now, it is your turn. Only passionate people can create a passionate nation. Celebrate Canada, and the achievements of Canadians, every day of the year. Make those celebrations glorious, showcasing your love for Canada. When a Canadian in your community does something wonderful, don't just put a medal on their chest, build a larger than life statue of them with a plaque telling their story. Create a permanent legacy of glorious Canadian deeds that will be there to inspire future generations of Canadians.

We have the privilege to be the citizens of the country that the United Nations has ranked as number one in the world for several years. Many people in under privileged countries would risk their very lives for the chance to become a Canadian. So I ask you to stop... look in the mirror. Tell me, what will you do to make Canada a better country than when you found it?

Chris Robertson

Two Decades Later...

Where do I start? After completing the To The Top Canada Expedition, my wife Carol, my son James and my dog Smooch were thrilled to have me home in Hamilton, Canada. My rest was short-lived as media outlets scrambled to do interviews and invite me to be a guest on television programs and radio talk shows. I knew that, for the rest of my life, I would be an ambassador of pride and patriotism for Canada. I'm reminded of the line from the movie "Spiderman": "With great power comes great responsibility." I was a Canadian role model now and for every Canadian child that I may inspire, I had to be a shining example of a good Canadian who strived to make Canada better every day. Epitomizing this high standard would be a challenge that I would meet with the same determination as completing the expedition itself.

One day, working in my backyard, I realized that the To The Top Canada Expedition had changed me. I was raking the lawn, when behind me I suddenly heard the crackling sound of an animal approaching, leaves softly crunching underfoot. Instinct suddenly took over and, as if on auto-pilot. I immediately turned to face the intruder, my arms in a defensive position ready to fight! It was just a grey squirrel running across the backyard. My body, with heightened sense of sound and instant reflexes, had reacted as though I was still on the Dempster Highway, hearing what sounded like an approaching bear. Returning to the safety of southern Ontario almost seemed surreal as the constant vigilance, required for survival in Canada's north, could now be turned off. I wondered if I could ever really turn it off again...

My face had also changed. A slight redness in my cheeks and some scarring that are the marks of frostbite. I would carry these marks with me for the rest of my life. For me, these scars are badges of honour, reminders that I had gone the distance, and would forever be the first person in history who had travelled from the bottom of mainland Canada 6,520 kilometres to the top!

One of the first orders of business was taking my hand written diary from the expedition and typing it on my personal computer. I had to ensure that the account of the first journey to the top of Canada was preserved so this historic Canadian journey could be remembered. I got a quotation from a major Canadian book publishing company to publish a book of my complete diary of the To The Top Canada Expedition. The quotation came back just under $10,000 to publish 2,000 copies of the book. Now, the To The Top Canada Expedition had not only drained RRSP's (retirement funds) but had also left me just over six figures of debt. I didn't have $10,000 to publish the "To The Top Canada" diary. I wrote a letter to the federal government inquiring if the Department of Canadian Heritage would award me a grant to publish the book. Their answer was "no". Why, I wondered. I thought to myself, if there was ever a project that was deserving of a grant from Canadian Heritage, it would be the record of the first journey from the bottom of mainland Canada to the top. I was never given a reason why my request was declined.

Perhaps, in the bureaucratic scheme of things, my To The Top Canada Expedition was not important. Or did a Liberal Government want to downplay a To The Top Canada Expedition and the Quebec Referendum that inspired it, fearful that they would highlight the fact that our nation was almost lost during the Liberal government's watch. Or, maybe the government was simply being good stewards of our tax dollars.

A few short weeks later there was a story in the news that broke my heart. The same department that had said "no" to my request had awarded a grant to a Quebec company to publish a new book, but not the mere $9,000.00 I had asked Quebec for. They were given $98,000.00 of taxpayers' money to publish a book about dumb blond jokes. I was angry. How could this book be chosen and mine declined. Why would this Quebec company need an obscene amount of money when it only costs $10,000.00 to print a book? This was an injustice. I had to speak out and clearly say that I thought Canada's government could do better! The media jumped on the story. The Toronto Star made my Letter to the Editor the Letter of the Day and included my picture, making it the most prominent story in the Editorial section. The CHUM radio and television network nationally told the story of this injustice. There was no greater advocate on my behalf than Roy Green, an On-Air Host of a major talk-radio program on Hamilton's 900 CHML. Roy is a champion for justice on many issues in Canada and when he grabs an issue he is like an angry pit bull that bites you and doesn't let go! Roy not only had me on his program but he kept inviting me back until justice was done. Now, the government never did change their decision, but because of the public's outrage, people starting sending in their money to buy the book even before it was printed. Soon, enough money arrived in the mail that "To The Top Canada" was published. In a short seven weeks, the first edition was sold out. After that, the Canadian public still wanted to hear this story. The second, third and fourth editions were exhausted leading to a 20th Anniversary Special Edition countless book signings later, the book is now in your hands and sharing this very special Canadian story and more important, its message that every Canadian has a responsibility to make our country better through acts of positive citizenship. This was another mountain conquered, proving once again that you should never, ever give up until your goal is achieved.

My message has been heard, through the media, by millions of Canadians but there are still millions of Canadians who have never heard my story. I continue to seek new ways to share the message to make Canada better. I'm always looking for new vehicles to tell my story and take Canada to the top of its potential. I've been successful on several fronts. A short-version of my story was chosen from over 6,000 inspirational Canadian stories to be in the popular book Chicken Soup For The Canadian Soul. This book was soon the number one bestselling non-fiction book in independent bookstores in Canada. My story was also told in the international coffee table book Hope & Heroes: Portraits of Integrity where I was featured with international heroes of the world like Nelson Mandela. My inspirational story was also presented on the Billy Graham Worldwide Radio Network. I've released a CD called Canada's Christmas Story where I tell the To The Top Canada story set to popular Christmas music. I have written a movie screenplay about the To The Top Canada story. I've contacted Canadian television networks to see if they are interested in the movie but quickly learned networks, including CBC, don't make movies. They buy the right of movies from independent film production companies but there are no commitments at this time. In the screenplay, one scene answers the question that all my female readers ask about... What happened before the expedition, when I came home one day and said to my wife: I am going to try to become the first person in history to travel from the bottom of Canada 6,520 kilometres to the top under my own power, that I was leaving home for almost a year to do it and I would be cashing in our life savings to make it happen! What would your spouse's reaction be? (Anyone who would like the answer to this question, is asked to write CBC www.cbc.ca and encourage them to get this movie into production!) Everyone who reads the script says they love it, but there are no takers yet. This is just one more mountain I'm still climbing.

There was a promise I made during the To The Top Canada Expedition on Thursday October 2, 1997. I promised I would help Rev. Larry Robertson (no relation) raise some money to help make the dream of a permanent Anglican Church in Inuvik come true. Upon my return home from the To the Top Canada Expedition I created a To the Top Canada presentation and I added it to my list of professional speaking topics that I offer in my business. Soon, "To The Top Canada" became my most popular presentation with business, associations, institutions, schools, foundations and government agencies lining up to hear it. My peers in the professional speaking industry presented me a trophy honouring the To The Top Canada presentation as the "Best Keynote Speech of the Year".

Remembering my promise, I distributed business cards with the inscription, "BE AN ARCTIC MIRACLE", to all of my audiences at the end of each To The Top Canada program. The card asked audience members to help build a church in Inuvik by sending $10.00 directly to the church address in Inuvik. Soon, to the amazement of the people of Inuvik, thousands and thousands of dollars starting arriving in the mail just ten dollars at a time.

Now, I didn't know how the fund raising efforts were coming so I would call Rev. Larry Robertson from time to time for an update. On one call I learned that a volunteer church treasurer in Inuvik had to resign due to exhaustion from trying to keep up with sending out charitable receipts. Larry explained that the sheer amount of donations had caught them off guard. The Inuvik Church had reorganized with a new committee structure. Many people were now involved to ensure charitable receipts were sent out so no one volunteer would be exhausted. Enough money was raised and construction soon started. In late 1999, as construction was nearing completion, I was invited to the dedication. I had to decline as I knew first hand how expensive return airfare from Toronto to Inuvik was. It was something I could not afford. Although I was working now and had income, all my income went to my family living expenses and the debt service from the expedition.

Even though I wanted to go, there was no possible way I could afford it. Then I got a call from Larry one night. He told me everyone in Inuvik had chipped in to buy me a plane ticket so I could be there for the dedication taking place on Sunday January 9th, 2000. I flew up to Inuvik for the weekend. On the first night, the members of the Parish Council took me out to dinner. It was interesting to hear what happened from their perspective. Before I had started my Arctic Miracle Campaign, the church had almost lost hope. The cost of building a new permanent church was just under half a million dollars. In a community with high unemployment and a population of only 3,200 people this was not a place that you would target with a fund-raising campaign. Then the money started arriving in the mail and hope was rekindled. At one meeting, a church member stood up and said these words: "WE'VE GOT TO BELIEVE WE CAN BUILD A CHURCH, THE WAY CHRIS ROBERTSON BELIEVES WE CAN BUILD THIS CHURCH!!!" From that moment, everyone in Inuvik was behind the church building project. Volunteers were working hard seeking donations and materials to be used in the construction. Their faith was rewarded with the dedication of the church. During the service that Sunday I shared the story of the words I had read in the Bible on the final day of the To The Top Canada Expedition. These words, written over 2,000 years ago, described Canada's Arctic perfectly and touched the hearts and souls of all present. There was also some bittersweet joy on this dedication weekend. There had been a tragedy in the community. A Gwich'in man's house had suddenly caught fire. To escape the flames, he ran outside without time to grab his winter jacket. He quickly started his snowmobile and raced towards Inuvik for help. Unfortunately, in the treacherous cold of the Arctic winter, he succumbed to hypothermia. There was sorrow that the man had died but there was joy that, for the first time, the entire community could come together under one roof in their church and grieve together as one. Several times that weekend I heard people refer to their new church as the "Miracle Church"... Rev. Larry Robertson is now the Bishop!

Every day it seems I hear more stories of how the To The Top Canada story is touching lives. One day I was at Ivor Wynne Stadium in Hamilton attending a Tiger-Cat football game together with another professional speaker friend of mine. Since I bought the tickets, Timothy asked if he could get me a snack at halftime. While Timothy was away, I was standing up in the stands and stretching. A man walked up to me and said: "You're Chris Robertson, aren't you?" I indicated yes I was. The man explained that although I did not know him, he wanted to shake my hand. He said he had attended a To The Top Canada speech and was tremendously inspired. Shortly after my speech, he learned that he had cancer. He was afraid of going to the chemotherapy treatments but finally said to his wife: "If Chris Robertson can make it to the top, I can fight and get through this". He wanted me to know that the To The Top Canada story had given him the courage to fight cancer and that I had "saved his life"!

I speak in many schools across Canada. In a given year, I address thousands of students about my journey to the top of Canada and my message of positive citizenship for all Canadians. I've spoken across Canada, from inner city schools in the core of Toronto to country schools in rural communities including one in the heart of a Mennonite village. At one elementary school in a rural community, I was assigned a young girl Debbie (not her real name) as a student assistant to help me set up in the gym and work the lights during my presentation. I was told by the teacher that Debbie's mother had recently died and she was now living with her father who was battling alcoholism. I let Debbie hold the Canadian flag I had carried during the expedition. Debbie and I then got a basketball and shot some hoops, playing 21 in the school gym. To thank Debbie for her assistance in setting up, I gave her an autographed copy of my book To The Top Canada. I wrote an inscription that let Debbie know she had the power to make any dream in her life a destination and make her life better. While I was packing up my equipment, the teacher came up to me and said: "You made quite an impression." I acknowledged that the students really seemed to enjoy the presentation. The teacher then told me she was talking about Debbie. After the presentation, when Debbie was heading out for recess, she told the teacher that this was "the best day of her life". I have now spoken at well over 1000 schools in Canada from coast to coast to coast. There is a generation of "glowing hearts" that I have touched that are going to make Canada better as Canadians committed to personal deeds of positive citizenship. I could have no finer legacy.

On the fifth anniversary of the beginning of the To The Top Canada Expedition, I organized a celebration called the "Canada Victory Tour". On this tour, I started at Point Pelee and revisited all the 51 communities I had travelled through during the To The Top Canada Expedition. This time I drove my car! My wife Carol and our son James came along to experience my full route for the first time. In each community I gave a complimentary presentation of the To The Top Canada story. Many people in the communities enjoyed seeing the slides of themselves in the presentation. The Global Television Network, one of the media networks covering the Canada Victory Tour, loaned us a television camera so we could film footage as we drove to the top. My son James was now 16 years old. He was the designated camera man for the trip. At one point in the Canadian North James saw a heard of caribou for the very first time in his life. He jumped out of the car and started running after the caribou herd filming the whole encounter. Carol and I looked at each other, wondering how soon he was going to be coming back. For the rest of the trip, we gave him the nickname "Caribou Dundee". As this was summer, we could only drive as far north as Inuvik. We had to then fly from Inuvik to Tuktoyaktuk, as the ice had now melted. A Global Television team had flown into Inuvik to join us and flew with us to Tuktoyaktuk to film my first visit back since the completion of the expedition. It was an incredible experience for me to revisit all the communities again. The best part was that this time I could share the experience with my family. They now understand and appreciate how incredible a challenge it was. You can talk about it, but until you see the Dempster Highway and the Arctic for yourself, you can never fully comprehend the danger, the obstacles and the sheer determination needed to undertake the journey to the top. Still, though my family is in awe of the expedition, they know my work is not finished. They see me working every day to take my message to make Canada better to even more Canadians. My family does keep me down to earth with their sense of humour though. My son kids me, asking when am I going to get around to making "To The Top Canada-

On Ice" with real skating bears. James is an adult now, studying at university in an MBA program. The little boy, who you see on the back cover of my book standing mid-chest to me, on our way to the Montreal Rally in 1995, now towers over me at six foot four, to my five foot eleven.

Back in 2003, we started to celebrate and mark the final day of the Expedition with a celebration called To The Top Canada Day on January 8th. On this date and before it, when making New Year resolutions, we encourage all Canadians to set a personal and specific goal to make Canada better in the coming year. You can visit the website at www.tothetopcanada.ca to get more information. To The Top Canada Day has grown and we now invite Canadians to nominate a previously unrecognized hero for the "To The Top Canada Award". Here comes the favour I would ask you, right now, to think about a person who is the most deserving hero in your community and go to the www.tothetopcanada.ca website and nominate that person so they can be honoured. This will take only five minutes of your time and you'll be making Canada better right now by doing this. You can read about the heroes we've honoured to date on the web-site. You can also view pictures and see the award is actually pretty unique. The To The Top Canada Award is mounted on an authentic traditional Huron snowshoe.

In the last 20 years Canada has changed... Over 20 years ago, it seemed liked Canadians needed to be given "permission" to speak proudly about Canada. I remember 48 hours prior to the 1995 Montreal Rally before the last Quebec Referendum, in preparation to leave for Montreal from my home community of Hamilton, Canada. I went to mall after mall and store after store and I could not find a shirt, jersey or coat that said "Canada" on it or even had a "Maple Leaf" on it (I finally secured one by driving out of town). Now, Canada shirts are everywhere and my heart beams every time I see a Canadian wearing one. More recently a CNN news story identified the Nation Branding of the Canadian Maple Leaf as one of ten things Canada does best. Today, Canadians have given themselves permission to say and shout: "I'm proud to be Canadian" or "I am Canadian!"

Time has also made the book TO THE TOP CANADA a historical document. I remember my frustration as a consumer paying more than double the price of gas in Inuvik. The shocking price I was paying was 93.9 cents/litre. I'm sure there have been students reading an earlier edition of TO THE TOP CANADA without this special edition chapter, who thought what is the problem? Today gas is about $1.35 cents/litre and any gas station in Toronto charging 93.9 cents/litre today would have cars lined up for kilometres hoping to get such a low price. I'm sure as time goes by gas will jump again to over $2 or $3 per litre and $1.35 will seem like a bargain. Maybe we won't need gas as electric cars are just becoming available now. They are expensive, but as their price drops I'm sure they will become more common place. Speaking of history, I have donated many items from the To The Top Canada Expedition to schools. The best collection is owned by the Hamilton-Wentworth District School Board. My bike was donated to Ray Lewis Public School which is a school on the Hamilton mountain in the

Hamilton-Wentworth District School Board. In 2014 a new head office was built and opened for the Hamilton-Wentworth District School Board and in the building is a Special Time Capsule where artifacts from the To The Top Canada Expedition are stored. This Time Capsule will be opened in the year 2114. I won't be there when it opens, but my grandson may be... He'll be 102 at that time! Canada and the world have changed so much since the 1995 Quebec Referendum that motivated me to undertake the quest of the To The Top Canada Expedition in 1997-1998. I can only imagine what changes will happen socially, technologically and medically to make the world a better place in the next 20 years. I do know this... The Best Canada is yet to come! So let's roll up our sleeves and turn on our ipads (a form of technology that may be obsolete 20 years from now) and make the Best Canada our destination! The sooner we start on this journey, the sooner we'll arrive at our destination! All Canadians have a responsibility to help us achieve the Best Canada! Hope is like riding a bicycle... If you just keep pedalling, it will take you anywhere you want to go!

Finally, I want to wish you the very best of success in setting your own personal life goal to make Canada a better country. When you think about all the wonderful blessings we enjoy living in Canada, doesn't this country deserve your commitment to do ONE PROJECT that makes Canada a better country than when you found it? Start today!!! Transform your heartfelt feelings for Canada into real goals and real action steps.

Thank You & Proudly Canadian,

Chris Robertson

Canadian Heritage   Patrimoine canadien
Parks Canada   Parcs Canada

Point Pelee National Park
1118 Point Pelee Dr., R.R.#1
Leamington, Ontario   N8H 3V4
Tel. & TDD (519) 322-2365
Fax (519) 322-1277

November 3, 1998

Chris Robertson
395 Sanatorium Road
Hamilton, Ontario
L9C 2A7

TO WHOM IT MAY CONCERN,

This letter is to confirm that Chris Robertson left Point Pelee National Park, which is the most southern point of mainland Canada, on his To The Top Canada expedition on March 1, 1997. Bicycles are not allowed down at theTip area and Chris Robertson was given special permission to take his bicycle down to the Tip, to begin his To The Top Canada expedition. We understand from national media reports that Chris Robertson successfully arrived in Tuktoyaktuk on the Arctic Ocean on January 7, 1998. Since Point Pelee became a national park on May 29, 1918, no one has ever left from Point Pelee National Park, on an expedition to the top of mainland Canada under their own power. We congratulate Chris Robertson on his Canadian achievement.

Yours Sincerely,

Fedela Falkner
Acting Park Superintendent
Point Pelee National Park

Canadä

If you haven't heard "Canada's Ambassador of Positive Citizenship" Then you haven't heard Canada's story!!!

Award Winning Professional Speaker Chris Robertson wants to speak at your school, company or organization and tell you the inspirational story of the To The Top Canada expedition!

To contact Chris Robertson to speak at your next meeting, convention or special event please contact your local Speakers Bureau or contact Chris Robertson directly at chris@chrisrobertson.ca.

Here are just some comments from people who have heard Chris Robertson speak to their organization:

My heartfelt thanks to you. Your inspiring presentation not only warmed and energized the room, but also helped to "break the shell of Canadian pride". Thank you for helping to "draw out" the passion for our great country!

The experiences you encountered during your journey across Canada were inspiring and your ability to relate the lessons learned to the audience was much appreciated. You picked up the energy level of the room and left everyone thoroughly entertained and invigorated!

Thank you very much for your excellent "To The Top Canada" Presentation. It was apparent from the reaction of the audience and from the feedback that everyone was inspired by your message. You are a living example of what can be achieved by the powerful combination of goal setting and a positive attitude!

Thank you for your incredible presentation at our Professional Development Day. Your keynote on "Exceeding Expectations Forever" and sharing the adventure of the "To The Top Canada" expedition was truly inspirational. Most important was your skilful facilitation that taught us how to bypass limitations and take our programs to the next level. Your program should be mandatory for everyone interested in maximizing their potential. Thank you for giving us a day we will never forget!

Acknowledgements

I would like to say thank you to the following, who have my special appreciation.

1. I especially want to thank God, who watched over me, kept me safe and brought me to the final destination of my impossible journey. He taught me that when all you have is God, God is enough...

2. Thank you to the many Canadians who were like angels watching over me with food, shelter and smiles along the way. I learned that, in Canada, there are no strangers but just friends I haven't met.

3. Thank you to Hometown Radio CHML Talkline Host, Roy Green, who started a campaign that made this book possible. If pride in Canada makes a great Canadian, then Roy Green deserves a badge of honour.

4. Thank you to the corporations who shared their services and support including Business Depot, Magna International, Comfort Inn, Holiday Inn, Novotel Hotels, Best Western, Venture Inn, McDonalds, Harveys, Swiss Chalet, Subway, Mr. Submarine, Pizzaville, Robin's Donuts, Husky, Baskin Robbins, Dairy Queen, A&W, Pizza Hut, Bonanza, Cyclepath, Energizer Batteries, NWT Air, Air Canada, Dofasco and, especially, the small business owners, too numerous to mention, but who proportionately gave even more to help me than the larger corporations. God bless you all.

5. Thank you to my volunteer editors including my wife, Carol Robertson, my sister Cathy Morrison, and my friends Leslie Lorette, Dr. Thomas Gerry and Margaret Jones.

6. Thank you to my friend, Barry Shainbaum, for his enthusiasm during the To The Top Canada expedition and for his permission to publish three of his photos in this book.

7. Thank you to all the literary critics who will read this book and realize that if you asked Canada's best authors to cycle with 500 pounds of total weight, up mountains and through storms for twelve hours and (for those still living) had them write their daily diary by flashlight at the end of the day, that in comparison, I did a reasonable job of documenting the first journey from the bottom of mainland Canada to the top.

8. Thank you to all the people in all the crowds and audiences across Canada who came out in person to support the To The Top Canada expedition. Yours cheers, good wishes and prayers gave me the power to go the distance.

9. Thank you to you the reader who bought this book. Your investment with other patriotic Canadians has allowed this story of a great Canadian achievement to be told for generations to come.

Chris Robertson

To The Top Canada expedition

Minister
of Foreign Affairs

Ministre
des Affaires étrangères

Ottawa, Canada K1A 0G2

As Minister of Foreign Affairs and Minister of the Atlantic Canada Opportunities Agency, and on behalf of Canada, I wish to commend Chris Robertson for his dedication to our great country. His journey from the bottom of mainland Canada to the top, as recorded in his powerful book, *To The Top Canada*, is evidence of the power of one individual to inspire a country.

To The Top Canada is a must-read for every Canadian that wants to witness true courage and perseverance. The gruelling journey across such a vast and beautiful country is both commendable and moving.

I truly believe that this story captures the true heart and soul of our country and its people. Thank you, Chris, for your passion for Canada!

Peter G. MacKay

Canadä